RACE, CRIME
and RESISTANCE

SAGE has been part of the global academic community since 1965, supporting high quality research and learning that transforms society and our understanding of individuals, groups, and cultures. SAGE is the independent, innovative, natural home for authors, editors and societies who share our commitment and passion for the social sciences.

Find out more at: **www.sagepublications.com**

RACE, CRIME
and RESISTANCE

Tina G. Patel and David Tyrer

Los Angeles | London | New Delhi
Singapore | Washington DC

First published 2011

SAGE Publications Ltd
1 Oliver's Yard
55 City Road
London EC1Y 1SP

SAGE Publications Inc.
2455 Teller Road
Thousand Oaks, California 91320

SAGE Publications India Pvt Ltd
B1/I 1 Mohan Cooperative Industrial Area
Mathura Road, New Delhi 110 044
India

SAGE Publications Asia-Pacific Pte Ltd
33 Pekin Street #02-01
Far East Square
Singapore 048763

Library of Congress Control Number: 2010936933

British Library Cataloguing in Publication data

A catalogue record for this book is available from the British Library

ISBN 978-1-84920-398-2
ISBN 978-1-84920-399-9

Typeset by C&M Digitals (P) Ltd, Chennai, India
Printed by CPI Antony Rowe, Chippenham, Wiltshire
Printed on paper from sustainable resources

Contents

About the Authors

Dr Tina G. Patel joined the University of Salford in September 2008, as Lecturer in Criminology. Her research and teaching interests relate to 'race', racism, exclusion, police and violent behaviour. She is currently undertaking work into the policing of racist violence in Northern Ireland, and use of racial profiling within the context of the war on terror.

Dr David Tyrer is a member of the Centre for the Study of Crime, Criminalisation and Social Exclusion and Senior Lecturer in Sociology at Liverpool John Moores University. His research interests are broadly concerned with race, racism and postcoloniality, and his recent work has focused on relations between states and racialised and ethnicised minorities. He has a long-standing research interest in Islamophobia on which he is currently preparing a monograph.

Acknowledgements

Tina G. Patel: Thank you to colleagues at the University of Salford – especially those in Sociology, whose guidance, support and space for development allowed this book to be written. For your love, care and encouragement, dedication is reserved for my family (Patel and Hamilton), especially my partner (David).

David Tyrer: I would like to record my thanks to those friends and family members whose support has meant so much to me. I owe a particular debt of gratitude to the following: B.A. and O.W. Tyrer; A.K.B.; colleagues in Criminology and Sociology at LJMU for providing institutional and intellectual support (especially Joe Sim, Liz Sperling, Margaret Edwards, Jenny Van Hooff and Bryan Scott); Shai; Bobby; A.K.V.; Antonio; Federica; Danielle; Gareth, Helen Churchill Charlie; and Tina G. Any shortcomings are mine, and not a result of the support offered by these individuals.

We would also like to thank all those involved in the research studies mentioned, including the funders, colleagues and those participants who so willingly gave up their time to discuss their experiences. Our thanks go also to our respective colleagues and collaborators who have supported the development of our work, and especially to Gillian Hall. We would like to thank our anonymous reviewers for their insightful comments on earlier drafts, and to express our gratitude to staff at Sage – especially Caroline Porter and Sarah-Jayne Boyd. Finally, we wish to acknowledge all those who have kept up the struggle when others have faded.

1

Introduction: Constructing the Race–Crime Problem

This book is about the continued and subtle ways in which crime is constructed as racialised in post-Macpherson UK. Macpherson (1999) is a report on an inquiry following the 1993 racist murder of Stephen Lawrence, a black African Caribbean youth in London. The report highlighted failures of the Metropolitan Police Service and problems of institutional racism, making a number of recommendations for criminal justice institutions. Consequently, there are seemingly more entrenched systems for reporting, monitoring and combating institutionalised racism, and yet the modalities of racism seem to have articulated with this, ostensibly hostile, institutional framework in order to persist in ever more ambiguous and nebulous forms. This book argues that notions of 'black criminality' are often reworked in new ways and have fed into the wider policy on community cohesion and citizenship (Khiabany and Williamson, 2008) that often directly takes black and minority ethnic people as objects of state intervention, while claiming not to be racialised. An important theme of the book is the ways in which ideologies of 'scientific racism' which were in the past woven into state policies on crime control in countries such as Britain, USA, South Africa and Germany have resurfaced, articulating in new ways with forms of cultural racism, and being expressed in new ways, for example through calculations of risk rather than strict biological hierarchies. The key issue being highlighted is that, in spite of claims that we are in a post-racial age, problematic construction of crimes as racialised persist, illustrated more recently, for example, by moves towards increased racial profiling, meaning that older notions of 'black criminality' and the dangerous 'immigrant other', undeserving of a right to a place in Britain, are once again appearing. The book will consider how and why certain racialised groups are vulnerable to the discriminatory practices of criminal justice agencies. In doing so, it will also highlight how their claims to knowledge and experience have been marginalised, presenting the argument that this urgently needs to be replaced by practices that are underpinned by an ethos of access, equality and empowerment. The aim therefore is not only to shed critical light on the continued utility of 'race' in what are sometimes described as 'post-race' times, but also to highlight how this thinking and its impact on crime has been, and continually needs to be, challenged.

Before we continue, some clarification is needed for the terms that are used in the text. Terms of reference are constantly changing, being negotiated and updated on a variety of local and global levels. It is acknowledged that 'race' talk is in itself a complex, political and contested process. The term in itself is problematic and contested, highlighted in some sources by the use of inverted commas (Mason, 2000: 8). Debates run about its continued use in social science disciplines, with valid arguments being presented about the responsibility of academics being to replace it with other preferable terms of reference, such as 'ethnicity'. However, our studies tell us that 'race' is still treated by many in society as a real entity, by which lives are organised and behaviour is constructed (Mason, 2000). We therefore use the term 'race' here not descriptively to refer to a given attribute, but instead as an analytical term to describe a process of power which impacts upon all of us in different but significant ways, for example how Muslims as a seemingly religious community are still racialised as a group. So, even though 'ethnicity' is often preferred over 'race', the latter is still a term that is analytically relevant, especially in terms of the matters discussed in this text. Although we view the use of the term in inverted commas as relevant, the regular use of the term in this text means that encasing it in inverted commas would hinder readability flow. The reader should therefore take our use of the term (*race*) as representing our acknowledgement of its contested and problematic status.

The term black is often used in the English language as something crudely associated with negative connotations. During the USA Civil Rights Movement of the 1960s, and later activism in Britain, it became mobilised a political term, and came to be used with a capital letter as 'Black', to indicate the unified inclusion of all those people who suffered inequality, discrimination and racist violence because of their non-white skin colour, for instance largely those of African, Caribbean and South Asian origin. It also indicated political solidarity against such racial discrimination. However, we argue that the term can no longer be viewed as a singular political label which brings with it the same set of meanings. As such, the term is used in lower-case typology: *black*. In addition, our critique of essentialised identities means that the term is rarely used on its own. For example, *black and minority ethnic* is also used as a preferential term of reference, alongside more detailed terms of reference. This highlights labels that have been re-negotiated and moved away from an essentialised notion of a singular or universal black identity. For instance, *South Asian* is used to refer to those with recent origins in any of the Asian countries and, more specifically, *British Asian* is used to refer to those individuals with recent origins in South Asia, who were born, raised and now living in Britain. *African Caribbean, African,* or *Caribbean* is used to refer to those with recent origins in the Caribbean and/or Africa. More specifically, *British African Caribbean* is used to refer to those with recent origins in those countries, who were born, raised and now living in Britain.

The terms *white* and *white European* have often been presented in race talk as neutral, for instance in referring to all those who reside in a cultural space that is unquestioned and positioned as the 'norm'. Furthermore, those who are included in this space enjoy a position of power and privilege. We recognise that the terms are also bound up by the similar implications that are associated with essentialised notions of blackness. We therefore use the terms reluctantly to refer to all those who are of non-black minority and ethnic status. In doing so, we recognise that it too is a problematic term that is in reality something of complex and multiple entities. It is thus not a singular racial entity, representative of whole nations, such as the UK and USA. We do, though, argue that in crime matters discussed within these contexts the term represents a majority view. We therefore use it to point to the ways in which it is considered the norm and so is rendered invisible, as well as being an entity that is able to reproduce its position of power and authority (Garner, 2010).

Racialised others and the roots of a racist rationale

The concept of the 'other' allows 'us' to create 'ideals and typifications and the other present us with tests and measures for these ideals' (Spencer, 2006: 8). This is a way of creating definitions, maintaining boundaries and constructing hierarchies based on difference. When race enters this othering process, particularly within the context of crime and deviancy, it is important to consider the roots of racially loaded concepts, common usage and persistence. Within the context of racial othering, a good starting point would be the European global expansion from the late fifteenth century onwards, which saw scientific explanations about race becoming popular (Mason, 2000). By the mid-nineteenth century, there was firm support of *Enlightenment thinking* and the discipline of *race science*. Its key contributors included Immanuel Kant (1724–1804), David Hume (1711–1776), Charles Linneaus (1707–1778), Charles Darwin (1809–1882) and Francis Galton (1822–1911). Such thinking proposed hierarchical ideas about race, which were in themselves tied to mistaken ideas about the human biology.

These racist ideas gained widespread support, becoming linked to 'a notion of hierarchy in which all differences, both of history and future potential, were seen as a product of biological variation' (Mason, 2000: 6). Dominant in political discussions, such ideas also filtered through to lay understanding, meaning that they became normalised and unquestionably accepted. This led to the creating of boundaries between groups of peoples, who were distinguished on rather a crude biological basis of colour, whereby white equals being of a good and pure nature, and black is associated with evil (Mason, 2000; Tizard and Phoenix, 2002). This then became converted to the rationale that all those who were non-white were 'degenerative, falling away from the true nature of the (human) race' (Dyer, 1997: 22). Sociological understanding of the construction of race has found that over time the continued racial polarisation of blackness and whiteness in this way has not only been justified by making references to the supposed natural order of the human race, but has also been maintained via political and religious testimonials. For example, Johan Boemus in 1521 proposed that all humans 'descended from the sons of Noah, these being Ham, Shem and Japeth, and argued that the descendents of Ham degenerated into "blackness", whereas those civilised descended from Shem and Japeth, and so remained "white"' (Fredrickson, 1981, cited in Dyer, 1997: 22).

However, it is argued here that race is socially constructed via a power relationship in society, where being white equals privilege and superiority, and being black equals disadvantage and discrimination. These terms can therefore be seen as socio-politically loaded concepts. Their meanings and usage are based on ideas that are developed and maintained in social human interaction. This is supported, not least by the vast amount of sociological work which also disproves the dated ideas from the Enlightenment period around the so-called problematic nature of black and minority ethnic people, for example as having poor IQ levels, a proneness to violent behaviour, untrustworthiness, sexual promiscuity, and so on. However, these crude, offensive and outdated ideas continue to dominate and show themselves in a variety of discriminatory practices and attitudes. In suggesting reasons for this, many have pointed to the deeply embedded racism and discriminatory practices of wider society and institutions within that society, practices that are both intentional and unintentional. Thus a combination of the persistence of inaccurate stereotypes and a power in-balance means that racism continues to exist and perpetuate itself.

The result is the unequal treatment of certain groups at the hands of another, for instance global slavery, lynching, the Ku Klux Klan, Jim Crow and segregation in the USA; apartheid in South Africa; and institutional racism, racist violence and the war on terror (Islam). We can see that, for some, race is in fact a matter of life and death, for example the treatment of Jews in Hitler's Final Solution. In more recent years, the killings of Stephen Lawrence and Anthony Walker suggest that even within modern society and a post-Macpherson criminal justice system, one's race (or perceived race) acts as a precursor to abuse and death, sometimes even at the hands of the state, as we saw with the shooting of Jean Charles de Menezes. The terror emerging from such a form of white domination is seen to set the norm; it is accepted and largely goes unchallenged by white-majority mainstream society, who maintain and perpetuate it for social, political and economic reasons of self-interest. They hold, in their white terror (hooks, 1992), the position of power in processes 'of naming, defining, decision making and the use of symbolic and physical violence' to exercise control (Garner, 2007: 15).

In contemporary society, this racialised unequal treatment continues, albeit in more masked and reworked forms. This means that black and minority ethnic people continue to be seen as 'flawed psychologically, morally and socially' (Owusu-Bempah and Howitt, 2000: 95), not only as individuals, but also in terms of their cultures and family life, and indeed every aspect of their lives. For example, consider the focus in more recent times of media images, lay stereotypes and even political commentary on 'baby-fathers':

> David Cameron has urged absent black fathers not to neglect their responsibilities, in an interview addressing the issues of family and social breakdown … The issue has previously been identified by political figures as a source of society's ills. Last year, Justice Secretary Jack Straw said the 'continuing problem' of gang violence was due to the absence of fathers in black communities. (BBC News, 16 July 2008)

Also consider the recent flurry of news stories around strict Asian parents who force their young daughters into arranged marriages and abuse them when they fail to agree, followed by the eagerness with which the Forced Marriage Unit was set up in 2009, as a joint initiative between the UK's Foreign and Commonwealth Office and the Home Office. It is not disputed that such cases exist, or that victims of such arrangements require assistance, but the close links made in the media between these cases and Islam as a faith sends out a problematic message about all Muslim and Asian communities.

These presentations would certainly have us believe that black and minority ethnic people, their families, communities and entire culture, are feckless and problematic. This leads to the problem of white being accepted as the norm against which everything is then measured against, although nothing is able to be superior to it. As Dyer argues, 'in other words, whites are not of a race, they're just the human race' (Dyer, 1997: 3). The imaginary of the black and minority ethnic dangerous 'other' also serves to create a white victimhood rationale, which is then used to justify further discriminatory attitudes and behaviour. Indeed, it is used as a form of public support for increased measures of protection, via control, surveillance and removal, of 'them' for the safety of 'us' and 'our' identity, culture, health, space and land. This was most evidently seen during the 2005 general election and the local elections of 2006 (Sinha, 2008), where political campaigns focused on the 'immigration problem', and in doing so made direct links between the country's decline and the 'influx of migrants' whose supposed predisposition to have lots of babies caused overpopulation and 'welfare scrounging', which then led to a drain on an already strained NHS, housing and schools. These migrants were also seen to import diseases, for example, HIV/AIDS and TB, and, more dangerously, were seen as posing a security threat to Western ideals, through terrorist activity and religious extremism (Sinha, 2008). It is not surprising, then, that a new dangerous 'other' became the focus of racialised panics amongst some white populations (Gilroy, 2004), as was seen with the rise in support for groups located on the far-right political spectrum, such as the British National Party.

The problem with racialised constructions of crime

Crime is racialised when individual criminal behaviour is viewed as being indicative of the racial traits of the wider black and minority ethnic community, meaning that 'whole categories of phenotypically similar individuals are rendered pre-criminal and morally suspect' (Covington, 1995: 547). Gilroy argues that the view of black and minority ethnic groups as 'innately criminal' became 'common sense' in the 1970s and 1980s with the muggings moral panic, and is crucial to the development the 'black problem' (Gilroy, 1987: 109). Here, such crimes were identified as expressions of a black and ethnic minority culture (Gilroy, 2002), and played a significant role in shaping public fear and anxiety about crime in general and, in terms of fears of the British national decline, via the creation of crisis and chaos, which then fuels hostility about their presence and supposed criminal tendencies.

Black and minority ethnic people are easily accepted as a reference point for crimes, though crimes may be blamed on completely fictitious black and minority ethnic characters. For example, Garner asks us to consider the case of Charles Stuart in October 1989, Boston, USA, who along with his brother murdered his pregnant wife, and identified a black African American man as being guilty of the attack. Although Stuart's brother finally confessed to the crime, admitting that it was a murder driven by a life-insurance claim, what is of interest is the response of the local community and criminal justice system, which carried out an intense police operation, and saw media and political talk of restoring the death penalty (Garner, 2007: 20). One wonders whether such a response would have been made if the victim had been of black and minority ethnic background and the suspect white. Certainly in the UK, the initial absence of media, public and political attention to the racist murder of Stephen Lawrence suggests not. The idea that Stuart was treated as an individual, and the supposed black African American perpetrator as a representative of the black community, and part of a pathologised black collective at that, illustrates the common thinking: that any one of these black men could have killed the white woman because it is in the nature of black men to do things like this. The rationale was that black men are innately savage, animalistic, destructive and criminal. They are fiends or sociopaths, a social menace who prey on helpless white bodies.

This imagery is also supported by 'factual' representations in the news, which presents Britain as a society where the black and minority ethnic population poses a problem. Indeed, Pilkington's (2003) analysis of the British press in the 1980s found that black and minority ethnic groups are portrayed as a 'foreign other', who pose a problem in their immigration to this country and then, when here, pose a law and order problem. For example, consider the negative representations of black and minority ethnic people in the press, which is ill-informed, stereotypical and presented as comical at best, and full of blame, hate and suspicion at its worst (see Malik, 2002 for an in-depth discussion on this). In recent times this has taken a more sinister turn as black and minority ethnic people, especially those of Asian Pakistani and Islamic background, are now seen as being of a particular 'terror' threat; for example, 'the enemy within' and self-segregation claims, underlined by views of white victimhood and the idea that the British people have done all they can to support these people, but they have actively rejected and attacked British society. For example, in an article headed 'The enemy within', the story reads:

> ... home-grown terrorists ... The danger seems ever present ... there is an enemy within Britain who wants to destroy our way of life. Most of this relatively small group of fanatics are British-born Muslims who have been educated here and brought up within our tolerant democracy ... The great challenge for Britain is how to stop this and minimise the future risks. Nobody should underestimate the scale of the problem or the time needed. We already have a generation of disaffected Muslims who see any excuse, whether it is war in Iraq, Afghanistan or Lebanon, as a reason for killing their fellow citizens. (*Sunday Times*, 13 August 2006)

This, then, also serves 'to obscure the extent of "white-on-minority" violence' (Russell, 1998, cited in Bowling and Phillips, 2002: 108). Such selective reporting also detracts from the high numbers of racially motivated attacks against black and minority ethnic people. Even more dangerous, it supports the claims of the right-wing press that these black and minority ethnic people are dangerous others that pollute British society, and therefore they need to be controlled and removed. For example, consider the claims of the British National Party about supposed Asian rape gangs who were preying on white girls (*Sunday Times*, 18 January 2006). This is achieved through the power of language and imagery, in terms of its word association, its selectivity and complete fabrication. For example, consider the images published in the press following the Toxteth disturbances in 1981, and the selective use of photography, depicting the aggressiveness of rioters. The problem here is that no pictures or reference to the heavy-handed policing methods, or to the white looters, were made. Such media selectivity is common today, as demonstrated in what has now been widely recognised as the two racially biased 'looting' and 'finding' images following Hurricane Katrina (*New York Times*, 5 September 2005). The cumulative effect of stereotypical and negative representations of black and minority ethnic people in this way clearly serves to promote a discourse of 'racist commonsense'. It is true that media presentations can be negotiated by its audiences, but that interpretation is severely limited when that audience does not have direct experience or accurate information.

Racial profiling in a post-Macpherson era

It is argued that the relationships between criminality and race are actually mythical and, as we have seen, are based on socially constructed political motivations and economic interests. Gilroy, writing in the late 1980s, argues that the ancient images of black lawlessness reoccurred in modern forms with the muggings moral panics of the 1970s and 1980s. They therefore not only echo, but also draw upon, the biological and cultural racism or earlier eras (Gilroy, 1987, cited in Bowling and Phillips, 2002: 77). These images and representations are still here today, with for instance images of gangs and gun-crime. For example, consider Greater Manchester Police's use of a 'wanted' style poster in their search for suspect Moses Mathias in August 2009, where it was reported that:

> Huge billboards containing a photograph of Mathias have been projected onto the walls of a building outside Piccadilly Station in Manchester and on a large screen in Piccadilly Gardens in the city centre in an unprecedented move by detectives. Additionally, a £15,000 reward has also been offered to help find Mathias after detectives spent months searching for him. (*Guardian*, 17 August 2009)

They present to us views of all black and minority people as being the result of a problematic culture, located in deprived inner-city neighbourhoods, and having been raised in households where fathers were absent. All this, it has been argued by commentators, politicians and the media alike, leads young black African Caribbean men to adopt 'a subculture of machismo and violence' (Smith, 2009: 32) that is anti-police, anti-education and as a whole against any legitimate authority, and where violence is commonly used in attempts to resolve disputes. In the eyes of the public, the vast majority of whom have no experience of these crimes, such panics appear legitimated when supported by the claims of Home Office research, or met with the setting-up of specialist committees, whose task it is to address the problem. For example, the Street Weapons Commission (2009) not only called for the establishment of a Violence Reduction Unit, but also called for, in its language of urgency and panic, immediate action on all our parts: 'This report represents a call to action. If we don't act – now – then the implications are serious for our future individual safety, community wellbeing and our society. Therefore we believe tackling gun and knife crime should be an urgent national priority for everyone ...' (Street Weapons Commission, 2009: 8). Although in their review of knife crime policy and evidence Eades et al. (2007) highlight the need to be cautious here, especially given that the crime data is limited, we nevertheless see the continued demonisation of black and minority ethnic groups as dangerous, criminal and in need of control. Such rationale is used to not only justify increased police attention, but also for the demanding of more police powers.

The dominance of such racial profiling is clearly ever more present, despite suggestions by the state and various agents of the criminal justice system, for example, claiming otherwise. Here, especially since the 9/11 atrocities, the Muslim population in Britain, including anyone of Asian or Arabic appearance, has faced a new kind of exclusion; one that sees them being viewed as extreme fundamentalists and terrorists. It could be suggested that the racial profiling and increased surveillance of this group is *in addition* to that still experienced by those of black African Caribbean origin. Kalra (2003), however, argues that there is now a growing shift of target from black African Caribbean to South Asian Muslims. Indeed, it seems that the current criminalisation of this group has intensified to such an extent that to belong to this group, or even to be perceived as belonging to this group, stirs up images of the 'Islamic fundamentalist terrorist', which is responded to with increased surveillance, not only by the police and the state, but also by lay members of society who are constantly encouraged to inform on friends, neighbours, work colleagues, family member and strangers, should they suspect anything suspicious. For example, consider the recent media campaign which showed a photograph of a garage storage lock-up containing what appears to be a huge number of bottles, and ran with the heading: 'Handyman? Pest Controller? Bomb Maker?' It went on on to state:

> They're making bombs, so naturally terrorists will try to conceal their activities. But sometimes they can leave signs. Signs we need your help in spotting. They may load up their vehicles with large amounts of chemicals, fertilisers or gas cylinders, all of which can be used to make bombs. These may be bought with cash. They'll also have to be stored somewhere like a house, a lock-up or a garage. You might even see discarded material. If you notice anything suspicious or out of the ordinary CALL THE CONFIDENTIAL ANTI-TERRORIST HOTLINE ON 0800 789 321. We don't believe any call is a waste of time. If you suspect it, report it. (*Metro*, 17 March 2010: 21)

The idea is that 'responsible citizens' should actively observe and report not only as part of their national duty to Britain, but also as responsible global citizens. In comparing the criminalisation of black African Caribbean people in the 1970s and 1980s with that of Asian Muslims in the 1990s and 2000s, Hudson (2007) argues: the 'Muslim Asian is now well established as an "Enemy within"; in the light of recent events, perhaps as *the* enemy within' (Hudson, 2007: 163).

While it is often claimed that the post-Macpherson context is one marked by increasing state awareness of the need to challenge racism through formal legal means, an expanding literature has emphasised that this has also gone hand in hand with the emergence of new forms of racism. These new forms of racism, for instance Kundnani's (2001) 'new popular racism', or the 'xeno-racisms' of Fekete (2001) and Sivanandan (2006), are seen in terms of, on the one hand, cynical reference to legalistic measures for combating racism, and on the other hand, the securitisation of race relations as anti-asylum racism and the militarised border controls with which it is associated articulate with the war on terror to produce a new mode of racism that is closely associated with intensified forms of control and new modes of profiling and constructing racial categorisations. Here racialised ideas of crime and deviancy are presented to the wider public, for example through political speak, urban myths, the mass media and news coverage of current affairs, and even through the storylines of movies in the entertainment industry.

This has continued in more recent times, for example with the racial profiling of South Asian and Muslim young men in the period since 9/11, which has intensified since 7 July 2005, which has seen an unprecedented increase in the stopping and searching of South Asians under sections 44 and 45 of the Terrorism Act 2000: this enables the police and the Home Secretary to define any area in the country as well as a time period wherein they can stop and search any vehicle or person, and seize 'articles of a kind which could be used in connection with terrorism' (Terrorism Act, 2000, section 45).

The literature on racial profiling as a disciplinary practice emphasises its role in 'filtering' urban space (Khoury, 2009) by constructing some racialised subjects as 'invisible' (white) and so passed over by profiling regimes, or as is the case for some black and minority ethnic subjects, as hyper-visible (racialised) and 'out of place' to be picked up and constructed in terms of expected criminality (Khoury, 2009; Romero, 2008). The specific practices of racially profiled stop and searches authorised under section 44 of the Terrorism Act 2000 are also centrally concerned with intersections of raciality/spatiality since the practice involves the authorisation of blanket stop and search powers in designated areas without the need to prove any real grounds for suspicion. The practice itself therefore is centrally concerned with the racial marking of subjects as being 'out of place' (and undesirable) within the terms of a regime of racial spatialisation, and the sheer volume of racially profiled stop and searches under section 44 raises important questions about belonging, inclusion and marginality. Read against these statistics, which show, for instance, between January 2003 and December 2004 there was an increase of around 300 per cent in stop and search operations performed on South Asians, the following quotes themselves highlight the challenges we face in analysing race and racism post-Macpherson:

> Terrorists are likely to be linked to sectors of the community that, because of their racial, ethnic or geographical origins, are readily identifiable. (Lord Hope to the House of Commons Home Affairs Committee Sixth Report of Session 2004–2005: Terrorism and Community Relations, cited in Moeckli, 2007: 663)

> We should not waste time searching old white ladies. It is going to be disproportionate. It is going to be young men, not exclusively, but it may be disproportionate when it comes to ethnic groups. (Ian Johnston, Chief Constable, British Transport Police, 2005, cited in Moeckli, 2007: 662)

As Gabbidon et al. (2009) note, Chief Constable Johnston's plea not to waste time searching white older women makes no mention of the fact that elderly South Asian women are no more likely to pose a terrorist threat to society than are whites, and in so doing underlines both the empirical paucity of arguments in favour of racial and ethnic profiling and the racist nature of the practice. Despite, the Macpherson Report, the Race Relations (Amendment) Act 2000 and a government which denies that the state carries out racial profiling (or if it does it is somehow justified), the justifications of Lord Hope imply acceptance of racial profiling as necessary, and suggest that the provisions under which it is occurring override race equality legislation, as the following comment illustrates:

> Stop and searching under section 44 [of the Terrorism Act 2000] 'might require some degree of stereotyping in the selection of the persons to be stopped and searched and arguably, therefore, some degree of discrimination … [which would be] validated [under sections 41 and 42 of the TA 2000 to override the Race Relations Act 1976 and RRAA 2000]'. (Lord Scott to the House of Commons Home Affairs Committee Sixth Report of Session 2004–2005: Terrorism and Community Relations, cited in Moeckli, 2007: 663)

Indeed the problematic use of stop and search by the police has been recently highlighted, when in July 2010, the Home Secretary, following a ruling by the European Court of Human Rights, issued new guidelines which stated that the police would only now be able to carry out stop and searches if they had 'reasonable suspicion of terrorist activity' (*Guardian*, 8 July 2010). The new guidelines reflected concerns about the broad interpretation of sections 44 and 45, possibilities of racist victimisation and the threat to civil liberties. However, similar forms of racial profiling continue, and we suggest that these practices are able to work as a central mode through which regimes of racial spatialisation operate, and in so doing they highlight central tensions in these post-Macpherson times which fly in the face of the conservative literature which underplays the racist nature of profiling (Waddington et al., 2004), and which challenge the official rhetoric of formal equality. The allure of this racial profiling derives from the idea of protecting 'us' from the supposed 'dangerous others'. And, as Yuval-Davis et al. (2005: 515) rightly notes, following 9/11, 'we have seen an intensification of the criminalization of irregular migrants and asylum seekers, who can be portrayed as threatening and undermining core values of European societies. This supposed danger allows for the suspension of human rights and indefinite imprisonment'. This is despite there being a lack of evidence to suggest the fulfilment of this promise. Moeckli (2007: 661), for instance, notes that while tens of thousands have been searched as 'part of a concerted effort to focus law enforcement resources on certain ethnic groups', to date not a single South Asian has been charged with terrorism-related offences after having been searched under section 44 of the Terrorism Act (2000).

The racial profiling with which we are concerned therefore emerges from a wider field of power relations between black and minority ethnic people and the state, and is not specifically concerned with the war on terror per se, but rather with wider processes of racialised governance. For instance, it takes place against a rising tide of ethnic and racial profiling across Europe (De Schutter and Ringelheim, 2008), which has included cases such as the racial profiling of Roma passengers at Prague airport which were undertaken by UK immigration officials in the months prior to 9/11 (Moeckli, 2007). This has been a context marked by Europe-wide developments in the securitisation of immigration and asylum (Fekete 2004), in which the militarisation of anti-immigration surveillance has been linked to the suspension of basic human rights (Yuval-Davis et al., 2005). Within this context, the war on terror has converged with wider trends in the 'management' of immigrants and minorities across Europe, as the following comment illustrates:

> The war on asylum in fact predates the events of September 11. But after the London bombings of July 7, the two trajectories – the war on asylum and the war on terror – have converged to produce a racism which cannot tell a settler from an immigrant, an immigrant from an asylum seeker, an asylum seeker from a Muslim, a Muslim from a terrorist. We are, all of us Blacks and Asians, at first sight terrorists or illegals. We wear our passports on our faces or lacking them, we are faceless. (Sivanandan, 2006: 2)

But, it would be ignorant of context to suggest that the current expansion of racial profiling is taking place solely in response to the terrorist attacks of 9/11 and 7/7. Rather, it can be argued that this is part of an even longer historical trajectory regarding the 'demonisation' or 'criminalisation' of Asian Muslims, for example during colonial practices in the Subcontinent (Quraishi, 2005; Runnymede Trust, 1997; Wardak, 2000; and, Webster, 1997). Fekete (2001) notes that there has been a wider process of securitisation of minorities and immigrants in Europe which, mobilised around a 'xeno-racism', is focused and directed by security agencies, supranational bodies and intergovernmental organisations. However, at the same time, the figure of the hyper-criminalised South Asian (and Muslim) male did not emerge in response solely to the terrorist atrocities witnessed in 2001 and since. The discursive construction of South Asian youth in terms of criminality and the potential to pose an existential threat to 'mainstream' society predates 9/11, as we have seen earlier in this chapter, and certainly draws reference to discussions about the supposed lawlessness and inassimilability of these groups.

In particular, this criminalisation has occurred side by side with the government's 'community cohesion' policies, both as they resonate with older racist arguments about assimilationism (Worley, 2005) and as they intersect with the trajectories of the wars against asylum seekers and terror (Sivanandan, 2006) to articulate new forms of racialised governance, for example centring on 'xeno-racism', which are concerned with race and spatiality. This 'new popular racism' (Kundnani, 2001) is one which is concerned with raciality and spatiality, and yet it is one in which these dimensions frequently go under-explored. This is because the state, and its ideological apparata, has played a key role in demanding that we de-contextualise these discussions by focusing not on specific spatial and structural contexts from which the social problems sustaining this discourse emerged, but rather on the essentialised, pathological nature of black and minority ethnic subjects.

In terms of the concerns of this book, these being matters relating to crime and justice, it is important to recognise though that the black and minority ethnic victims of such a racist discipline do not passively accept their marginalised position. Rather, at different points and to varying degrees a form of resistance often takes place. This resistance, whether it is at individual or group level, aims to correct the wrongdoings of a racially biased criminal-justice system. It seeks to free its victims from a system that is dominated by agents of a state whose aim it is to maintain white power, regulation, control and authority over the black and minority ethnic body. Methods of resistance vary, and not all result in the desired outcome. However, what is of significance is the attempt to challenge the injustice and dominant power through the mutual reciprocity, agency and struggle that black and minority ethnic groups in marginalised positions pursue.

Discourse, method, race, crime and resistance

In this book we draw from a range of material, including (though not restricted to) pieces of fieldwork data, media representations, political discourse, and official reports and statistics. This approach reflects our express decision to offer an anti-essentialist account of race, crime and resistance based on a recognition that race is discursive. As such, we are concerned with discourse not simply as being textual, but rather as being bound up with all meaningful activities (Howarth and Stavrakakis 2000: 3) and interactions. The simplistic criticism that any consideration of discourse is simply about textual or imaginary practices is wide of the mark: discourse reflects the material conditions in which it emerges and takes in all meaningful social practices, and is even reflected in the organisation and functioning of institutions. For example, if a police officer stops and searches a black and ethnic minority person because s/he believes black and ethnic minority people are more likely than others to be guilty of certain forms of crime, this encounter does not occur completely outside of discourse. In other words, we are not dealing with pre-existing racist knowledges which exist outside the encounter between the police and the citizen, but rather a process through which these racist knowledges are simultaneously constructed through the encounter. Discourse is what constitutes the positions of different social actors engaged in any interaction, in relation to grammars for speaking about – constructing, in all senses, not merely speech or text difference. Discourse theory is not about denying the real conditions in which racism occurs, but is rather concerned with a recognition that there is no way of accessing the real other than through discourse. For example, when we speak of black and ethnic minority people, there is ultimately no way of avoiding the 'fact' that the various categories which we will use, and which will be operationalised by the state (for example), are all discursively constructed: IC1, Muslim, Asian, white, terrorist. We cannot access these without using language.

It is precisely because these are not fixed, essential categories that they are so contested: as Sayyid (2004) notes, the various categories for identity which dominate the British ethnoscape all emerge through processes of struggle and contestation. These contests are discursive – and of course, they are also material in so far as they occur in specific material contexts, using particular resources, and so on, although as Howarth and Stavrakakis (2000: 4) note:

> The distinctions between political, economic and ideological practices are pragmatic and analytical, and strictly internal to discourse. This is worth stressing because it distinguishes our approach from those approaches ... that use the concept of discourse, but regard discourses as little more than sets of ideas or beliefs shared by policy communities, politicians or social movements.

Our recognition of the importance of discourse to race informs the way in which we thus approach the subject conceptually and methodologically. As Sayyid and Zac (1998: 249–50) note, the decision to draw from discourse theory is not necessarily about its advantages over other empiricist approaches, but rather a recognition of the different perspective that can be gained from looking at the world in a slightly different way. We have deliberately avoided drawing into this work an in-depth and very technical approach to discourse, for which readers can easily turn to a range of other works (Howarth 2000; Howarth et al., 2000). Nor are we focusing this book on an engagement with 'cultural criminology'. As critical criminologists we are primarily concerned with the ways in which the conceptual horizons of discourse theory provide us with some alternative ways of exploring questions around race, crime and resistance which we believe are complementary to our commitment to critical criminology. This approach frames our understanding of the contested and contingent nature of the categories with which we are dealing, and leads into our emphasis upon the political nature of identities. It helps focus our attention on the hegemonic practices which stabilise the various conflicts, contradictions and contests which ensure that all social orders – even the most thoroughly racialised – are always unsettled. This approach is therefore implicit to our consideration of the immanence of counter-hegemonic practice which unsettles that racial order. Finally, our approach assists us in tracing out the ways in which discourse about race, crime and resistance is articulated across multiple dispersed and often unexpected sites or 'nodes', and how it organises these different articulations into a coherent racial politics concerned with governing racialised populations. For example, this approach allows us to consider the continuities and discontinuities between state practice and, for instance, the racial politics of the far right which is formally disavowed by the state without offering a totalising conception of a 'continuum' of racism or hate. Within this approach, the range of material from which we draw reflects different nodal points within a particular hegemonic discourse of race and crime in Britain today. This approach does not lead us to assume that some of these nodes should carry more weight than others; for example, as nodal points within a particular discourse, we are as concerned with particular political discussions as we are with 'empiricist' artefacts. Questions about the different empirical status of this material would therefore be second-order questions in our book: they would be pertinent had we drawn from a different conceptual vocabulary and adopted a different methodological approach. However, these are expressly not the terms of our approach. In fact, we believe that breaking out of the traditional empiricist focus which has dominated criminology provides us with additional opportunities to offer an account of race, crime and resistance by looking to some of the different nodes organised by the dominant discourse.

Book structure and content

One of the aims of the book is to allow its readers actively to self-reflect and critically engage with its content. To assist this process, each chapter finishes with a set of revision questions. Guidance on what your answers to these should cover can be found at the end of the book, and can be consulted once you have attempted to work through the revision questions for yourself. Also accompanying the book is a companion study website. This site can be accessed via SAGE, and contains the following material:

- Chapter summary
- Further reading
- Case study material

Although the book can be read in isolation from this material, it is envisaged that these additional sources will provide further background details on the main cases discussed in the chapter, as well as guidance on further reading material (accessible via SAGE) should you wish to read more on the subject matter.

In referring to contemporary case studies, including those from the authors' own empirical research, a critical consideration is given in the following chapters of the roots and modes of reproduced racial inequalities within the criminal-justice system, including other mechanisms of state and social control. This not only maps key issues in race and crime debates, identifies mechanisms of discrimination and exclusion, considers processes of discrimination and the assigning of stigmatised labels, for example 'deviance', 'black criminality', 'Muslim extremism', and so on, but also explores forms of mobilisation and resistance to these processes of racialisation. In considering the contemporary challenges to the critical analysis of race, crime and criminality, we unpick not only the persistence of race, but do so while paying critical analytical attention to its continuities and discontinuities in a specifically post-Macpherson context. To do this, the framework of analysis adopts a critical criminological standpoint and an anti-essentialist theoretical approach, which includes utilisation of post-modern critiques, such as Critical Race Theory and Black Feminist Critique.

Chapter 2, Crime Science?, considers how racialised ideas of crime and deviancy are presented to the wider public through urban myths, the mass media and entertainment industry, and in the news coverage of current affairs. The reader will be invited to reflect critically on the purpose and persistence of such views, and to assess the degree to which discussions on crime and criminal types can ever be free from processes of racialisation.

Chapter 3, The Politics of Hate, examines the use of hate as a common mode of racism. In doing so it questions the attempts that are routinely made to conceal and localise such racialised hate, which allows it not only to be hidden, but also legitimated, not least by state policy and practices themselves, which maintain a racialised order.

Chapter 4, Policing Racism or Policing Race?, critically examines the police and their troubled relationship with the black and minority ethnic community following publication of the Macpherson Report (1999), and asks to what degree have *real* changes been made, particularly in matters regarding the racist victimisation of black and minority ethnic people. In doing so, we consider whether the police can ever remove themselves from discriminatory ideas about racial hierarchy, especially when those ideas are commonplace in wider society.

Chapter 5, Courtin' Justice, provides a focus on the areas of prosecution and sentencing. Consideration is given to black and minority ethnic people's representation in the court docks, regarding their vulnerability and differential outcomes in comparison to their white counterparts. Their position as courtroom personnel is also considered, with the question being asked: is there fair representation and does this necessarily mean fair justice? It is argued that the courtroom is not a separate, neutral domain, but rather a crystallisation of societal power relations and a reflection of wider challenges facing the criminal justice system.

Chapter 6, Proportionate Punishment?, uses the case of asylum-seeking detainees, and in particular, the problematic practices of 'housing' and detention centres, to focus on the areas of punishment, prisons and probation. The chapter expands its analysis of biopolitical racism, by highlighting the dominance of racist biopower in punishment regimes.

Chapter 7, Victims' Rights and the Challenge of Discrimination, considers the issues of rights and citizenship. The chapter goes on to examine how certain groups are assigned labels, for example worthy victim or non-worthy victim, based on crude and biased racialised ideas, which go on to influence service delivery, and the enhanced risk of deviance presentation or experiences of secondary victimisation. The chapter considers how forms of collective mobilisation can be used to engage with institutionalised racisms and to promote change.

Chapter 8, Forms of Resistance, provides a consideration of both the individualised and collective forms of resistance to discriminatory practices. It discusses the ways in which these modes of resistance to racism can also be used to obtain positive outcomes. The chapter considers how now, more than ever, we have the existence of sub-groups and categories, who continue to collectively fight discrimination, but do so on a more flexibly defined basis. These forms of action, it is argued, are still underpinned by notions of resistance to racial discrimination and disadvantage, but are also diversified by factors such as religion, ethnicity and nationality.

Chapter 9, Researching the Agenda, gives a critical criminological coverage of some of the issues entailed in undertaking research into race and crime, for example gate-keeping, power and authority, accessing a marginalised group, undertaking research with over-researched groups, negotiating disclosure of findings, especially those that are critical of agency practices, and so on. A consideration is then given of how criminological knowledge about the issues is then constructed and utilised.

Finally, Chapter 10, Re-constructing Race and Crime, brings together the main arguments of the book and concludes with a call for critical criminology and other social science disciplines to re-construct the problematic messages that are presented about race and crime, and to examine critically the mechanisms of social, state and crime control.

REVISION QUESTIONS

1 In crime matters, why do we talk about the racial profile of suspects/offenders?
2 How is the notion of 'black criminality' sold to us?
3 Does 'white governmentality' exist in the criminal justice system? If so, where can it be found? How is it allowed to exist? What are the repercussions of its existence?
4 What are the key forms of 'race talk' in a post-Macpherson era?
5 What do criminologists seek to offer to the study of racism?

FURTHER READING

Bowling, Benjamin and Phillips, Coretta (2002) *Racism, Crime and Justice*. Harlow: Longman.
Gilroy, Paul (1982) 'The Myth of Black Criminality', in Martin Eve and David Musson (eds), *The Socialist Register*. Monmouth, Merlin. pp. 47–56.
Sivanandan, Ambalavaner (2006) 'Race, Terror and Civil Society', *Race and Class*, 47(1): 1–8.

2
Crime Science?

Age-old notions of 'black criminality' have been debunked. Their racist assumptions and discriminatory agendas have been revealed by criminology and anti-racists. For example, we know that the muggings moral panic of 1970s and 1980s Britain was based on unreliable data and racial stereotypes delivered by an over-zealous media and manipulated by those in power for their own political purposes. Yet, the muggings legacy remains, in that young men of black African Caribbean descent, who were its folk devils (Cohen, 1973), are still the focus of heightened police attention. For example, UK stop and search figures from 2007/2008 show that there were 1,035,438 stop and searches, of which 13 per cent were Black people. This is an increase of nearly eight times more stops and searches of Black people per head of population than of White people (Riley et al., 2009: 11). Their status of innocence or as victims of crime themselves is overlooked. Indeed, the consideration of the police as a force whose behaviour is problematic and biased is overlooked by a society which is ready to accept without closer scrutiny the idea of the 'black dangerous other'. This is despite the 'institutionally racist' findings by Macpherson (1999) and numerous other cases highlighting black vulnerability within the criminal justice system. In examining this racial bias, it is argued that such views of black criminality are presented through the mass media and by politicians. It is then legitimated in the eyes of the public, with the support of selective crime data and the statements of authority figures. For example, consider the outburst of Judge Ian Trigger in 2010 who, in sentencing an offender originally from Jamaica for drug offences, embarked on a tirade, in which he told the offender: 'Your case illustrates all too clearly that completely lax immigration policy which exists and has existed over recent years in this country ... People like you come to these shores from foreign countries to avail themselves of the generous welfare benefits which exist here' (*Liverpool Daily Post*, 10 May 2010). All this combines to further the crime agenda and wider societal agenda of a state whose interests are served by the existence of a racial hierarchy that places whiteness in a position of power and authority. In the past, state policies utilised those scientific racist ideologies to achieve a status of domination and control. For example, in Britain this related to the immigration of 'coloureds';

in the USA we saw Jim Crow and slavery; in South Africa there was apartheid; and in Germany there was the Final Solution under Nazi rule.

It is argued in this chapter that these racist ideas continue to be woven into state policies (albeit in more palatable ways) around crime control and other areas of social policy, such as immigration, education and mental-health services. For example, consider the plans proposed in the UK by Philip Holbone, Conservative MP for Kettering not only to ban the wearing of burkas in public (as is now the case in France), but also making it a criminal offence to wear a burka in public (McSmith, 2010). Similarly, consider the withdrawal of the UK's National Identity Card scheme in May 2010, yet the continuation of a separate but very similar scheme run by the UK Border Agency, which requires migrant workers, foreign students and family members from outside the European Economic Area to carry identity cards (BBC News, 27 May 2010).

The continued influence of racist ideology on state policy is based on expanding the 'black dangerous other' category, more so to an extent than had even been done in the past. This has meant moving beyond the image of the black African Caribbean deviant to include other black and minority ethnic groups who are not only defined solely in crude racial terms, but in addition are discussed under a array of ethnic and cultural categories, giving the appearance of a discounting of race. Here it is argued that these are attempts to mask a form of 'race talk' which still uses as its base the idea of a 'white norm'. This chapter considers how these racialised ideas of black deviancy and white victimhood are presented to us and legitimated by selective use of crime data, and then used by a state whose politically motivated interests are served by a positioning of white privilege. In doing so, it considers how such ideas have gained support in a society that at the same time has come to be obsessed with gene-mapping, criminal profiling, white victimhood, increased surveillance measures and pre-emptive policing strategies against those it views as suspect bodies, these being people of black and minority ethnic backgrounds.

The presentation of black criminality

The process of criminalisation is rooted in social reaction theory. It refers to the various 'institutionalised process through which certain acts and behaviours are labelled as "crimes" and "outlawed". It reflects the state's decision to regulate, control and punish selectively' (Chadwick and Scraton, 2001: 69), for example, as we have seen with the recent use of control orders against people of black and minority ethnic background, South Asians especially. Critical theorists in criminology have developed this analysis further, arguing that criminalisation does not occur in a vacuum. Rather, it is influenced by contemporary politics, economic conditions and dominant ideologies and is contextualised by variables of social class, gender, sexuality, age, race, religion and ethnicity. Indeed, black and minority ethnic people are far more likely to be perceived as criminal suspects, as opposed to victims (or non-participants) of crime as, for instance, we saw by the way in which officers from the Metropolitan Police Force treated Duwayne Brooks at the scene of the Stephen Lawrence attack. In this sense, crime is racialised. This is because the actions of deviant black and minority ethnic individuals are explained in racial ways, or are presented as the racial traits of an entire black and minority ethnic community. This is problematic, not only in its accuracy, but also because of the ways in which such groups are selectively monitored and disciplined. Gilroy (1987: 109) argues that the view of the 'blacks as innately criminal' is crucial to the development of new definitions of the black problem. It is important to note that this is not to deny that some black and minority ethnic people have sometimes been identified as the perpetrators of crimes which resemble the stereotyped images of which their populations are assigned to; rather the durability of these images and their remarkable ability to act both as a focus for popular anxiety about crime in general and as a sign for national decline, crisis and chaos is questioned (Gilroy, 2002). Similarly, in the USA during the same time, we saw a number of Latino and black African American drivers being stopped, following the release of law-enforcement guidelines encouraging officers to be suspicious of drivers who, amongst other things, drove rental vehicles, wore lots of gold jewellery, whose status didn't 'fit' the car they were driving and who represented (in their unsubstantiated and biased view) 'ethnic groups associated with the drug trade' (Harris, 1999, cited in Bartol and Bartol, 2005: 337).

The actual relationship between criminality and race in terms of race being a marker for criminal tendency has been debunked. Yet its ideas remain. Here the histories of race and crime show that the idea of 'the racial other' is a reoccurring theme dominant in European thinking. For instance, long before extensive contact between Europeans and people from other parts of the world, certain groups were portrayed as having a specific set of psychological attributes and character flaws which are attached to their skin. Here black, African or African Caribbean peoples were attributed characteristics of stupidity, laziness and violence; Asians were attributed characteristics such as deviousness and insularity; and those designated 'white' were given attributes of honesty, integrity and superiority of mind and character. However, it is argued that the older images of black lawlessness, for instance in the form of stowaways, drifters, pimps and drug dealers, are once again recurring. Gilroy writing in 1987 (cited in Bowling and Phillips, 2002: 77) used the examples of muggers, illegal immigrants, black extremists and criminal Rastafarians to illustrate the reproduction of black lawlessness. More contemporary images of reproduced black criminality include gun- or knife-toting gangsters – recall, for example, the Moses Mathias 'wanted' poster (BBC News, 17 August 2009). Here black (African Caribbean) men are presented as animalistic and savage criminals – consider, for instance, the depiction of the deviant subject in the 1992 film *Candyman*, whose blackness was key to the presentation of his terror and the vulnerability of his (white) victim. Even in the 1995 follow-up

Candyman: Farewell to the Flesh, when we learn of the deviant's background, of how he had engaged in a love affair with a white woman and for doing so was chased, tortured and attacked by an angry mob, the character is denied our sympathy as the story sees him continuing to chase and attempt to kill his white victim. Such depictions subconsciously send out the message that black and minority ethnic people are a threat and are in need of surveillance, control and removal. This is especially heightened within the context of 'white fear'. In comparison, constructions of Asian criminality were associated with a supposedly problematic community that was 'inward looking', 'tightly knit', self-regulating, passive and ordered by tradition. Their crimes were then often associated with dishonesty, fraudulent behaviour and incest. This too is often presented as deviant, if we take, for example, the panics surrounding arranged marriages which, following the Forced Marriage (Civil Protection) Act 2007, saw the use of Forced Marriage Protection Orders. It is suggested that the government's interest in forced marriages, accumulating most recently in 2009, with the UK's setting-up of the Forced Marriage Unit, is in this case opposed not so much on the basis of the harm it does for the women involved (and it is recognised that there is a problem – as discussed in the previous chapter), but rather because of the immigration panics surrounding Asian men. Asians have also been criminalised in the areas of fraud and assault. This group faced additional resentment as they were seen by some members of the white population as having imported a foreign culture into the country – a culture which in recent years is being presented as anti-western and an attack on Britishness. In particular, since 9/11, the Muslim population in Britain has faced a form of exclusion which presents them as extreme fundamentalists and terrorists.

It is argued that traces of the types of racial stereotypes that we have so far discussed can still be detected today. These characters are clearly based on nineteenth-century basic crude images of the black dangerous 'other', who is primitive and characterised by 'deep ambivalence' and savagery 'lurking just below the surface' (Hall, 1995, cited in Pilkington, 2003: 182). Pilkington (2003) argues that black and minority ethnic people have of course moved in the post-war period and diversified. But they are still seen as the 'other' – the problematic, different and dangerous 'other' who threatens 'us'. They are seen as different from white majority gaze, because this gaze is taken as the norm against which all others are measured (Ross, 1996, cited in Pilkington, 2003: 183). It is therefore 'a Eurocentric standard of measurement' (Park and Green, 2000: 15). One difference in more recent images is the shift in location and use of language. Here attempts are made to mask 'race talk', with a narrative that instead talks about *urban conflict* rather than *race and ethnicity* (Pilkington, 2003: 185). This is even more dangerous as it can be viewed as a more palatable way of still talking about black and minority ethnic groups and the supposed problems that they pose without appearing directly racist.

A powerful way in which such images of black criminality are so convincingly presented to us are in the abundance of negative stories that are found in media representations of black and minority ethnic groups – a simple internet search of key words such as 'black crime' or 'black culture' throws up examples of such stories. This is coupled with an ignorance of their experiences of racism, both everyday and structural, at the hands of a white majority society. In the media, they are presented as sub-normal. This was recently found in the work of Fawcett (1998), who looked at racist assumptions held about black and minority ethnic groups in Northern Ireland, which amongst others found the persistence of the view that 'ethnic minorities are different, inferior, uncivilized' (Fawcett, 1998: 112). In other media representations, they are presented as problems or deviants, in need of control, regulation or removal, as opposed to members belonging to society (Pilkington, 2003). Here black and minority ethnic groups are portrayed as a toxic foreign other, who are a 'threat ... first through their immigration to this country and then, when settled here, as posing a law and order problem' (Gordon and Rosenberg, 1989, cited in Pilkington, 2003: 184). This view remains today, although it has now taken a more sinister turn. This is the presentation of black and minority ethnic 'others' as 'the enemy within', whose presence now constitutes a serious level of indiscriminate terror threats. This has been generated by claims of British-born Muslims embarking on self-segregation strategies, fuelled by anti-British hostility. Here there is a majority view that Britain has supported *these* people, but *they* have actively rejected this help and chosen instead to attack British society. This also serves the purpose of validating self-imposed notions of white victimhood. Consider for example, the numerous news reports presenting these views, such as that given by the *Sunday Times* in 2006, which ran with the headline 'The Enemy Within', and commented:

> It is now self-evident that there is an enemy within Britain who wants to destroy our way of life. Most of this relatively small group of fanatics are British-born Muslims who have been educated here and brought up within our tolerant democracy. Those looking for the outward signs that identify them as full of hatred would be hard-pressed to find them. Many seem all too ordinary ... The great challenge for Britain is how to stop this and minimise the future risks. Nobody should underestimate the scale of the problem or the time needed. We already have a generation of disaffected Muslims who see any excuse, whether it is war in Iraq, Afghanistan or Lebanon, as a reason for killing their fellow citizens. (*Sunday Times*, 13 August 2006)

The message sent out in such news reports generates fear and panic, through the use of image distortion and emotive language. It should be noted though that African Caribbean people continue to be subjected to similar media distortions. Here they are still presented as belonging to a pathological culture, prone to criminality, and whilst other ethnic and religious groups are also now more readily seen as deviants, the important point to realise is that black and minority ethnic people are still judged to be incompatible with authentic forms of Britishness. Their difference of race, religion and ethnicity, and their status of the foreign 'other' are seen as a cause of their deviancy and criminality. A thematic examination of how black and minority ethnic people are presented and how this influences attitudes in lay society has shown the power of language and imagery, in terms of its word association, its selectivity and complete fabrication. For example, consider the Toxteth disturbances in 1981 and the selective visual presentations, which were largely of the 'rioters' armed with 'weapons' and the police in positions of bravery and defence. Some of the most common images associated with these events are those that represent the (black) rioter's aggressiveness and violent unruliness and (white) police defensiveness and brave pursuit of upholding law and order.

These 'representational strategies', which involve 'blurring the line between fact and opinion' (Malik, 2002: 87), appeared once again in the 1995 Brixton riots, where again images of black criminality were seen in abundance, and similarly no attempt made to humanise or contextualise the death of Wayne Douglas – the black African Caribbean man who died in police custody (Malik, 2002: 88). More recently, these racialised strategies were also present in the reporting of human displacement following Hurricane Katrina, which hit the New Orleans area of the USA in 2005. Here Katrina news reporting made representations of black criminality and used against it markers of white victimhood and heroism, evidenced not least by the white 'finding' and black 'looting' press images. Sommers et al. (2006) analysed three key aspects of media coverage of Katrina, focusing in particular on how race shaped the story. In doing so, Sommers et al. argued that media portrayals had the potential to both shape and reflect societal attitudes. It did so first in its use of language, when it described the survivors, most of who were of African American background, as 'refugees'. This was a problem because they were American citizens still within the USA borders, and, because the term 'refugee' is racially biased. Also of interest was how in articles where 'refugee' or 'evacuee' was used it appeared within ten words of 'poor' or 'black'. Second, there is the story angle of the Katrina reporting. Here there was a focus on violent crime, for example looting and 'violent crime wave'. In particular, reports described sniper fire aimed at rescuers, rampant homicide and roving gangs of youths committing rapes against teenage victims and even babies. On one occasion, there were even allegations, including those made by the CNN news channel, that gunfire was directed at helicopters which halted a hospital rescue mission. In fact it was later revealed by National Guard officials that no such attack took place (Piere and Gerhart, 2005, cited in Sommers et al., 2006: 6). The third illustration of the powerful relationship between media reports and lay attitudes was most powerfully reflected in the blogs and personal narrative accounts found on the web. Evidence of the influence of these types of new media resources to present racially discriminatory ideas is not new; for example, consider right-wing use of blogs on the web. In the case of Katrina, white supremacists responded by not only blaming the survivors for their fate, and proposing that aid strategies should just target the white survivors, but they also used the web to give 'warnings' that the African American evacuees would start a crime wave spree across the country.

However, of particular interest is that these discriminatory views were not restricted to extremist sites. Several mass e-mails began to circulate by people claiming to give 'first person' accounts (Sommers et al., 2006). Many of these described the African American survivors in stereotypical and racially discriminatory ways (Heldman, 2007; Voorhees et al., 2007). The cumulative effect of stereotypical and negative representations of black and minority ethnic people in this way, in the news especially as well as popular culture, is that it promotes 'racist commonsense' which serves and maintains racial inequality. True, media presentations can be negotiated by its audiences, but that interpretation is limited when that audience does not have first-hand experience. And let us not forget that sometimes those communities actually have no reason to challenge them, and in fact may benefit from not doing so.

However, it is also important to recognise that such forms of criminalisation are not always just about race, in its crude biological sense of the term. Often processes are intertwined with religion, culture, nationhood and ethnicity. Hence we also have a hierarchy of whiteness (Webster, 2008). This means that not all those referred to as white escape the portrayal as a criminal type, for example Irish, Maltese, Russians, Jews and others who have, at specific times, been thought of as a problem for the social order of England (Bowling and Phillips, 2002: 77). Consider also the work of O'Nions (1995), who argued that members of the travelling community have persistently suffered discrimination and prejudice from the rest of society. For example, the Criminal Justice and Public Order Act (1994) contains provisions which will reduce the number of traveller sites available in an attempt to discourage the nomadic way of life which has been central to the lives of many travellers for over 500 years. These are exclusionary practices aimed at forcing the traveller community to abandon their culture and traditions, by labelling them as 'work-shy' travellers, 'criminal' travellers or 'social parasites', and hence criminalising them (O'Nions, 1995).

Science, genetics and racial profiling

In the past, social scientific ideas about race were widely used to legitimate a racist discourse, and were used to gain support for the politically motivated exploits of state policies. In the UK, scientific racism was woven into immigration policy. Here there was the Alien Restriction Act (1919), which was used to prevent immigration into Britain, and the Commonwealth Immigrants Act (1962), which in particular and more overtly restricted immigration from the 'new' Commonwealth, for example, India, Pakistan and Caribbean – and not the 'old' Commonwealth which included Canada and Australia (Kundnani, 2007). Such immigration preference for white subjects was also seen in the case of the Bosnian refugees in Australia for whom the Australian government, and its people, has a 'humanitarian preference' based on the view that they would be more likely to integrate into the wider Australian community, and thus not disrupt social cohesion, due to their (white) European background. In comparison, at the same time, 'Iraqis, Iranians, Sudanese, Ethiopians, Eritreans and Afghanis also arrived in Australia as "quota refugees", but in considerably smaller numbers' (Colic-Peisker, 2005: 617). As it turns out, the Australian government's rationale about the Bosnian refugees has proved problematic given that, despite their 'white appearance', they are now experiencing discrimination, racism and xenophobia, often associated with the terrorism moral panic following 9/11 (Colic-Peisker, 2005).

Scientific racism can be found in the overlapping relationship between the eugenics movement and biological criminology, which were most popular in the USA and Europe from 1900 to 1930 (Webster, 2007). The eugenics movement in particular based its work on an attempt to improve the quality of human stock, which for them involved reducing the numbers of lower classes, the physically and mentally unfit, the criminal types and others who were considered as socially undesirable (Garland, 1985, cited in Webster, 2007: 14). In the USA and Europe, those of non-white background came under this last category. The result was a move towards forced sterilisation and genocide, both utilised in Nazi Germany. However, such sterilisation programmes were also widely supported in the USA, as a 'solution' to its 'race problem' which, as it argued, saw the 'negro' contaminating its 'high mental qualities' (Rentoul, 1906, cited in Black, 2003: 208–209). Here we saw social scientific ideas about race starting to be used in criminological explanations on crime and criminality, as a way of giving weight to views about 'black criminality'. For example, Lombroso (1899, cited in Bonger, 1943: 48–49) stated about the black African American men:

> ... the stifling of the primitive, wild instincts. Even if he is dressed in the European way and has accepted the customs of modern culture, all too often there remains in him a lack of respect for life of his fellow white men, the disregard for life which all wild people have in common. To them, murder appears as an ordinary occurrence, even a glorious occurrence when it is inspired by feelings of vengeance. The mentality is furthered in the Negro by his scorn of his white fellow-citizens, and by bestial sexual impulses.

Often these 'scientific' ideas were linked to religion, as a way to further 'legitimate' their claims; for example, consider Charles Carroll's publication of 'the Negro a Beast' and 'In the Image of God', both published in 1900, claiming that African Americans were not only genetically inferior, but also non-human, more like apes, and that the white race was naturally superior, as desired by God (Webster, 2007: 15).

Today such forms of 'genetically based racism' (Parrott et al., 2005: 3) have gained popularity, especially following the Human Genome Project, which ran from October 1990 to April 2003 in the USA, although with input from an international body of scientists (Bonham et al., 2005). This is one of the most notable human genetic research projects whose publically stated aim was to identify, for health and life insurance purposes, the genes associated with diseases. However, although the project also commented that it sought to prove once and for all that biological races did not exist, the project actually became known for adding weight to previously discounted claims about racial inferiority. As a consequence it was used to heighten racism, so much so that it has been described by some as having been used as a form of 'genetic colonialism' (Dodson and Williamson, 1999, cited in Mccann-Mortimer et al., 2004: 412). Even UNESCO's International Bioethics Committee in 1996 argued that its findings could be 'misappropriated for racist ends by those seeking whatever scientific support they could find to legitimate discriminatory beliefs' (Gannett, 2001, cited in Mccann-Mortimer et al., 2004: 412).

Today, a variety of legislation offers protection from many of the above practices, meaning that some of our basic rights are incorporated into law. On an international level, this includes a number of measures introduced to protect from the most dangerous consequences of racism, such as murder, genocide and enslavement, and includes the Convention on the Prevention and Punishment of Crime of Genocide (1948); Supplement Convention on the Abolition of Slavery and the Slave Trade (1956); United Nations Declaration of the Elimination of All Forms of Racial Discrimination (1963); United Nations Declaration of Human Rights (1948); International Covenant on Civil and Political Rights (1966); European Convention on Human Rights (1950); American Convention on Human Rights (1978); and African Charter on Human and People's Rights (1986).

In the UK, such rights are absolute, limited and qualified under the Human Rights Act (1998), and give us rights and freedoms that might not be covered by discrimination legislation, for example Race Relations [Amendments] Act (2000). In terms of race matters, human rights refer to issues around safety, dignity, society and our private life. It is about the right to equal treatment, and freedom from discrimination on (perceived) grounds of race, religion, ethnicity and nationality: 'People have the right not to be treated differently because of race, religion, sex, political views or any other status, unless this can be justified objectively. Everyone must have equal access to Convention rights, whatever their status' (Human Rights Act, 1998, article 14).

However, in reality, violation of legislation occurs on a regular basis, for example in terms of the victimisation of people of black and minority ethnic background, often at the hands of the state in the form of white governmentality. Here, the research evidence suggests that being of black and minority ethnic background is associated with a higher probability of receiving negative and discriminatory police treatment (see, for example, the work of Robert Reiner, 2000). Until recent years, young Asian men in general (Indians, Pakistanis and Bangladeshis) were underrepresented in all offence categories except assault. However, the late 1990s and early 2000s saw some changes. 9/11 and 7/7 were considered by many to be the responsibility of all Muslims not just the fundamentalists who carried out the attacks in the misguided view of Islam. This created a racist backlash directed against Asian Muslims (and anyone of Middle Eastern descent), who were consequently labelled as extremists, fundamentalists, terrorists and anti-Western/British. Despite the British government and some media efforts to point out that the enemy is terrorism and not Islam, and despite Muslim organisations condemning the attacks as un-Islamic (Pilkington, 2003: 277), far-right groups such as the British National Party gained a seats in elections, and the 2001 disturbances in Northern England revealed growing tensions between young British Asian Muslim men and the police. Kalra (2003) argues that there is now a growing shift in the targeting of black African Caribbean people to those of Asian Muslim background. However, this may be disputed if, for example, we remind ourselves of the UK stop and search figures from 2007/2008 provided at the start of this chapter, from which we can see that '13% were of Black people, 3% of people of Mixed ethnicity, 8% of Asian people and 1% of people of Chinese or Other ethnic origin' (Riley et al., 2009: 11).

However, some maintain that people of Asian background are now being significantly over-policed. Illustrating this are the disturbances that occurred in Oldham, Bradford and Burnley in 2001, involving Asian youth. Here we were presented with the idea of 'the enemy within', whose particular cultural, ethnic and religious difference was incompatible with British society. This made reference to Enoch Powell's ideas, in his calls for repatriation in the aftermath of the 1980s riots. Here Powell argued that as the black population in Britain would grow, they would not become part of British society but would instead remain distant and alien in ungovernable inner-city areas. From this would result violence and disorder. For Powell these were the 'facts' behind the 1980s riots. Years later, following the 2001 disturbances, we had the same panic, but different demons, in that black African Caribbean people were seen as having achieved some sense of integration into British society but the Asian Muslim community had not. This, the media, police and politicians argued, was now the root of divisions and troubles.

To further present the ferociousness and inhumanity of the 'rioters' of the 2001 Northern disturbances, as well as the urgency of the situation, it was argued that whereas earlier generations had risen up against the police and discriminatory disadvantage as a community, united in their anger, the behaviour of the 'young rioters' and the condemnation of the community leaders, who had failed in their role to control *their* people (Kundnani, 2007: 54), were illustrative of these communities falling apart from within, as well as from without. This created a panic that was based on the idea of the extremist and anti-British Muslim faith, a culture so alien to Britain that its violent actions were, therefore, all the more desperate. These groups were choosing to self-segregate, it was claimed, and in doing so they were also attacking British culture and values. This panic was heightened following the terror attacks of 9/11 in the USA and 7/7 in Britain. These events tied in to the whole anti-Islam feeling within British society – a feeling which not only the British National Party harnessed for support and popularity, but also the current New Labour government used to control, regulate and remove people of black and minority ethnic background.

These events were also used by the state in their push for a stronger and united British identity. Part of this involved not allowing migrant communities in the UK to establish themselves as separate and distinct cultural groupings that proceed to live in sub-isolation from mainstream British culture (McGhee, 2005). As Kundnani notes, 'a people that had been discarded for their class, excluded for their race, stigmatised for their religion, ghettoised and forgotten, was now blamed for refusing to mix' (2007: 54). What was inadequately considered though were factors such as segregation in housing and education, racism, discrimination, and racially motivated deaths (including lack of adequate policing) and deaths in police custody (including Ricky Reel, Steven Lawrence, Chris Alder, Michael Menson, Harold McGowan, Stellios Economou, Harold 'Errol' McGowan, and Jason McGownan, Leon Marshall, Liaquat 'Bobby' Ali, Alfonso Coley, Zahid Mubarek, Edita Pommel, Jan Marthin Pasalbessy and Colin Salt).

In such debates, British Asian Muslims clearly become the focus of the self-segregation claims. In addition, though, asylum seekers and others who are subjected to immigration controls, such as those from a black and minority ethnic background or from non-western countries who are viewed by the state as posing a threat to European values, have also been targeted, via restricted access, suspension of human rights, imprisonment, increased surveillance and identity checks (Yuval-Davis et al., 2005). These groups have been subjected to specialist measures in an attempt to be kept out of the UK. The most recent of these was an announcement made in June 2010 detailing a UK cap on the immigration of non-European Union workers (Watt, 2010). When access in wider Europe has been granted, they have been subjected to attempts to be forcibly assimilated, for example citizenship tests and forbidden dress codes (Fekete, 2004). Fekete (2001) highlights the particularly dangerous nature of this new form of 'xeno-racism', which is a form of 'racism against asylum seekers, (which) marries up the worst racist practices throughout the western world' (Fekete, 2001: 39).

Occurring also at a time when we were being told to fear and suspect terrorist behaviour, those of Asian background, such as international students, are now being increasingly put under surveillance in the likes of Denmark, Germany and Norway (Fekete, 2004). Indeed, more recently in the UK, plans were announced at a national admissions conference hosted by UCAS in April 2009, which saw lecturers in universities being asked to 'monitor' the movements and identity of international students, which the immigration authorities claim may be using their student visas as a cover for terrorist activity. This form of 'structured anti-Muslim racism' and 'institutionalised xeno-racism' (Fekete, 2004: 3–4) or, as Sivanandan refers to it, a form of 'xenophobia that bears all the marks of the old racism, except that it is not colour coded. It is racism in substance, though xeno in form. It is xenoracism, a racism of global capital' (2006: 2), was further highlighted by the new criminalised profiling regimes of the state, supported by the police and immigration officials (Fekete, 2005), with an increase in the use of predictive profiling measures, which now used in an attempt to identify terrorists before acts of terrorism, characteristics such as nationality, age, education and family background as markers of risk (De Schutter and Ringelheim, 2008). The racially discriminatory undertones of these are clear, regardless of whether they are presented under the euphemisms of ethnicity, nationality, community cohesion, British identity, and so on. Such ideas and policy interventions were able to gain support via notions of white victimhood. Thinking about whiteness in this way, as a system of privilege, is a huge source of anxiety for individuals who consider themselves white. Media coverage, political thought and indeed lay thinking embedded in us tells us that scrutiny of the dominant (white) rather than the minority (black and minority ethnic) racialised group is invalid.

Questioning 'race talk'

A variety of theories have been used to explain the apparently high rates of 'black crime', for example subculture of violence (Comer, 1985; Silberman, 1980; Wolfgang and Ferracuti, 1967); underclass thesis (Calvin, 1981; Wilson, 1987); new left realism (Lea and Young, 1984). However, it can be argued that all these theories 'needlessly assign criminal propensities to many non-criminal Blacks' (Covington, 1995: 560). It is argued here that, rather, critical analysis must consider the racist underpinnings of state policies on crime control, not only to highlight the continued existence of racist practices, but also in order to offer a more informed analysis of race matters. Here Critical Race Theory would be of use. Critical Race Theory emerged in the mid-1970s, in the USA, primarily, as a number of lawyers, activists and legal scholars realised,[1] more or less simultaneously, that 'the advances of the 1960s USA Civil Rights Era had stalled and, in many respects, were being rolled back' (Delgado and Stefancic, 2001: 4). Building on the insights of two previous USA-based movements, Critical Legal Studies and Radical Feminism, the Critical Race Theory movement was interested in the relationship between race, racism and power, with a particular concern for 're-addressing historic wrongs' (Delgado and Stefancic, 2001: 5).

Such a re-examination would first involve a critical analysis of why the state responds the way in which it does when faced with particular forms of deviant behaviour. For example, its view of the urban unrests (riots) is to explain it with a view that the Islamic and Christian faiths were so different that there was a 'clash of cultures', which led to 'self-segregation' and 'parallel lives' (Cantle, 2001; Denham, 2002). Furthermore, British Asian Muslims were now seen as 'the enemy within'. This leads the state to respond with harsher forms of policing and punishments. This was illustrated with the events in Bradford in 2001 where approximately 500 British Asian Muslim youth, most of whom were male, fought with more than 1,000 police officers (Alexander, 2005). However, what must be questioned is 'the (state's) attempt to legislate and control cultural bodies through the inscription of highly racialised institutional violence' (Alexander, 2005: 200). For example, the state responded to the 'Bradford rioters' by sending in over 1,000 police officers, many of whom were from riot patrol, and releasing a number of statements condemning the actions of the Asian rioters. In terms of sentencing also, there were stark differences and over-sentencing of the Asian youth. For example, consider the case of Asam Latif, who received a sentence of four years and nine months for rioting, after he threw six stones at the police; that of first time offender Shazad Ashraf, who had handed himself in to the police and was personally supported by Councillor Ian Greenwood, but later imprisoned for five years for throwing two missiles and waving his arms in a manner that would encourage others to participate in riot behaviour; and, that of Mohammed Manir, who received a prison sentence of four years and nine months for hurling two stones (Allen, 2003). As a consequence, it was claimed that a form of community sentencing was taking place (Allen, 2003: 47), in which the judge had been concerned with setting an example and sending a message to others in the community (Allen, 2003; Alexander, 2005).

What is of interest, though, is the way in which the Asian youth had been the focus of attention which laid the blame for the estimated £11 million worth of damages (Allen, 2003, cited in Alexander, 2005: 201) firmly at their door. No real analysis was made of the pre-riot context. It is also interesting, although of little surprise, that the Asian youth then became the 'folk devils'. Their behaviour was explained in crudely inaccurate and offensive ways. They were explained solely in terms of *their* supposed racially based (which incorporated religion, ethnicity and culture) deficiencies. As had been the case with other disturbances before, no serious acknowledgement or consideration was given to the underlying causes of their situation, which had led to their behaviour, for example their experiences of segregation in housing, education and employment; racism; discrimination; racially motivated attacks and in some case deaths; heavy-handed and over-policing methods; a failure to be protected from the regular presence of far-right groups, such as the British National Party and the National Front. Thus, whereas their elders had also previously resisted via other means,[2] this generation were unwilling to accept this second-class status. They felt that as born and bred British citizens, they and their parents and grandparents before them had contributed greatly to Britain, not least in terms of economic prosperity. The 'riots' could therefore be seen as an accumulation of frustration, despair and result of the constant racisms experienced by this group. They were *not*, as the media and politicians would have us believe, mindless acts of violence.

We therefore need to consider the social injustice element of the causes of riots. Here Benyon and Solomos (1987) make exactly this point, when they argue that we must view such disorders in terms of broader social injustice issues that are related to the political, social, cultural and economic contexts in which they occur.

This must be done in place of the idea of 'human wickedness' or a 'greed for looting' or 'black criminality' (Benyon and Solomos, 1987). This is because such unrest arises within the context of certain social, economic and political conditions, such as those stated above. They argue that these are conditions under which unrest may occur, but it is also important to recognise how there are in addition a series of other factors involved that help to explain the outbreak of disorder and the use of violence at a particular given time. Here, the tinder is created by these underlying conditions, but it lies dormant until it is ignited by a particular sparking event (Benyon and Solomos, 1987: 182). The sparking ignition in the Bradford case was not only the racist murder of the local Asian youth, but also an accumulation of despair at the social injustice felt by the 'rioters', some of which was rooted in racism, as well as having class and gender factors.

Second, this analysis must take into account the use of white victimhood notions, via a deconstruction of Western whiteness as the norm, and blackness (including all others such as non-Western whites) as a 'dangerous' label. Not only in relation to crime, but also in terms of general 'race talk', where a white rationale is used to justify discriminatory attitudes and behaviour. For example, consider the backlash of discriminatory behaviour against British Asian Muslims following 9/11. Here, the idea that black people have culture, and a problematic one at that, and that white people have civilisation is perpetuated and it is this perpetuation that needs to be challenged and changed (Khan, 1979, cited in Ely and Denney, 1987: 12). But the question is: how can these ideas be challenged, especially when ideas of white norm and even hierarchal ideas about white supremacy are so embedded in societal attitudes? Some of these important questions are present in British race-related studies that have incorporated critical whiteness analysis, which, designed by Critical Race Theory, asks us to re-examine the invention and use of whiteness (Delgado and Stefancic, 1991).

It is argued here that whiteness needs to be questioned and dislodged from its centrality and advantageous position. Its invisibility needs to be questioned in lay thought, political debates and even media messages (Dyer, 1997). Dyer sees the norms of self-control, rationality and order as white qualities. This also then creates the norms of 'others' as sensual, vivacious and of childish disorder. For example, consider the film *Dangerous Minds* (1995) which 'demonstrates a sustained attempt to devalue and homogenise minority urban experience, and inculcate white middle-class values, presenting them as rationale vis-à-vis irrational inner-city youth' (Garner, 2006: 261). The film, Henry Giroux contends, 'functions mythically to rewrite the decline of public schooling and the attack on poor, black, and Hispanic students as part of a broader project for rearticulating whiteness as a model of authority, rationality and civilized behaviour' (Giroux, 1998, cited in Garner, 2006: 261–262). So here we have the myth of the colonial saviour or even the white messiah, who saves his or her white people and also is able to provide charismatic leadership for the oppressed other. This fiction is to present whiteness (and virtually always maleness) as benevolent and selfless, and the people of colour encountered as in need of uplift and direction. Indeed, as Sivanandan states: 'White racial superiority is back on the agenda – in the guise, this time, not of a super-race but of a super-nation, a super-people, a chosen people on a mission to liberate the world' (2006: 1). This status of whiteness, in that it is rendered invisible, left unmarked, and associated with numerous privileges, must be questioned.

REVISION QUESTIONS

1 Given a lack of evidence, it is argued that the relationships between criminality and race/ethnicity are mythical. Yet these ideas persist. Why?
2 How has social science been used to legitimate racist oppressive practices?
3 What legislative protection is offered against racism? Does this prevent racist human rights violations from occurring?
4 What key theories and concepts have been used to explain data showing high rates of 'black crime'?
5 How can Critical Race Theory contribute to the study of race and crime?

NOTES

1 Prominent Critical Race Theorists include Derrick Bell, Alan Freeman, Kimberle Crenshaw, Angela Harris, Charles Lawrence, Mari Matsuda and Patricia Williams.
2 For example, in 1925, the West African students' association saw a student response set up to campaign against exploitation and racial prejudice and an end to colonialism. In October 1945, the Pan Africa Congress in Manchester met to pledge to fight for the complete and absolute independence of the colonies and an end to imperialism. In 1951, the West Indians' organised response to discrimination in the workplace at a factory in Merseyside met secretly in lavatories at first to take up cases of discrimination. In 1965, there was the first important immigrant strike which took place at Courtauld's Red Scar mill in Preston over the management's decision to force Asian workers to work more machines for less pay. In the 1980s Southall Black Sisters campaigned against virginity testing (Sivanandan, 1982: 3–6).

FURTHER READING

Covington, Jeanette (1995) 'Racial Classification in Criminology: The Reproduction of Racialized Crime', *Sociological Forum*, 10(4): 547–568.
Fekete, Liz (2001) 'The Emergence of Xeno-racism', *Race and Class*, 43(2): 23–40.
Garner, Steve (2010) *Racisms: An Introduction*. London: Sage.

3

The Politics of Hate

John: I've heard that if any white person goes down there [Deptford High Street] they gets mugged. The niggers just hang about all day sunning themselves, which is a waste of time for them, but then some poor kid comes along on his way home from work and they nick all his money.

Paul: My mum went over there [Deptford] once and she was nearly mugged. There's a video shop where they all hang out.

Mark: Me and John are going to school in Deptford, and that is a black area, you know. A blacks' paradise over there! (Research participants in Cohen, 1997: 262)

Britain is developing ghettos – literal black holes into which nobody goes without fear and trepidation, and from which nobody ever escapes undamaged. (Trevor Phillips, Chairman, Commission for Racial Equality, 19 September *Guardian*, 2005)

Hate crime is central to our understanding of the relationship between race and crime, because its commission and the responses of the state reveal much about the relationships between victimisation, marginality and nodes of power (Perry, 2001). Hate and its responses reveal the racialised boundaries underwritten by the rationalities of government, as they structure the moral and political limits of the social. In this chapter we explore some of the challenges this poses by considering two lacunae in discussions of race hate: the tendency to consider hate in terms which render it void of affective content, and the absence of a conception of the political in mainstream criminological theorising of hate crime. Our argument is that in order to understand the place of hate in contemporary racism, we need to reconsider its centrally affective nature, and acknowledge that hate is above all a political relation.

Contextualising the politics of hate

The recognition of hate crimes as a specific form of criminal activity has been a key element of rights-based campaigns by black and minority ethnic people, and it has tended to be the case that legislation governing hate has been passed in response to campaigns and resistance instigated by members of ethnically marked communities. For example, the campaign which followed the racist murder of Stephen Lawrence ultimately led to an official inquiry which revealed institutional racism in the Metropolitan Police Service's mishandling of the investigation and in turn led to legislative changes. However, new challenges have been posed by a context in which the war on terror has been accompanied by increased levels of race hate directed towards Muslims and those felt to resemble them (Frost, 2008; Poynting and Mason, 2006). This trend has witnessed increased politicisation by far-right groups around anti-Muslim sentiment (Githens-Mazer and Lambert, 2010), particularly in ways which emphasise white Britons as the real victims of the encounter with the Muslim other. At the same time, Muslims have been ambiguously positioned in relation to race relations legislation, and have engaged in campaigns for improved recognition and protection against anti-Muslim racism (Tyrer, 2011). These complexities of contemporary anti-Muslim hate illustrate the contestedness of hate and pose a number of challenges with which we are concerned in this chapter.

Any social scientist wishing to engage with the question of 'hate' must at some point address the founding question: 'what is hate?' The question is challenging: if we fall back upon legal definitions of hate then we are beginning from the premise that current legal definitions of hate are unproblematic. However, as we have just seen, we cannot rely on such assumptions. To begin from an uncontested acceptance of the state's understanding of hate is also problematic because of the ways in which the interests of the state can converge with the commission of particular forms of hate. For example, Pantazis and Pemberton (2009) have shown how the pursuit of the war on terror has been central to the demonisation of Muslims as an 'enemy within'. Another, more subtle, manifestation of this can be witnessed in the ways in which those who engage in hate crimes often tend to justify their actions through appeals to hegemonic norms and ideals, such as a defence of the 'nation' and 'race'. In other words, the state is not removed from the wider social relations which produce hate crime. At the same time, it is clear that hate is contingent, and socially constructed: what we understand as 'hate' is not necessarily what would have been thus understood a decade ago, and possibly not what will be understood as hate in another ten years' time. Chakraborti and Garland (2009) suggest that, among definitions of hate, Barbara Perry's (2001) conception usefully accounts for the impact of hate upon the participants in the encounter and their communities, and acknowledges the contingency of hate and its relation to power, bigotry and marginalisation:

> Hate crime ... involves acts of violence and intimidation, usually directed towards already stigmatised and marginalised groups ... it is a mechanism of power and oppression, intended to reaffirm the precarious hierarchies that characterise a given social order. It attempts to re-create simultaneously the threatened (real or imagined)

hegemony of the perpetrator's group and the 'appropriate' subordinate identity of the victim's group. It is a means of marking both the Self and the Other in such a way as to re-establish their 'proper' relative positions, as given and reproduced by broader ideologies and patterns of social and political inequality. (Perry, 2001, cited in Chakraborti and Garland, 2009: 5)

This definition has its strengths: it foregrounds struggles over power and subjectification, and it emphasises the radically intersubjective nature of hate. It also implies that the adoption of an anti-essentialist conception of identities as socially constructed can be a precursor to properly understanding both hate and the identities against which it is targeted. It also implicitly recognises the political nature of hate, in turn pointing to a further series of questions about how we can conceptualise the political, and how the political relates to the radical antagonisms which define hate crime. We add to Perry's definition a single emphasis, which we place upon hate as a mode of antagonism, in order to frame hate as fundamentally political. To establish this conception of hate, we return to the anti-essentialist grounds of Perry's conception of identities, to elaborate the ways in which 'self' and 'other' are accounted for as being negatively relational. In anti-essentialist terms, this conception of identities is often articulated with the concept of 'constitutive outside' in order to emphasise how the construction of identities as negatively relational also entails their positive affirmation through an acknowledgement of their difference from each other. As Hillier explains: 'For instance, a woman identifying as Caucasian has several constitutive outsides (male, non-Caucasian ethnicalities and so on). We tend to create an identifiable "us" by the delineation of a "not-us" or "them"' (Hillier, 2007: 37). For instance, hegemonic conceptions of 'black' and 'white' are constructed around a series of binary oppositions and exclusions which associate whiteness with the essential traits which are constructed as lacking in blackness. Thus: white modernity/black backwardness; white decency/black criminality; white civilisation/black barbarism, and so on.

This attempt to 'close' identities through the construction of an external antagonist (Howarth, 2000: 105) forms the basis of the post-Marxist, anti-essentialist account of the political offered by Ernesto Laclau and Chantal Mouffe. Laclau and Mouffe (1985) develop a conception of the political centred on the recognition that all social relations are relations of difference which entail the construction of antagonisms, an understanding of which is central to our ability to grasp the political itself. Thus, what puts the political into the contemporary politics of hate is the social construction of white racial identities through the social construction of opposing non-white (increasingly, Muslim) identities which are represented as an external antagonist interrupting the expression of white national identities. This conception is important to this chapter for three reasons. First, it centres the political nature of all modes of antagonism rather than leaving it implicit to hate but undefined. Thus, it builds into our conception of hate an understanding of the political itself. Second, forms of race thinking are naturalised and hegemonic, and as such frequently go unproblematised. To frame our exploration in terms of a politics of hate sutures the cleavage which is established in popular discussions of race between respectable, everyday, hegemonic racisms, and the exceptionalised racisms of hate crimes. Third, as a result, the introduction of a conception of the political allows us to explore the politics of hate. In other words, since the political reflects struggles over social boundaries (Howarth 2000: 106), our conception of hate as a centrally political relation helps us to analyse the hegemonic practices employed to maintain a stable racialised order. Race hate is centrally political because it entails a radical intersubjective relationship articulated through antagonism.

I hate you so much right now: affect and hate

'Hate', 'fear', 'threat', 'panic', 'anxiety', 'terror', 'guilt', 'belonging', 'patriotism': racisms are steeped in the lingua franca of affect and emotion in a way surprisingly under-theorised in even the most excellent discussions, such as that offered by Bowling and Phillips (2002: 118–127). Unsurprisingly, the legal framework surrounding hate, for instance the Racial and Religious Hatred Act (2006), also voids it of affective content, with 'hate' not even of itself a prerequisite for hate crime (Chakraborti and Garland, 2009: 4). But far from being a nebulous and fuzzy distraction from the business of dealing with the 'real', 'material' business of dealing with hate, affect and emotion complement analysis of the governmental rationalities they infuse. In order to establish this, we first need to briefly consider hate in relation to racialised governmentality.

Hate crime is often associated with white working-class disadvantage, both in the political discussions about the contemporary rise of the far right which tend to pathologise white working classes as racist to exceptionalise racism, and in the rather different academic treatments (Ray and Smith 2004). In respect of the latter, Paul Iganski's (2008) research in London suggests that although political economies of hate crime illustrate important socio-economic factors, there is not a uniform relationship between deprivation and race hate. In this light, it is important to note the attention paid by an established literature to the idea of a 'continuum' of hate (Frost, 2008: 567) which is established across different structural positions and in varying relationships to institutions of state and civil society. We find this helpful in illustrating the links between the state and hate which we noted earlier in the context of the war on terror. However, we seek to modify this notion of continuum based on a recognition that any racialised order is always an unstable equilibrium (Omi and Winant, 1994), open to critique and riven with contradictions such as side-by-side state practices of ostensibly challenging racism while in reality perpetuating it. To effect a conceptual shift away from an implied linear continuity towards a recognition of these discontinuities enables us to better understand the politics of hate for two reasons. First, rather than glossing over the similarities between different actors with a superficial unity, it allows us to consider how the fraught alignment between them arises. For instance, it would be superficially attractive, but ultimately simplistic and empirically unsustainable, to read our opening quotes and conclude a *de facto* equivalence between race hate on the streets and an argument expressed by the head of the Equality and Human Rights Commission. Second, the hegemonic struggle to unify these divergent positions in spite of their discontinuities reveals sites of real-world resistance and symbolic spaces opened by critique (such as those to which we turn in later chapters). If we find idea of continuum essentialist, then we are concerned with how social actors in different structural positions can become aligned through the exercise of white governmentality. For example, we are concerned with how social actors who themselves experience marginality can enact forms of hate which, during the war on terror, have converged with the interests of the state. This line of analysis places under scrutiny routine attempts to conceal technologies of power by exceptionalising and localising hate as an aberration at the margins, among the socially excluded and those on the extremist fringes of politics (Hesse, 1997). Instead, we prefer to emphasise the role of hegemonic practice in stabilising the contradictions and challenges (Howarth, 2000) faced by a racialised order, and creating the sense of stability across multiple dispersed and often contradictory nodes.

We thus re-emphasise a politics of hate partly because its seeming imprecision is in fact a reflection of the ways in which it works to suture a wider repertoire of racist rationalities and techniques across varying structural positioning and in differing relationships to key institutions of the state and civil society and loci of power. Hate is not an ill-defined concept, but a loose depiction of a political relation of racism which bears witness to the centrally affective and emotional terms that structure racist discourse. Following Deleuze (1992), recent work on biopolitics has increasingly focused on the radical dispersal of governmental power across civil society, rather than its condensation within particular disciplinary enclosures (for example, school, prison, police). This is seen as entailing a shift from the Foucaultian notion of discipline through discursive construction (as 'mad' or 'bad') towards control through the direct accessing of the body via affect and emotion (Clough, 2003). While it is beyond our scope here to explore the wider implications of this, we are concerned with how the mobilisation of an affective politics aligns subjects and subjectifies them as an expression of racialised governmentality. This reading of affect as central to biopolitical practice has tended to be associated with the influence of Deleuze's re-reading of Foucault (Deleuze, 1992).

Any Foucaultian reading of surveillance practices implies, for example, the ways in which subjects practise self-surveillance as a result of the anxiety caused by their awareness of the panoptical powers of surveillance. Thus, emotion works as an economy which links the state with its subjects, as Sara Ahmed (2004) has argued. Noting that the 'love' of race and nation expressed by white supremacists is closely linked to the hatred they display towards racialised others, Ahmed suggests that affective and emotional states are not essential and immutable, but that as they work to align bodies and subjects with each other (and against others), they circulate between subjects and are subject to slippages. For example, to Ahmed, hate is figured for white supremacists who construct the other as interrupting their own love for nation (Ahmed, 2004: 117). But these affective and emotional states also travel: to Ahmed they slip from one object of hate to another, so that those who are hated come to resemble one another (2004: 118). In turn, this politics aligns subjects, precisely because they appear so fluid:

> In such affective economies, emotions do things, and they align individuals with communities – or bodily space with social space – through the very intensity of their attachments. Rather than seeing emotions as psychological dispositions, we need to consider how they work, in concrete and particular ways, to mediate the relationship between the psychic and the social, and between the individual and the collective ... emotions work by sticking figures together (adherence), a sticking that creates the very effect of a collective (coherence), with reference to the figures of the asylum seeker and the international terrorist. My economic model of emotions suggests that while emotions do not positively reside in a subject or figure, they still work to bind subjects together. Indeed, to put it more strongly, the nonresidence of emotions is what makes them 'binding'. (Ahmed, 2004: 118)

In the context of contemporary politics of anti-Muslim hate, fear and anxiety about Muslims – Islamo*phobia* – are central to the ways in which Muslim otherness is constructed in contrast to white normalcy, as we noted earlier. Meanwhile, fear of the other has been mobilised by the state during the war on terror in a discourse appropriated by far-right groups such as the British National Party and the English Defence League (Githens-Mazer and Lambert, 2010). Thus, a broader emotional and affective politics of victimhood emerges, with attachment to nation appearing to work alongside fear, resentment and hatred of the other in the emergence of a contemporary politics of hate. Whether we agree with Ahmed's (2004) conceptualisation of a slippage between affective states, or whether we instead emphasise the idea that hatred of the other is discursively overdetermined into fear as a means of attempting to justify this politics and make it appear a proportionate response to the threat posed by the other, it is clear that a politics of affect is central to contemporary struggles to maintain the racial order, and that part of its success is based upon the resignification of hatred as anxiety as a means of justifying racism.

The progress made by the state in challenging the racisms of the powerful appeared to have reached its zenith with the recognition of institutional racism in the Macpherson inquiry (1999) into the Metropolitan Police Force's handling of the murder of Stephen Lawrence and in the attempts to combat institutionalised racism through the Race Relations (Amendment) Act (2000). New offences of racially and religiously aggravated criminal damage and assaults were created under the Crime and Disorder Act (1998), and an offence of religiously aggravated assault was created when the Act was amended by the Anti-Terror Crime and Security Act of 2001. At the same time, the broadening of working definitions of race-hate crimes employed by the police has emphasised victims' perceptions. These measures were intended to impact not only on the perpetrators of hate, but also on the state agencies whose abilities to deal with them were hampered by problems of institutional racism. Thus, the powers granted to police to deal with such crimes, and the expectation upon them to meaningfully act, were issued in parallel with increased sentencing powers for courts to deal with such crimes.

However, the superficial impression of significant progress by the state in recognising the extent to which it had become ravelled up in the problem of race hate has been challenged on a number of levels. First, these gains were accompanied by a counter-trend through which the state itself engaged in a radical critique of its 'multiculturalism' strategy, along with a process of increasing securitisation of integration (Birt, 2009) and asylum which came to coalesce during the war on terror with the emergence of a widespread anti-Muslim racism (Fekete, 2004) and the construction of a new suspect community (Pantazis and Pemberton, 2009). Second, during this period the political far right was able to capitalise upon this wider construction of 'aliens' and 'Muslims' as posing an existential threat to Britain by mobilising around a specifically anti-Muslim racism. In doing so, far-right groups emphasised the idea that the true victims of race hate in Britain were the white working classes, and they focused on trying to mobilise members of white working-class communities in a politics of hate directed against Muslims. For example, although critics of the far right English Defence League have highlighted its links to known extremists and focused on its racism (Taylor, 2010), the group has been keen to brand itself as simply defending against the threat posed by Muslims (Townsend 2009). We have selected this case study as the focus for this chapter because it perhaps best exemplifies the importance of being aware of the complex politics of hate which frames the context in which hate erupts in its criminalised forms on the street (and elsewhere). On the one hand, the emergence of Muslims as a focus for racism – or even as a proxy through which to undertake racist acts against non-Muslims – reflects a series of wider tensions and contests over the regulation of racialised social boundaries, and merits consideration in its own right. On the other hand, the attempt by far-right groups to mobilise white working classes in a politics of Islamophobia has led to an increasing panic about 'working-class racism' which requires further unpicking to explore the ways in which the racisms on the margins are framed by the decisions and hegemonic moves made at the centre of society to stabilise contested social boundaries. Thus, we need to move away from essentialist conceptions of race which discount Muslims' experiences of anti-Muslim racism, and interrogate essentialist accounts of 'white working-class racism' at the margins to recognise its links to hegemonic practices at the centre.

By 2009, it seemed that a moral panic was emerging around white working-class race hate. This had been some time on the horizon, but had been overshadowed by government priorities in focusing anti-extremist work against Muslims, rather than white racists. This focus had resulted in warnings that the state needed to deal with the rise of far-right extremism (Local Government Association, 2009). By late 2009, the concern over the emerging politics of hate had turned into a moral panic about the radicalisation of the white working classes, and led Communities Secretary John Denham to announce action in October of that year which was targeted against the spread of far-right extremism into working-class communities, to tackle the alienation and disaffection assumed to be making white working classes vulnerable prey to the racist far right (Communities and Local Government, 2009; Verkaik, 2009).

The moral panic was fuelled by the continued growth of the far-right British National Party, and by the emergence of a second, smaller group, the English Defence League. These groups had both been keen to emphasise their respectability, and to distance themselves from less savoury aspects of the far-right extremism scene. For the British National Party, this included playing down a number of key incidents in its recent past, including Holocaust denial by its leader Nick Griffin and Griffin's 1998 conviction under section 19 of the Public Order Act 1986 for publishing or distributing racially inflammatory material. The task was challenged, though, by a series of other incidents which have demonstrated the far right's continued espousal of a politics of hate, including the 2009 arrest of over 30 people when a far-right terrorist plot was foiled amid the largest haul of weapons and bombs on the UK mainland since the Irish Republican Army was active in the early 1990s (Birt, 2009: 57). Another huge cache of bomb-making equipment had been uncovered in 2006, and led to the arrest of a former British National Party council election candidate in Lancashire in connection with a far-right terror plot (*Nelson Leader/Pendle Today*, 2006; *Burnley Express*, 2007). That case almost exactly coincided with the trial in Norwich of three racists who had planted a nail bomb in a house inhabited by migrant workers (BBC News 2006). Such cases resonated with David Copeland's 1999 terror campaign, in which he had planted a series of nail bombs targeting gay people and ethnic minorities, with the intention, among other things, of causing a race war.

Activism by far-right groups was also involved in creating tensions which spilled over into violent disturbances in towns and cities across the north of England during the summer of 2001, as first Oldham, then Burnley and finally Bradford went up in flames as diasporic BrAsian communities responded to social exclusion and provocation by taking to the streets and engaging variously with the state and the racists. Amid the division and disorder, the British National Party gained a substantial number of votes in the Oldham West constituency in June 2001, just days after the riots (and just days before an Asian family was burnt out of their off-licence business in an Oldham arson attack) (Renton, 2003; 2005).

Far-right activity following the 2001 disorders continued to target Muslims, and although the growth of the Islamophobic far right has been increasingly associated with increased suspicion fostered by the war on terror (Githens-Mazer and

Lambert, 2010), it was also facilitated by the ambiguous positioning of Muslim communities vis-à-vis Britain's race relations legislation. For instance, in a number of incidents during 2008, far-right supporters appeared to be testing the limits of the law through a series of incidents in which anti-Muslim leaflets would be distributed, members arrested, and then activists would stage protests which would neatly coincide with the release (without charge) of the arrested activists. In November 2008, British National Party leaflet distributors were arrested in Liverpool city centre, and later released uncharged. This followed the controversial clearing just months earlier of a British National Party councillor from Pendle in Lancashire, who had distributed leaflets entitled 'Islam – a threat to us all', stereotyping Muslims as responsible for the British heroin problem. In June 2009, the British National Party tried similar tactics in London, distributing an Islamophobic leaflet which depicted an old photograph of white people to bemoan the end of the way 'London used to be'. By September of that year, it was leafleting in Essex with a very blunt message: 'No mosques in Loughton.' Other cases involved the arrest of a British National Party campaigner for allegedly calling a woman a 'nigger' while distributing Islamophobic leaflets in Wanstead (*Wanstead and Woodford Guardian*, 2009).

By targeting a group ambiguously positioned by the legislation, the British National Party was able to raise its profile and publicise its message in a year in which the 2008 European Parliamentary elections saw Griffin and a second candidate, Andrew Bron, elected to represent constituencies in the north of England. Closely associated with these forms of activism was the increasing prominence of a loosely structured group of far-right activists called the English Defence League. Reported to have links with soccer-hooligan groups, the English Defence League (Booth et al., 2009; Taylor, 2010) has played a largely complementary role to the British National Party with which it claimed to have no connection, by mobilising white working class people around an anti-Muslim message. English Defence League 'marches', often focused on highly symbolic causes such as an end to mosque building, or claimed to oppose the Islamification of Britain and the spread of Islamic law. Despite a lack of evidence that Britain is being Islamified or subsumed under an Islamic theocratic regime, these represented highly symbolic ways of representing the idea of a Muslim threat to British ways of life. A number of English Defence League protests occurred during 2009, many of which appeared to be associated with disorder, including a violent protest in Birmingham (Hines and Pitas, 2009). The focus of the protests was Muslims, although they were facilitated through social networking websites with seemingly innocent names such as 'British Citizens Against Muslim Extremists'.

Cases such as these reflect the growing activism of the far right amid a contemporary politics of hate which has entailed pursuing racist agendas against Muslims in the knowledge that members of this group lack the level of legal recognition provided to members of other minorities. This included outlandish claims made by the leader of the British National Party that white Britons had become victims of a 'genocide' (Taylor, 2009); that black and minority ethnic Britons should be regarded as 'resident foreigners' (*Daily Mail*, 2009); and that he no longer considered London to be a British city because of the extent to which it had become 'ethnically cleansed' by these 'resident foreigners' (Hazelton, 2009). The rising appeal of the far right also coincided with an economic downturn, as Britain's economy slumped into recession from 2007 onwards. The potent cocktail of increasing unemployment, a far-right demagogue with an elected mandate and mob frenzy were enough to convince the state that action needed to be taken. In 2009, the government announced that a programme would be put into place to deter young working-class whites from being influenced by the far-right politics of hate. This bore an ironic parallel to the state's attempts to prevent the radicalisation of the sworn enemies of the far right (Muslim youth) under its Prevent strategy.

From the centre to the margins ... and back again

Anti-Muslim racism (Islamophobia) emerged in the early 1990s following the increasing movement among British Muslim communities to define themselves in terms of what Meer (2008) sees as a quasi-ethnic Muslimness, rather than on the grounds of ascribed racial or ethnic categories. The condition of possibility for the emergence of Islamophobia was the prior emergence of 'new racism' (Barker, 1981), a form of racism which disaggregated phenotypal markers of racial difference and resignified them in cultural terms to emphasise notions of essential 'cultural' difference rather than immutable biological characteristics (Barker, 1981). Islamophobia reflects these logics both because it has seen the repackaging of racism directed against groups racialised as phenotypically different around ideas of the (racialised as) culturally alien Muslim, and because it has been the focus of new stereotypes about the cultural alienness of Muslims as a group who are racialised as being discretely bounded in themselves (and existing in opposition to other racial groups, such as Griffin's 'indigenous [white] Britons'). Islamophobia reflected changes to the nature of racism, but also became the focus of a series of contests over the nature of the racial order itself. These were played out in a curious, and at times rather cynical, set of discussions which attempted to fix the meanings of racism in essentialist terms around a static and essentialist conception of race which worked to deny Muslims legal protection against Islamophobia as a form of racism (Meer, 2007, 2008). This hostility to the notion of Islamophobia reflected an important line of defence of the contours of the established racialised social order (Tyrer, 2011), positioning Islamophobia ambiguously in relation to the law and framing the far right's increasing emphasis on mobilising around anti-Muslim racism as a defensible form of prejudice in line with its attempts to reposition itself as respectable. Opposition to legal protection against anti-Muslim racism *qua* racism was an important component of Islamophobia (Khan, 2006; Meer, 2007; Tyrer, 2011), and worked hand in hand with the claim that to protect against Islamophobia would stifle free speech. As such, the struggles over the extent to which anti-Muslim racism should be recognised and subject to legal coverage took the basic form of a struggle to maintain the shape of a particular racial order, and an ideological rearguard which was mobilised in defence of the idea of the immutability of essential notions of race (Sayyid and Vakil, 2011).

The emergence of the contemporary politics of hate occurs in this context as a mode of contesting and protecting that racial order, which is precisely why it has so self-consciously drawn upon the hegemonic discourse of the war on terror to emphasise ideas of a Muslim threat. This reframes our understanding of this politics of hate, since by adopting an anti-essentialist perspective which emphasises the political nature of hate, we are able to acknowledge the contingent and contested nature of racialised identities. This includes recognition of the fluidity of Muslim identities and a recognition that essentialist moral panics about a stereotypically white working-class racism are problematic: the contemporary politics of hate is played out on a terrain shaped by wider hegemonic struggles over the nature of the racial social order. The far right's attempts to mobilise socially excluded members of white working-class communities in a politics of hate do not constitute the distinctly working-class project that today's moral panics would assume, but are another locus in a hegemonic struggle to regulate racialised boundaries, in which the far right has capitalised on fears of the other whipped up by the media and the state in the war on terror (Afshar et al., 2005: 263), and reflect a 'mainstream mood' involving a 'culture of unashamed questioning of the cultural practices and national allegiances of British Muslims' (Amin, 2003: 460). The far right has mobilised this politics of hate by appealing to familiar and hegemonic symbols and representations of Muslim otherness, and by cynically capitalising on the ambiguous positioning of Muslims vis-à-vis race relations legislation.

There is nothing new about the idea of working-class racism: Enoch Powell's famously racist 'rivers of blood' speech was greeted, for example, by trade-union marches of support. What makes the contemporary politics of hate so significant are two features. First, it is framed by the emergence of wider hegemonic operations to stabilise the challenges to the established racial order. In this light, the contemporary politics of hate (as it is played out by actors appealing to the white working classes) is significantly not essentially working class, but rather there is a politics at play through which white working classes are the proxy through which hegemonic notions of racialised social boundaries are being regulated. Second, it is significant because the dominant modes for recognising working-class racism is itself, in its pathologised, caricatured and exceptionalised forms, working-class racism, fascism, and so forth.

The emergence of the moral panics around working-class racism takes its form precisely at a point at which the state appears to have made some progress in dealing with the 'race' question. But there has not been dramatic progress by the state (Bourne, 2001), for gains were almost immediately accompanied by a reversal, as the state engaged in a far-reaching critique of official modes of dealing with minorities. This critique coalesced around a series of deeply conservative policies framed by conservative, Putnamesque notions of social capital which mistook cause and effect for racism, and perpetuated the myth of self-segregating communities through the adoption of community cohesion policies (Worley, 2005), as the state began to question as having been too radical the very model of multiculturalism which had been gradually adopted some 20 years earlier precisely because of its conservative potential to depoliticise black and minority ethnic youth. This has been supplanted by wider processes of securitisation/militarisation of immigration and asylum (Fekete, 2004) and by the securitisation of integration (Birt, 2009). With the state's claims to be progressing in combatting racism undercut by its wider positioning within the context of a heavily securitised 'new popular racism' (Kundnani, 2001), the impression of being serious about racism is attained by focusing solely on exceptionalised forms of racism – the racisms at the margins, which can be disavowed as fascistic or working class.

Working-class racism associated with far-right mobilisation thus emerges on the margins to echo the discourse of the centre which has represented various racialised others, most notably Muslims and asylum seekers, as undermining Britishness and threatening 'ordinary' white Britons, but is demonised as aberrant in order to disavow the centre's own racism. It is not, then, part of a continuum of hate, but rather another nodal point in the articulation of a variegated and often contradictory politics of contemporary racism. This is important, for racial boundaries are policed not only by the construction of a racialised non-white other as deviant and different, but also by shoring up the boundaries of whiteness itself, where those deemed to be furthest from the ideal white liberal subject, the socially excluded, for instance, are part of a terrain being fought over at the boundaries. We see this with the ways in which American eugenics against 'poor white trash' went hand in hand with anti-miscegenation measures aimed at policing racial boundaries and keeping African Americans subordinate. In today's politics of hate, sections of the post-industrial sub-proletariat are deviantised as a way of recuperating a pure sense of liberal whiteness at the centre, one unencumbered with the question taint of racism.

How those at the margins are mobilised in this politics of hate is also part of a more significant process. While the far right has been keen to allude to the similarities between its racial politics towards immigration, and those of the mainstream parties, the latter have found their only defence to be by reconstructing the British National Party as unreconstructed Nazis. This strategy was most noticeable during Nick Griffin's appearance on the BBC's *Question Time* programme in October 2009, when he was questioned over his Holocaust denial and his links to the Ku Klux Klan by panellists. This was a way of disavowing the racism of the British National Party in the face of its appropriation of the state's language of fear and anxiety. The British National Party's politics therefore emphasise the fallacy of the idea of a simple continuum of hate. While mainstream parties may have legitimated its racial politics by fuelling the wider context of anxiety about the other and constructing immigration as a serious problem, the British National Party has distanced itself from this mainstream politics of race through its anti-establishment rhetoric. But the ability of the British National Party to hegemonise is based not only upon the role of mainstream political projects in politicising the 'Muslim' question and pursuing wholeheartedly the wars on terror and on asylum, but also on the role played by the mainstream parties in creating the political vacuum within which this politics of hate can be articulated and can appeal to white working classes.

Chantal Mouffe (2005) has explored the broader post-political context which frames this process, pointing out that the growth of the European populist far-right has been facilitated by the emergence of a post-political consensus politics which seeks to suppress traditional left–right distinctions in the pursuit of a post-adversarial politics. In Britain this was reflected in New Labour's occupation of centre-right territory through the pursuit of neo-liberal policies to which it added a marginal 'social' edge. The 2010 general election similarly brought to power a Conservative–Liberal Democrat coalition government which has softened traditional right concerns by articulating them with some concern for causes such as social justice and environmentalism. Although there remain differences between the parties, the overarching ideological split which traditionally generated the left–right distinction is softened by the hegemony of neo-liberal consensus. An impression of wider choice is created, because groups likely to benefit most from neo-liberal policies now have a range of parties occupying the centre-right ground from which to choose, but in real terms there are actually fewer distinct political projects and identities on offer. This is particularly true for those who are less likely to benefit from neo-liberal consensus politics: working classes who most need the welfare state which has been diminished by both New Labour and its successor coalition government, for instance. The crowding of the centre-right ground creates a political vacuum which is filled by a populist far-right which positions itself as anti-establishment in order to capitalise on political disillusionment, and which claims to be the true representative of 'ordinary' people. Not without irony, the chief source of their populism is the hegemonic anti-Muslim, anti-immigrant popular racism they espouse: a form of racism which has been fed by the policies pursued by the New Labour government (Younge, 2009a, 2009b). The fates of white and black and minority ethnic working classes have become strangely intertwined, as they have been politicised by the discourse of the centre. They are racialised differently: one group (Muslims) as insufficiently British, the other (white working classes) as inadequately white (given its distance from white privilege), and thereby the locus of attempts to regulate the racial boundaries of our social system, through a politics of hate and division at its boundaries (a politics then blamed by state policy on the working classes themselves, on account of their failure to integrate, lack of social capital etc, in the emergence of a wider neo-liberal pathology of the poorest segments of our society).

This helps frame in terms of contemporary biopolitical racism, or control racism, as we term it, the continuities and discontinuities between different modes of contemporary racism amid the politics of hate. The noteworthy feature about the contemporary politics of hate is not that it exists on the margins of society, among the socially excluded and the fascist, in spite of all that the state has done to achieve progress in the face of race hate, but rather that it is defined by hegemonic preoccupations with regulating racialised boundaries. In other words, dominant approaches which exceptionalise hate by blaming it onto a stereotyped and pathologised working class are deeply problematic and disguise the role of the state and its ideological arms (such as the media) in hegemonising the grounds for its appeal.

REVISION QUESTIONS

1   How does an understanding of hate as political help frame our understanding of its role in structuring the boundaries of the social?
2   What does it mean to suggest that hegemonic responses to 'racism' and 'hate' tend to exceptionalise them in order to conceal their importance?
3   How can an understanding of white governmentality help us to explore the complexities of the relationship between populist discourse on race and the commission of race hate at marginalised and exceptionalised sites?
4   How are emotions (such as hate, resentment) mobilised through the exercise of racialised power?
5   Why has white victimhood become such a powerful way of popularising racism?

FURTHER READING

Ahmed, Sara (2004) 'Affective Economies', *Social Text*, 22(2): 117–139.

Chakraborti, Neil and Garland, John (2009) *Hate Crime: Impact, Causes and Responses*. London: Sage.

Colic-Peisker, Val (2005) 'At Least You're the Right Colour': Identity and Social Inclusion of Bosnian Refugees in Australia', *Journal of Ethnic and Migration Studies*, 31(4): 615–638.

Hesse, Barnor (1997) 'White Governmentality: Urbanism, Nationalism, Racism', in S. Westwood and J.M. Williams (eds), *Imagining Cities: Scripts, Signs, Memory*. London: Routledge, pp. 85–102.

Kundnani, Arun (2001) 'In a Foreign Land: the New Popular Racism', *Race and Class*, 43(2): 41–60.

4

Policing Racism or Policing Race?

The troubled relationship between the police and the black and minority ethnic population has a much longer history than any state or criminal justice agency would ever want to admit. However, it was only really from the 1960s onwards, with reports of the police going 'nigger hunting' (Hunte, 1966, cited in Bowling and Phillips, 2002: 8), that serious recognition was given to the culture of racism that existed in the police. The racially discriminatory behaviour of the police and the impact of this on their policing role and status of legitimacy was widely documented by criminologists (Holdaway, 1983; Lambert, 1970; Smith and Gray, 1985), whose studies highlighted the various ways in which the police, as individual officers and as an organisation, had a racist culture which would filter through to the way in which it provided a policing service, especially when black and minority ethnic people were concerned. Unfortunately, it took the publication of the Macpherson Report in 1999, an inquiry into the killing of Stephen Lawrence, a black African Caribbean youth, in London in 1993, for there to be any real meaningful acknowledgement of the sinister impact of police racism for black and minority ethnic people, especially when they are victims of a racist crime. Even then, the report's findings were initially contested by the Metropolitan Police Force (Bourne, 2001). In outlining the ways in which police racism existed and how this negatively impacted on the black and minority ethnic community, the Macpherson Report (1999) was hailed as significant, not only for its 'exposé' element,[1] but also for its recommendations to deal with the evil of racism within the police. For instance:

> The process of implementing, monitoring and assessing ... Performance Indicators in relation to ... the existence and application of strategies for the prevention, recording, investigation and prosecution of racist incidents; ... achieving equal satisfaction levels across all ethnic groups in public satisfaction surveys; ... levels of recruitment, retention and progression of minority ethnic recruits; and levels of complaint of racist behaviour or attitude and their outcomes. The overall aim being the elimination of racist prejudice and disadvantage and the demonstration of fairness in all aspects of policing. (Recommendation 2, Macpherson, 1999)

Police Services should through the implementation of a Code of Conduct or otherwise ensure that racist words or acts proved to have been spoken or done by police officers should lead to disciplinary proceedings, and that it should be understood that such conduct should usually merit dismissal. (Recommendation 57, Macpherson, 1999)

Now, just over ten years since its publication there is an opportunity for a more detailed analysis to be made on the Report's legacy. The need to do this is especially urgent, given that we are, as discussed in previous chapters, living in times of new forms of racism and 'xeno-racism' (Fekete, 2001; Sivanandan, 2006), which allow the police, one of the frontline agents of the state and a key institution within the criminal justice system, to continue to *police* race.

Within the context of a post-Macpherson era, this chapter seeks to examine the degree to which the police have made progress in being able to undertake policing duties in a non-discriminatory, fair, accountable and legitimate way – as was called for by Macpherson (1999). It does so by providing an updated and context-specific examination of the impact and significance of the Macpherson Report in cases of racist violence, suspects in custody and police-officer representation. In focusing on research undertaken into the Police Service of Northern Ireland, the chapter asks whether a post-Macpherson police force functioning in a society organised around the hegemony of whiteness, whose service it is argued continues to protect the needs and interests of the powerful, can ever develop a policing practice that is genuinely and adequately free from racial bias. It seems not when we consider police abuse of black and minority ethnic groups when on and even off duty. For example, consider the case of the South Yorkshire police officer, PC Paul Dawson, who racially abused taxi driver Abdul Rafiq, who refused to take him home after a night out (*Sheffield Star*, 28 May 2010).

Strained relations and Macpherson

The police routinely exercise considerable discretion in their enforcement of the law. However, when talking about black and minority ethnic people, there is concern as to whether such police discretion actually means discrimination. Here research evidence suggests that being young, male, of a black and minority ethnic background, unemployed and economically disadvantaged is linked to a higher probability of being stopped, searched, arrested, detained in custody, charged, making complaints against the police (especially of assault) and failing to have these complaints substantiated (Lambert, 1970; Lea and Young, 1984; Skogan, 1994; Smith and Gray, 1985). Until recent years, young Asian men (Indians, Pakistanis and Bangladeshis) were underrepresented in all offence categories except assault. However, the late 1990s and early 2000s saw some changes. An accumulation of 9/11[2] in 2001, and the northern riots in the same year, demonised young Asians, seen ultimately with far-right groups such as the British National Party gaining a foothold and seats in the European elections of May 2009. All this saw growing tensions between young Asian Muslim men and the police. So much so that Kalra (2003) argues that there is now a growing shift of target from African Caribbean to Asian Muslim males, evidenced not least by increased police surveillance and use of stop and search of Asians under the Police and Criminal Evidence Act (1984) and Anti-Terrorism Laws (Riley et al., 2009; BBC News, 10 June 2010).

Police discrimination and black and minority ethnic people's vulnerability has been widely documented, and crystallised in recent years by the Stephen Lawrence and Jean Charles de Menezes cases. Often, racialised youths are here presented as the deviants, as opposed to wider social issues being considered, such as bias, marginalisation and incitement by racist organisations (Ray and Smith, 2004). Kalra (2003) argues that 'police lore', this being the routines and customs that the police apply when dealing with people, means that black and minority ethnic people are marked for special treatment. This then has an impact on how that group sees both the police and themselves (Apena, 2007). For example, the 1994 British Crime Survey on what the public thought after their encounters with the police found: 21 per cent whites, 39 per cent African Caribbeans and 40 per cent Asians were dissatisfied. Gaskell and Smith in their study found that 'young blacks do plainly see some good points about the police. They recognise the need for good policing, but object to the way it's done' (Gaskell and Smith, 1985: 261–263). Similar findings were more recently presented by Apena (2007), whose sample reported feeling as if they were not treated with fairness in their encounters with the police. This resulted in viewing them in a number of ways, which ranged from 'general indifference', as one respondent (Tony) commented, 'I don't really pay any attention to them', to some having a sense of hatred for them, as one respondent (Robert) noted: 'I hate them … I would never call the police.' The respondents were able to validate these views by making reference to experiences in which they felt the police had treated them differently because they were of black and minority ethnic background (Apena, 2007: 217).

It is argued that such problems are found in the particular culture found within the police. Such police 'cop culture' is defined by Reiner as: 'the orientations implied and expressed by police officers in the course of their work' (2000: 85). Some, such as Waddington (1999, cited in Reiner, 2000: 85) argue that there is a gap between police attitude and behaviour, suggesting that officers fail to enact in practice the attitudes they have articulated in the canteen or in interviews with the researcher, and so 'cop culture' in this way is not only harmless, but also performs an important 'stress release' function. However, of concern here is the view that attitudes and behaviour cannot be separated so neatly, and that cop culture regularly seeps into police practice, which is even more problematic for black and minority ethnic groups given that racism is a core part of that culture. The existence of this has been well documented; for example, Reiner's original work in

1970s Bristol found that many police officers would often give adverse comments about the city's black and minority ethnic population. Similar results were later found by the Gifford Report (Gifford et al., 1989) and Simon Holdaway (1983).

The scene today remains the same; see, for example, Holdaway (1996), Bowling (1999), Sharp (2002) and of course Macpherson (1999). The only difference is that many police officers do not openly express such attitudes.[3] Indeed, more recently, since the tragic events of 9/11, a 'new racism' (Fekete, 2001) which excuses focused concentration on black and minority ethnic groups has emerged, meaning that 'to be a Muslim is to be under suspicion' (Younge 2001, cited in Pilkington, 2003: 277). Although this relates to the wider public view of Muslims, it can also be seen as one that strongly manifests itself in the police force. Here, evidence shows an increase in the amount of police stop and searches of Asians, in particular young Muslim men. For example, Home Office figures show that in 2002/2003 nearly 3,000 Asians were stopped and searched under the Police and Criminal Evidence Act (1984) and Anti-Terrorism Laws, which is a 36 per cent increase – compared with a 17 per cent increase for whites (Home Office, 2004). More recent figures of stop and searches carried out in 2007/2008 tell us that of those stopped and searched, 13 per cent (20,273) were black. Indeed, there were almost eight times more stops and searches of black people per head of population than of white people. In addition, 16 per cent (12,360) of Asian people were stopped and searched, which is twice as many per head of population than of white people (Riley et al., 2009: 28). Indeed the Anti-Terrorism Crime and Security Act (passed in December 2001) permits the unlimited detention of suspected terrorists and gives the police new and extended powers, for example extension in the power of the police to remove and confiscate disguises. The fear within black and minority ethnic communities is that in the current climate, they will be especially targeted by the police and security services (Pilkington, 2003: 277). Figures of stops and searches from 2007/2008 certainly add weight to this fear. For example, under sections 44(1) and 44(2) of the Terrorism Act 2000, 117,278 searches of people were made in 2007/08 compared with 37,197 in the previous year, which is an increase of 215 per cent. Of this figure there was a 277 per cent rise in the number of Asians being stopped and searched (Riley et al., 2009: 29). Of interest is the actual number of arrests for terrorism related offences. For example, Home Office figures (2009: 9) show that of the 213 arrests made in 2007/2008 under anti-terror legislation, 74 went on to be further charged, 19 incidentally for 'non-terrorism related criminal offences' and another four for 'failure to comply with duty at Port and Border Controls', with 136 being 'released without further charge' and another 11 being 'transferred to immigration authorities'. These figures certainly suggest that there is a racially based policing of citizenship. Considered even more disturbing in light of allegations of illegal searches being carried out following police misuse of section 44 (BBC News, 10 June 2010).

There are two main effects of police racism in this sense: (i) the criminalisation of black and minority ethnic populations, even though studies have shown that this group are less likely to commit crime than their white counterparts (Bowling et al., 1994 and Runnymede Trust, 1994, cited in Skellington, 1996: 163); and (ii) ignoring the crimes perpetrated on black and minority ethnic people, and even treating them as if they were themselves criminals – for example, note how there has been no 'moral panic' about racist violence on black and minority ethnic groups, despite the fact that in the UK, more than 61,000 complaints of racially motivated crime were made in 2006–07 (Ministry of Justice, 2008), a figure which no doubt is only a small fraction of true numbers. The police's lack of failure to protect black and minority ethnic people from racist violence, including data about their disappointment, low levels of trust and lack of faith in the police, has been widely documented; see, for example, Bowling's (1996) East London study. This was also evident in the context of the urban disorders which occurred in a number of northern English towns during 2001 (Kundnani, 2001; Rhodes, 2009). Black and minority ethnic groups report feeling as if the police fail to protect them from violent racism, even when it is clear that they are the victims, as we saw in the cases of the Stephen Lawrence (Lawrence, 2006) and 2001 urban disorders (Rhodes, 2009). Studies indicate the continued failure of the police to deal sufficiently with reports of racial violence; racist stereotyping by police officers themselves when dealing with members of black and minority ethnic community; the tendency of the police to deny or even play down the racial motive; and problems in what is reported to the police as racially motivated incidents and what is recorded by them as such (Bjorgo and Witte, 1993; Bowling, 1999; Bowling and Phillips, 2002; Gordon, 1990; Holdaway, 1983; 1996; Maynard and Read, 1997; Reiner, 2000; Skogan, 1994).

Such discriminatory policing is well known by social researchers and members of the black and minority ethnic community. However, with the Macpherson Report (1999) and television documentaries such as Mark Daly's *Secret Policeman* exposé in 2003, the problem has now been more publicly recognised. Our concern is with the legacy of Macpherson (1999), and the degree to which real changes have been made in the police force, especially in the policing of racist violence.[4]

Racial violence has a long history in the UK. For example in 1919, there were a number of serious attacks on black and minority ethnic people in the dock areas of Britain, including Liverpool. The late 1950s saw black people becoming a particular target for white racist youths. The 1960s saw 'paki-bashing' and attacks by white skinheads. The 1970s saw racial violence and harassment escalate – as illustrated in the *Blood on the Streets Report* (Bethnal Green and Stepney Trades Council, 1978) which reported on the violence suffered by Bangladeshi community in the Spitalfields area of Tower Hamlets. The 1980s and the 1990s saw the situation worsening; for instance, between 1988 and 1993, official Home Office statistics showed that 'racial incidents' rose by over 80 per cent – although care must be taken with the interpretation of a 'racial incident' which the police define as 'any incident which includes an allegation of racial motivation by any person' (Skellington, 1996: 82–88). Today, on top of the racial violence faced by

Britain's more established black and minority ethnic population, those from other backgrounds are also finding themselves targets, for instance members of the Muslim communities, Eastern European economic migrant workers and asylum seekers. This is evident in the daily reports of racially based attacks, such as 'Race hate murder man found guilty' (BBC News, 10 November 2009), 'Man jailed for repeated racist attacks' (*Halifax Courier*, 27 May 2010) and 'Man punched after racial abuse' (BBC News, 3 February 2010).

It is important to remember that the vast majority of racially motivated crime goes un-reported. Suggested reasons for this include: the victim's shame of their victimisation, fear and intimidation, attacks being too numerous to report, viewed as being part of life and the black experience (Bell et al., 2004; Gordon, 1990; Jarman and Monaghan, 2003; Skellington, 1996; Smith and Gray, 1985; Virdee, 1995). However, despite a variety of legislation[5] under which racist incidents can be prosecuted, an overwhelming reason for under-reporting points to the black and minority ethnic community's lack of faith in the police (Sharp and Atherton, 2007). Reasoning for this was evidenced in the case of Stephen Lawrence where Macpherson (1999) addressed the issue of racist violence and harassment, as well as its policing. He also highlighted the role that police discrimination played – for Macpherson, the failure of the police investigation into the murder of Lawrence was not attributable to overt acts discrimination by individual officers acting out of their personal prejudices, but stemmed instead from the occupational culture of the police (Pilkington, 2003: 255). Macpherson concluded that the Metropolitan Police Force in this sense were institutionally racist. Macpherson's definition is now taken as authoritative: 'the collective failure of an organisation to provide an appropriate and professional service to people because of their colour, culture, or ethnic origin. It can be seen or detected in processes, attitudes and behaviour which amount to discrimination through unwitting prejudice, ignorance, thought-lessness and racist stereotyping which disadvantages minority ethnic people' (Macpherson, 1999: para. 34).

Macpherson (1999) led to the Metropolitan Police as well as other forces making a number of changes, for example 'Policing Diversity: Protect and Respect' strategy (Metropolitan Police Force, 1999) and the ACPO Hate Crime document (Home Office, 2005). Some argue that improved policing is self-evident, as seen in the case of Anthony Walker, a black African Caribbean teenager in Merseyside, who was killed in July 2005. The Walker family themselves praised the work and sensitivity of Merseyside Police Force. However, given that from the very start parallels were drawn between the Walker and Lawrence cases, and following the high-profile coverage that the Walker case was given, not least by Merseyside Police Force's well-oiled public relations machine, it seemed that police forces are able to successfully police racist violence, one must ask whether the Walker case was indicative of real meaningful changes, or whether it was due to a carefully engineered investigation underpinned with the desire *present* the impression of change. This appears so when we consider Merseyside Police Force's eagerness to highlight the Walker family's praise for their work. This is illustrated in the following, an extract taken from the *Daily Post*:

> While an inquiry into the Metropolitan Police investigation into Stephen Lawrence's murder concluded the force was guilty of 'institutional racism' and had made a catalogue of errors, Anthony Walker's family have nothing but praise for Merseyside Police. Mrs Walker said: 'That was 13 years ago, when Stephen Lawrence was killed, and times have changed. The police's determination and efficiency in their investigation was there to see. We appreciated it. Detective Chief Inspector Peter Currie, who led the investigation, said shortly after Anthony's death, one of his sisters did express doubts about the police. He said: 'I asked her "What would give you faith in us?" and she said, "If you catch whoever did it". After we charged Taylor and Barton, I went to the Walkers' house and saw the same sister. I asked her "Have you got faith in us now?" and she put her arms around me and said "Yes, I have".' (*Daily Post*, 1 December 2005)

In comparison, the 2005 case of Jean Charles de Menezes suggests that little has changed in the police force. In this sense, it is maintained that the post-Macpherson changes have done fairly little to remedy the situation, as also illustrated in the findings of the Morris Report (2004) and the Calvert-Smith Report (Commission for Racial Equality, 2005). Indeed, a few years after Macpherson, the police force's emphasis is no longer on recognising institutional racism, but on factors such as self-imposed segregation, as seen in the official response to the 2001 riots in the northern cities of Burnley, Bradford and Oldham, which has been to lay much (but not all) of the responsibility on the Muslims (Pilkington, 2003: 277). It has also been seen in the arguments around a supposed intelligence-led policing approach, which continues to be defended despite the shooting of Jean Charles de Menezes. This policing approach tells us that members of the South Asian communities should now expect to be stopped by the police more often, not as an instance of racial profiling, but as a valid response to heightened terrorism, security threats and intelligence-led policing efforts (Rowe, 2009).

Black people within police environments: custody and career

Negative attitudes towards black and minority ethnic police officers indicate the firm presence of racist views. These have been widely documented. For example, in his study of police officer attitudes, Roger Graef (1989) reported the following:

Detective Sergeant: You know why there aren't more black coppers? They're too fucking lazy, that's why. I think they're scared of their people. And I don't think they've got the brain power for it either. I'm sorry but that's how I feel. You can get a whole community, you wouldn't get an O level between them. They're so bloody arrogant, they really are, certainly the people I come across

Police Constable:

in the West Indian community. I do know a couple who are quite nice guys, but 90 per cent of them – they really are arrogant. And totally 'anti'. Most of them are bloody born here. Yet they all live in their own communities, which is not right. What's the matter with other people? They think there's a war between them and us.

Police Constable:

What annoys me is the sheer arrogance of these arseholes who try and teach us Human Awareness Training. Theirs is the only one point of view. In my opinion, that coon with the ghetto blaster is a man who is terribly selfish. He doesn't give a monkey's about anybody else. He could be just as happy more quietly but, having no self-discipline, he doesn't give a shit about anything. Why is their point of view right and my one wrong? 'You're a racist'. It's absolute crap. It's become a moron's chant. (Respondents in Graef, 1989, cited in Rowe, 2004: 47)

Of concern is the way in which Graef's respondents claim that their views emerge *from* their own police-work experiences – suggesting that views are evidence based. However, we suggest that police work is pre-loaded with officers' racist assumptions and nourished within the discriminatory elements of 'cop culture' (Reiner, 2000: 85). They then use them to re-validate their views and embark on racist police work.

This was echoed in the undercover investigation undertaken by BBC journalist Mark Daly, who in 2003 spent a year at the Bruche Police Training Centre in north-west England, and then working as a probationary constable for Greater Manchester Police – a force which has previously launched 'Operation Catalyst' to implement the recommendations of Macpherson (1999). In purposely looking at the first-generation of post-Macpherson police training and their recruits, Daly not only revealed the prominence of racist views and sympathies for far-right political groups amongst trainees, but also trainees' intentions to act on those racist views once on duty:

PC Pulling:

A dog that's born in a barn is still a dog, a Paki born in Britain is still a fucking Paki.

PC Hall:

I'll stop him cos he's a Paki. Sad innit but I would. He's a Paki and I'm stopping him cos I'm fucking English. (*Laughs.*)

PC Salkeld:

Asian, Paki. It's fucking built in lad. It's built in since you were fucking two.

PC Harrison:

I class them as one thing and that's it, Pakis. (Officers in Daly, 2003)

Macpherson (1999) recommended that 'the Home Secretary and police authorities' policing plans should include targets for recruitment, progression and retention of minority ethnic staff ... [and] that the Home Office and the police services should facilitate the development of initiatives to increase the number of qualified minority ethnic recruits' (paras. 64–65). Although it can be argued that the Metropolitan Police Service is more racially and ethnically diverse than it used to be (pre-Macpherson), it remains a fact that only 8.2 per cent of its officers are drawn from black and minority ethnic groups, with those in high-ranking positions still largely being drawn from white backgrounds (*The Economist*, 2008: 72). This is surprising given the early presence of black and minority ethnic staff in the police, with Norwell Roberts being the first black and minority ethnic person to join the British police force in 1837.

In attempting to deal with the disproportionate representation of black and minority ethnic police officers, a number of recruitment campaigns and progression initiatives have in the past been launched, for example Nottinghamshire Police's 'Positive Action' (Nottinghamshire Police, 2010) Thames Valley Police's 'Community Recruitment Network Team' (Thames Valley Police, 2009) and the Metropolitan Police Force's 'Equip to Achieve' (Metropolitan Police Force, 2010). Forces have often sought feedback from black and minority ethnic people on such recruitment campaigns. For example, research into Lothian and Borders Police Force's use of photographs in specialist advertising and recruitment campaigns (Ramsay, 2006) consulted both police officers and community members from various black and minority ethnic groups. They found that although some good efforts were being by the Force to recruit underrepresented groups and improve community relations, sometimes they tried 'too hard to show everyone how diverse they are which can come across as unnatural' or deployed officers in 'tokenistic' roles (Ramsay, 2006: 10–13).

These not only sought to increase numbers, but in addition reflected the police's attempts to dispel the view that black and minority ethnic officers entered the police as second-class recruits, a commonly held view, as Holdaway (1996) found in his study. Post-Macpherson, specialist recruitment efforts are often accused of being a desperate and non-genuine attempt to meet recruitment targets and to fill equality and diversity criteria at any cost, even if it erodes the esteem of potential recruits, not least because they will be the target of ridicule or questioned about their merit, by colleagues and the public.

These ill-considered recruitment attempts have also been criticised for the way they fail to consider the retention and career progression of officers, and ultimately the removal of racism from the police. Indeed, landmark cases, some reported in the press, others not, have also illustrated that once a person of black and minority ethnic background makes it into the police force, their career is short lived or made difficult due to the racism of their colleagues and superiors. For example, in 1990 a Nottingham industrial tribunal found that PC Surinder Singh was unlawfully discriminated against by Nottinghamshire Constabulary in his training for the CID, and in the force's decision not to attach him permanently to the CID. The tribunal found that two other Asian officers were discriminated against in their transfer applications to Nottinghamshire CID.

The tribunal also found that racist language permeated most levels of the force, and that phrases such as 'come on coon, we've got work to do' and 'nigger boy, you are getting above your station' were commonly used (*Dispatches*, October 1990, cited in Skellington, 1996: 161). More recently we saw the case of Tarique Ghaffur, Britain's senior Asian officer in the Metropolitan Police Force, who announced in 2008 that he was taking legal action against the Metropolitan Police Force and its Commissioner, Sir Ian Blair, for racial discrimination. Also, there is the case of the Muslim woman Yasmin Rehman, a senior ranking police officer in the Metropolitan Police Force, who in 2008 took legal action against the Force for racial discrimination. Rehman claimed that leadership failure allows prejudice in the Metropolitan Police Force to continue and flourish. A similar claim was made by Commander Shabir Hussain, also from the Metropolitan Police Force, who stated that he had been sidelined for promotion because of his race (a case which in September 2008 Hussain lost).

In light of these critiques, it is argued that a more meaningful recruitment initiative is needed, which makes fundamental changes in the occupational culture of the police force. This will also lead to improvements in the retention and progression of black and minority ethnic staff, and address accusations of 'window dressing' (Cashmore, 2002) and tokenistic appointments (Bolton, 2003). This needs to move beyond superficial fast-tracking, or as Cashmore prefers to call it, 'accelerated action' of black and minority ethnic officers into high ranking positions (Cashmore, 2002: 339), and should be in consultation with not only specialist and support groups, such as the Black Police Association, as O'Neill and Holdaway (2007) argue, but also, we argue, the black and minority ethnic community themselves, in their capacity as service users and a pool from which future officers will be recruited.

When these officers face such racial discriminatory treatment, how then are black and minority ethnic suspects treated? Here, the disproportionate number of suspicious black and minority ethnic deaths in police custody has been held up as of particular concern, and in urgent need of examination, especially as occurs within the police-custody suite, a site away from the 'public gaze' (Britton, 2000: 641). This is a place of genuine fear for the black and minority ethnic population:

> The greatest fear most English people seem to have for their children, is that they'll be abducted or molested by paedophiles or something ... But I fear for my son's safety at the hands of the police. These people are supposed to protect us ... all of us. What am I supposed to tell him? Don't go out because the people we're expected to trust, the people governed to uphold the law, might kill you? What kind of life is that for a young man? (*Caribbean Times*, 3 April 1997, cited in Bowling and Phillips, 2002: 131)

Black and minority ethnic fear of police custody occurs not least because of the 'racist bias that has been woven into, and become an inextricable part of,

[its] culture and administration' (Sivanandan, 1991: 1). For example, figures from 2007/2008 show that there were 21 recorded deaths of persons who had been arrested or otherwise detained by the police, 18 of which involved white people and 3 of which involved deaths of black and minority ethnic people (Riley et al., 2009: 181), figures that are disproportionate to their numbers in the general population.

Here it is argued that black and minority ethnic deaths in police custody are to be seen in the context of unequal treatment before the law and due to 'official misinformation' that explains the deaths as accidental, or a misadventure or 'even the fault of the victim, because of his/her behaviour, drunkenness, abuse of drugs, or mental or physical condition', meaning that attention or blame is deflected away from police deviance and discrimination (Institute of Race Relations, 1991, cited in Bowling and Phillips, 2002: 133). This allows black and minority ethnic deaths in custody to occur, without questioning or accountability, such as in the case of David Oluwale, who in 1969 was found dead in a river after being beaten and chased by the police along riverbanks. The officers were convicted of assault, but cleared of manslaughter. Similarly, Clinton McCurbin died in 1987 when, after resisting arrest for alleged use of a stolen credit card, he was held in an arm lock around his neck for several minutes. Several witnesses said the police officer was 'practically strangling' McCurbin, yet an inquest delivered a verdict of 'death by misadventure'. Other cases include Richard O'Brien, Brian Douglas and Roger Sylvester. The very nature of these deaths needs to be questioned, not only for their racist nature, but also because they ultimately lead to instances of unlawful death, by an agent of the state which is supposed to undertake policing duties on the principles that police use of force must be essential, minimal, legitimate and accountable (Reiner, 2000).

In more recent times though, an erosion of these policing principles has further occurred, often in full public view. However, rather than being widely condemned, the aggressive behaviour of the police is being excused with an emphasis on the pressures that are now supposedly placed on police officers when dealing with new security and terror threats. Indeed, this was a claim made in the police shooting of Jean Charles de Menezes, where emotionally laden claims were made about the state's pressures of policing in an 'atmosphere of fear' (Independent Police Complaints Commission, 2007a: 16), presented the death as accidental and excusable, obscuring the alternative possibilities that incompetence, power and race were all somehow bound up in the tragedy. It is argued that the panic around 'new terror threats' is also used to informally justify the alleged heavy-handed treatment of suspected security threats and terror suspects. This includes torture by default, which is the police sanctioning others to use torture methods by transferring custody of the suspect over to an agent of state that is known for using torture, and by then turning a blind-eye to it when it does occur.

Learning lessons from Macpherson?

Despite a number of fair-policing changes introduced by the Police Service of Northern Ireland (PSNI) as part of its wider transgression from the Royal Ulster Constabulary to the PSNI, the force still remains a largely white, middle class, male-dominated policing organisation that is largely made up of officers of a Protestant faith. The force's name change and attempts to reorganise itself as a police force is yet in progress, and given the nature of it and Northern Ireland's wider historical problems, is likely to take some time. In matters relating to race, crime and policing, the PSNI is currently well situated to progressively learn from Macpherson (1999). However, given the historical, political and cultural development of both the PSNI and race relations in Northern Ireland, one must ask whether frontline officers are able to escape from the wider views of the society in which it exists (Bowling and Phillips, 2007), and if attitudes can ever be separated from policing behaviour (Sollund, 2007). For example, in the year 2008/09, there were 29 complaints of racism against the PSNI compared to 25 complaints of sectarianism (Police Ombudsman for Northern Ireland, 2009). Even more recently, there have been claims of racist victimisation by PSNI officers, such as that in the case of Coleraine taxi driver Ricardo Alavijeh (*Coleraine Times*, 17 December 2009).

A study by Patel (Patel, 2011) examined the incorporation of Macpherson's findings regarding racist incidents into policing ideology, approach and practice.[6] The study sought to examine the relationship between initiatives introduced on a senior-management level and their interpretation and execution on an operational level. It focused in particular on the impact on policing roles of perceptions held about race and racism in a distinctly transient society that is contemporary Northern Ireland. Data collection involved analysis of some PSNI internal and public documents on matters related to their policing of racist incidents. It also used semi-structured interviews as a means of allowing direct access to the voices of those undertaking policing duties, for example, operational police officers, such as 'beat' constables, as well as officers working within specialist units, such as Minority Liaison Officers (MLOs).

The study found that on a senior level, the PSNI had addressed anti-racist, equality and diversity matters and incorporated these into various training sessions. For instance, one officer, who had recently graduated from the police-training college, noted:

> It certainly was very prominent in the training, you know a lot of time and effort was spent on it. The first few days ... that's all about diversity, you know, you have sectarianism and racism and that sort of thing, you know about different cultures. The first four weeks was all human rights work, so there was quite a lot of focus ... [Did you cover Macpherson there?] Oh yes, yes, yes, yes, we did. Not in depth, but it was covered.

The PSNI had also attempted to improve their policing of racist incidents, as well as addressing under-reporting and the improving of community education, as documented in the *DCU Initiatives* document (PSNI, 2007b). Significant work included: a Vulnerable Persons Strategy; priority response within one hour; Hate Incident and Minority Liaison Officers; diversity training programme for officers; high visibility reassurance patrols; follow-up visits with all victims of hate crime; police representation on local forums and specialist community projects; aide-memoire cards distributed to operational officers; crime prevention and good business practice seminars with companies employing multiple numbers of migrant workers; officers learning languages, including Portuguese and Polish; shared use of an information terminal – 'G' Drive; and the production of a hate incident monitoring sheet and investigation pack. These initiatives were often met with positive efforts some MLOs; one commented: 'What I do is every morning I trawl through every single incident that has taken place … so I go through them individually because sometimes they are not flagged up as a hate crime.'

However, as the study progressed, it emerged there was still a view amongst the majority of officers that racist incidents and racism in Northern Ireland was something that was a fairly 'new' phenomenon. One operational officer said: 'It's only in recent years you know, with the influx of European ones from different European countries, that we've had really racial problems … um, uh, likes of attacks on the Portuguese house, possibly by Lithuanians or things like that.'

The implication of this racist commonsense is that it shifts the constructions of deviance, so that views of the typical offender and the typical victim become distorted. Not least this took away from the seriousness of the incident in itself. One MLO said: 'Yeah, it's kids … we've spoken to local shopkeepers and said "you know, wise up, don't be selling them eggs to kids, you know because they're going round the corner and throwing them at people's houses. You know, where's your Christmas spirit?"'

The problem of this last comment is the idea that the shopkeeper should avoid selling eggs to the young people who would then go on to throw them at the windows of black and minority ethnic residents – not least as a seasonal gesture of goodwill. This lessens the ability to understand the impact of victimisation, and seriousness of offender motives. For example, in talking about an Indian family's experiences, one officer said:

> But I have to say they don't really challenge it. [Why do you think that is?] I don't know … you know they're very meek that way … when I visited them they just said 'oh, we want to move now, we don't want any trouble, were going to move out of Northern Ireland' … the only thing is that I know that their son has just finished his GCSEs and they've not sent him back to school, and I said 'well, wouldn't he better off at school, you know instead of sitting at home vegetating and doing nothing for six months?

When asked about the perpetrators of such offences, one officer stated:

> It was the likes of the locals causing the damage, you see there was a time when they were annoyed that foreigners were coming in and taking their jobs … the big factories here, would be 90% foreign nationals, so they were using that as an excuse … but since then, there's been lots between the likes of the Portuguese and the Lithuanians, who have fallen out. I don't know what its about, a lot of the cases its about small things, you know having a drink and falling out over something that has been said, or whether they have fallen out at work or over work, and that is boiling over into the streets.

What this demonstrates is the victim-blaming rationale, part of which involves shifting the focus of racist incidents, by diverting attentions to 'black on black crime', and problematising black and minority ethnic people themselves, by placing them in the position of law-breaker. One operational officer stated: 'But then there's … some negative attitudes held by some people, that's just a personal view, some negative attitudes of people … I think because a lot of the foreign nationals are quite fond of the drink driving, you know, there have been some incidents of driving offences.'

Such views seem to be supported by some PSNI documents, which problematised black and minority ethnic people by first presenting them in the position of deviant, and then if at all, as a victim. For example, one PSNI presentation slide, titled 'Current issues surrounding the large number of foreign nationals in the Dungannon & South Tyrone area',[7] looked at crime of a particular area within Northern Ireland. It contained a list of eight crime-related issues prominent in the given area. These were (given in the order in which they were listed):

- Increase in drink/drive offences
- Increase in drugs/prostitution
- Knife culture
- Racial violence (internally/externally and cross-nationally)
- Emergence of Combat 18
- Threat from Loyalist paramilitaries
- Murder of/by migrant worker
- Being laid off at end of contract

Of concern is the way in which the slide's first three points relate to the idea of 'foreign national' (i.e. black and minority ethnic) crime. Only in the latter points does it make reference to their victimisation. So what this slide does is present black and minority ethnic presence for the wider white community as a problem. With this there is a hint of victim-blaming, for instance the suggestion that because of black and minority ethnic crime in drink/drive offences, drugs/prostitution and knife culture, the region has had to respond with racial violence and Combat 18. Such ideas about the black and minority ethnic criminal and 'foreign other' are also commonly found it other publicly available PSNI literature. For example, the following is an extract taken from the 2006/2007 Chief Constable's Annual Report (PSNI, 2007a: 6):

> BREAKING BARRIERS IN COOKSTOWN: Police in Cookstown faced up to the challenge of an influx of families from across the European Union and beyond with, amongst other initiatives, the production of an information leaflet in a number of languages. The leaflet highlighted four main areas: road safety, child protection, domestic violence and noise pollution. In addition to an English version for the indigenous resident population, the leaflet was translated into the main language groups of incoming workers – Latvian, Lithuanian, Polish, Portuguese, Russian and Slovakian.

Consider the problematic imagery created by some of the language (for example, 'influx'). In addition, the comment that leaflets are being produced/translated in the areas of domestic violence, child protection, noise pollution and road safety also sends out a more dangerous message: the criminalising of these black and minority ethnic individuals and the suggestion that their presence is at odds or of a threat to others. This narrative problematises them as individuals, as families and as communities in general, by representing them as deviants, both in the social and criminal context. This then justifies the police as regulators and controllers of them, over and above say presenting them as a service designed to protect their rights and needs (Patel, 2011). Indeed, when all the officers participating in the research were informed about the study aims and purpose, they immediately and predominantly spoke about this idea of black and minority ethnic deviancy and inter-ethnic crime between the new migrant community, as opposed to, say, their racist victimisation at the hands of some members of the local white community:

> It's coming to the surface a bit about extortion, maybe a bit of the Lithuanian elements being involved in that ... of their own community, you know give us money and we'll look after you ... but it's that element of what's acceptable in different cultures ... different cultures can certainly be very, very violent, you know they've had military training and the likes of that.

> I think Macpherson just highlighted the point that everybody knew, that there's was a slight problem with migrants coming in ... when it [Macpherson Report] first came out we didn't really have any migrants here, I suppose we didn't really pay that much attention to it cause we didn't have that much of a big a problem with migrants coming in, but since then with all those ones coming in to work in the different companies, I suppose we've had to step back and look at it.

The study revealed that the policing of racist incidents were being taken seriously on a senior-management level. Here organisational and structural changes were being introduced. Changes at this level had in some ways seriously considered anti-racist policing tools, such as the Macpherson Report (1999). These were primarily targeted towards protecting members of the black and minority ethnic community who experience racist incidents. Senior management had sought to filter these changes to MLOs and operational officers. However, underlying assumptions about a racial hierarchy were prominent amongst the officers interviewed. Here operational officers especially tended to equate policing in a racially diverse society with the need to police black and minority ethnic people themselves. Part of this racist commonsense discourse involves the tendency to view the black and minority ethnic people, especially newer migrant workers, as largely deviant and problematic. This was done via a process of racially based criminalisation. Concerns are therefore raised as to the degree to which these racialised ideas impacted on the actual policing of racist incidents on an operational level, especially in terms of considering the racist incidents they experienced at the hands of the local white community.

It could be argued that the police will always have elements of racism, not least because if they are 'to represent a cross-section of society, then it can be expected that some will be racially prejudiced' (Bowling and Phillips, 2007: 954). But we need to be concerned when racism in the police is far more that its wider societal representation, and instead when it is found in the majority of police officers' attitudes – especially when this impacts on their actual behaviour (Sollund, 2007) and continues to be embedded in the very institution and culture of the police. In reporting on the racialised views of officers, which at times were negative and problematic, wider consideration can be given to the possibility of Macpherson (fair and equal) policing in a time (war on terror and immigration panic) when a racist commonsense discourse is thriving, and where racialised profiling continues not only to be used, but also excused, legitimated and enabled by the state and its partnered criminal justice institutions and agents. Here, police (including the PSNI) use of Macpherson has seen the introduction of initiatives that allow seemingly more entrenched systems for reporting, monitoring and combating both institutionalised racism with the force, i.e. recruitment quota and diversity training, as well as dealing with cases of racist incidents in the wider community. However, it is argued that the modalities of racism still seem to have articulated with this institutional framework of the PSNI and other UK police forces. This means that racist policing, whether it be witting or (to use Macpherson's term) 'unwitting', persists. This not only occurs through the generation of fear, panic and hostility amongst the white-majority population about the supposed black and minority ethnic foreign dangerous other, as we saw in some of the PSNI officer quotes, but is also promoted within a discourse of 'racist commonsense'.

In this era of policing within a war on terror context, racist policing it is argued here persists in ever more ambiguous and nebulous forms. Consider, for example, the re-naming of race-based police work with more palatable terms, such as 'ethnicity', 'diversity' and 'cultural'. This allows the continued use of racist stereotypes and assumptions, in a way that is widely permitted by both lay public and the state. Furthermore, following 9/11, 7/7 and later the failed bomb attacks in London, racial-profiling strategies have been excused, accepted, legitimated and more worryingly enabled by the wider public and the state. Recall for instance, Lord Hope's comment: Terrorists 'are likely to be linked to sectors of the community that, because of their racial, ethnic or geographical origins, are readily identifiable' (Lord Hope to the House of Commons Home Affairs Committee Sixth Report of Session 2004–2005: Terrorism and Community Relations, cited in Moeckli 2007: 663).

So despite the Macpherson Report, the Race Relations (Amendment) Act 2000 and a government which denies that the state carries out racial profiling (or if it does it is somehow justified), racial profiling is presented as necessary, and suggests that the provisions under which it is occurring override race equality legislation. The allure of this racial profiling derives from the idea of protecting 'us' from the supposed 'dangerous others' (Yuval-Davis et al., 2005). This is despite there being a lack of evidence to suggest the fulfilment of this promise. This 'protection' rationale was also evident in the racist commonsense and crime pattern views in the PSNI study. The literature on racial profiling as a disciplinary practice emphasises its role in 'filtering' urban space (Khoury, 2009) by constructing some racialised subjects as 'invisible' (i.e. white) and so passed over by profiling regimes, or as is the case for some black and minority ethnic subjects, as hyper-visible (racialised) and 'out of place' to be picked up and constructed in terms of expected criminality (Khoury 2009; Romero 2008). This is the case for Asian suspects within the context of war on terror policing, or when addressing the needs of black and minority ethnic victims of racist incidents (in Northern Ireland by the PSNI), as the same racial profiling discourse is being used – one which emerges from a wider field of power relations between black and minority ethnic people and the state, and in particular the wider processes of racialised governance that they are subjected to.

The key issue being highlighted is that there is in post-Macpherson UK a revival in the problematic construction of crimes as scientifically racialised, illustrated by moves towards increased racial profiling, meaning that older notions of 'black criminality' and the dangerous 'immigrant other', undeserving of right to a place in UK space, are once again appearing. This is not only occurring at seemingly disparate local levels, i.e. PSNI and continued use of racist commonsense in the policing of racist incidents, but also at wider levels, i.e. all UK forces use of racial profiling in war on terror policing. What, then, does this tell us about the position and treatment of black and minority ethnic people by the state and its criminal justice agents, namely the police? The answer: it signposts the continued use of race as a marker for their treatment, either in responsive or pre-emptive policing. It is this continued form of policing that needs to be challenged, as well as the ensuing miscarriages (such as de Menezes) it produces.

1 Account for the existence of institutional racism in the criminal justice system.
2 What are the real consequences of the Macpherson Report (1999)?
3 Was the successful policing of the Anthony Walker murder driven by a police force genuinely free from racism or a police force wanting to appear to be free from racism? Does it matter?
4 What attempts have been made to deal with the lack of black and minority ethnic officers in the police force? What is the impact of these?
5 An inquiry into the police shooting of Jean Charles de Menezes in 2005 stated that officers were working under the state's pressures of policing in an 'atmosphere of fear' (Independent Police Complaints Commission, 2007a: 16). Is this response an acceptable reason for the series of police actions that took place on that day?

1 We are slightly cautious about giving the Macpherson Report (1999) too much credit in 'exposing' police racism. It is true that the report did highlight problems and that for some this was new information – a claim in itself we are also slightly suspicious about. However, we are eager to note that many had known and experienced police racism long before Macpherson.
2 9/11 was portrayed and seen by some as the responsibility of fundamentalist Muslims. This has generated a racist and discriminatory backlash against Muslims who are consequently labelled as extremists, fundamentalists, terrorists and anti-Western/British. This was despite the British government and some media efforts to point out that the enemy is terrorism and not Islam, and despite Muslim organisations condemning the attacks as un-Islamic (Pilkington, 2003: 277)
3 It is argued that this is partially due to small changes in the ethnic mix of police officers, more officers with higher education, the greater emphasis on multiculturalism in police training, and the official force ethos since the 1981 Scarman Report and more recently the 1999 Macpherson Report (Reiner, 2000: 99).
4 Racial violence is viewed as a physical or verbal hostility, which includes attacks on property, belongings and the person. It may be something that is suffered by individuals or groups. The action is motivated by a hate of colour, race, nationality, or ethnic or national origins. There does not necessarily have to be evidence of racism, as the victim can also claim this is the case when they believe that the perpetrator was acting on racial grounds.
5 There are several Acts, which can be utilised to resolve cases where racial violence or incitement is featured in the offence. These include the 1986 (and 1987) Public Order Acts; the 1988 Malicious Communications Act; Section 222 of the Local Government Act (which gives local authorities the power to intervene and prosecute to protect inhabitants in their area); section 5 of the 1936 Public Order Act; Sections 20 (on grievous bodily harm), 42 (common assault) and 47 (actual bodily harm) of the 1861 Offences Against Persons Act; the 1971 Criminal Damage Act; the 1953 Prevention of Crime Act; and the 1968 Firearms Act (Skellington, 1996: 91).

6 The study reported here examined the initiatives introduced on a senior level into the policing of racist incidents, and considered whether the existence of race-based assumptions at operational level may hinder execution of these initiatives. To access this data, an analysis was made of some of the PSNI's internal and public documents, regarding their equality/diversity and community safety strategies. In addition, nine interviews were carried out with those undertaking policing duties (operational police officers, such as 'beat' constables, as well as officers working within specialist units, such as Minority Liaison Officers). The officers interviewed were all 'white' and had been born and raised for the majority of their lives in Northern Ireland, although they slightly differed in terms of other variables (gender, age, religious background, policing experience and length in service, which ranged from just under a year to 26 years in the police).

7 Patel was informed by the sourcing MLO that this slide 'would usually be used when we are presenting information to our Policing Board or other outside agencies if we are trying to obtain resources or funding – most of the information was obtained from Dungannon Councils Website' (email correspondence to Patel from MLO, 12 March 2008).

FURTHER READING

Bourne, Jenny (2001) 'The Life and Times of Institutional Racism', *Race and Class*, 43(2): 7–22.

Kalra, Virinder (2003) 'Police Lore and Community Disorder: Diversity in the Criminal Justice System', in D. Mason (ed.), *Explaining Ethnic Differences: Changing Patterns of Disadvantage in Britain*. Bristol: Policy Press. pp. 139–152.

Rowe, Michael (2009) 'Policing and Race Equality: Thinking Outside the (Tick) Box', in H. Singh Bhui (ed.), *Race and Criminal Justice*. London: Sage. pp. 49–65.

5

Courtin' Justice

There is a mass of anecdotal data indicating that the court system (by which we mean pre-trial custody, courtroom processes and personnel, and post-trial sentencing) discriminates against those who are of black and minority ethnic background. Indeed statistics of sentencing and incarceration when factored by race seem to support this view, with disproportionate and increased rates of black and minority ethnic incarceration. For example, in 2003 black and minority ethnic people of British nationality accounted for 12 per cent of the prison population in England and Wales (National Statistics, 2005). In 2008 this had risen to 35 per cent (Tye, 2009). This is similar to data supplied from other countries, in the USA for example, over 40 per cent of sentenced inmates were black African American, which is a rate of incarceration that stands at seven times the rate of white males (Abrams et al., 2008: 1). However, research looking at *processes* of court discrimination and its wider relationship with the notion of justice is somewhat lacking, not so much because of the difficulty of proving court racism and its biased practices, but rather due to issues around access, data protection and the difficulty of holding a variety of variables constant enough for accurate and meaningful findings to be produced. This also isn't helped by the courts' lack of recording variables such as race and ethnicity. For example, in 2007/08, ethnicity was recorded in only 22 per cent of the magistrates' court data for England and Wales – although the recording of ethnicity at Crown Courts was better, indicating that the ethnicity of 81 per cent of all persons tried at Crown Courts in 2007 had been recorded (Riley et al., 2009). Some studies though have found that the perception of court racism is common; as one report stated: 'the poor image which black people have of the courts leads to the sense that if one is black in court, one has to prove one's innocence rather than the court to prove one's guilt' (NACRO, 1991: 23). Other research, both criminological and that commissioned by the government, has found that particular racial groups are disproportionately represented in the docks and are more likely to experience harsher penalties in comparison to their white counterparts (Hood, 1992; Riley et al., 2009). This reflects black and minority ethnic people's views of their experiences in the criminal justice system as a whole (Calverly et al., 2004). As victims too, recognition of black and minority ethnic victimisation and access to fair justice in the courtroom are less likely in comparison to their white counterparts.

This chapter will not outline the administrative practicalities of the court-system process. This is covered in depth elsewhere (see Crowther, 2007; Davies et al., 2005; Joyce, 2006). Rather, this chapter examines the power relationships and delivery of justice in matters of race. In doing so it argues that racism not only exists in the courts, but also works in such ways that it can hinder the levels of justice given to black and minority ethnic people, both as defendants and victims. It argues that the court system, like its fellow institutions within the criminal justice system, is filled with practices of discrimination and bias against certain groups, for example black and minority ethnic groups, women, the working class and homosexuals. For people of black and minority ethnic background in particular there is a unique type of vulnerability, which has persisted, despite a number of equality measures having been in place. This chapter not only considers the pattern of racial discrimination against black and minority ethnic people in terms of their differential outcomes, but also examines more closely the methods by which such forms of bias are able to continue. For example, it is argued here that equality measures and attempts to increase black and minority ethnic court staff are not a strong enough solution. This is because fair representation (for instance, more black and minority ethnic court staff) doesn't necessarily mean fair justice. Rather, serious attempts for fair justice need to move beyond 'tokenism' when dealing with the position of court personnel. Similarly, the equality in application of law when dealing with defendants and victims who are of black and minority ethnic background needs to be monitored as to ensure that they are adhered to. In making these arguments, this chapter invites you to consider the need to move beyond a simple conception of justice as a neutral process in the courts, and to conceive the court process as a crystallisation of societal power relations and a reflection of the wider challenges which face the delivery of justice by the criminal justice system. To illustrate these points, the case of Satpal Ram is discussed as a way illustrating the existence of such discrimination. It is argued that for Ram, following the widely criticised trial practices, the main obstacles to rectifying injustices were in fact created over a period of years by the subsequent practices of the Prison Service and Home Office.

Racial bias and the tipping of Portia's scales

When accused of a crime in a democratic society, defendants have the right to a fair trial (Human Rights Act, 1998: Article 6). This, is granted along with other rights, for example the prohibition of torture (Article 3) and the prohibition of discrimination (Article 14). Linked to the liberal political ideology of theorists such as John Locke (1632–1704), these rights are globally enshrined in key documents such as the Human Rights Act (1998), the Bill of Rights (1791), the International Covenant on Civil and Political Rights (1966), the European Convention on Human Rights (1950), the American Convention on Human

Rights (1969), the African Charter on Human and Peoples Rights (1981) and the United Nations Declaration of Human Rights (1948). The last of these, in particular, affirms that 'all human beings are born free and equal in dignity and rights' (United Nations Declaration of Human Rights, 1948: Article 1). The foundations of these rights are 'developed from the tradition of natural rights that sought to establish boundaries to protect an individual from unwarranted interference either by another individual or by the government' (Joyce, 2006: 311). These human rights principles, we are told, are incorporated into UK law as 'absolute, limited and qualified' (Human Rights Act, 1998). For those who feel as if they have been mistreated by the UK's criminal justice system, claims can be made to the European Court of Human Rights. Such applications are based on the view that the state has breached its obligations under the European Convention on Human Rights (1950). Regardless, the ideology at all levels is that we are to be protected from mistreatment and abuse.

The Human Rights Act (1998) states that 'everyone must have equal access to Convention rights, whatever their status' (article 14). Ideally, these are some of the key principles upon which justice in the UK works. For example, in the place where 'the administration of justice most visibly occurs' (Crowther, 2007: 173), a defendant has the right to have all the evidence against them to presented and the right to defend themselves. This occurs in a process that is underpinned by fair justice in accordance with established legal rules and procedures (Hudson, 2001: 104). Hence, we see the ethos of a fair trial and innocent until proven otherwise. However, in practice a very different picture appears. Here, accusations of bias and prejudice, the withholding or fabrication of evidence, and even the use of force to extract confessions, have been reported. For example, consider the now well-known cases of the Irish Republication Army terror suspects who were imprisoned for up to sixteen years in the early 1970s and released finally in 1991–1992. These two cases, that of the Birmingham Six and the Guildford Four, revealed how guilty verdicts and imprisonment were issued following false confessions, themselves extracted via violent methods, bullying and sleep deprivation, and the use of problematic evidence, which included false evidence and the practice of withholding evidence from the courts. Although the Criminal Cases Review Commission, set up in 1997 following the Criminal Appeal Act (1995), seeks to consider such suspect miscarriage cases, this does not prevent abuses such as forced confessions, torture whilst in custody, falsification of evidence, and so on, from occurring.

In matters relating to race, ethnicity and crime, human rights are about the right to equal treatment, and freedom from discrimination on (perceived) grounds of race, religion, ethnicity and nationality in the delivery of justice: 'People have the right not to be treated differently because of race, religion, sex, political views or any other status, unless this can be justified objectively' (Human Rights Act, 1998: Article 14). Within the context of pre-trial custody and courtroom abuse, it is clear however that some racialised groups continue to be discriminated against. Often this in itself occurs within denial of a racist context. It would be foolish to believe that patterns of black and minority ethnic economic, social, cultural and political exclusion that are born out of a history of racism and xenophobia would not continue to penetrate the walls of justice (Cole and Wardak, 2006). In talking generally about the existence of bias in sentencing, Hudson (1987: 95) argues:

> By and large, the criminal law is imposed by whites on blacks; by the advantages classes on the disadvantaged; by the elderly on the young, and by men on women. Most judges and magistrates are white, middle-aged, middle-class males. Moreover, even the small number of female or black judges must implement laws and administer sanctions formulated by legislatures which are unrepresentatively white, male, middle-aged and middle-class ... these characteristics – 'non-legal variables' – should therefore be made irrelevant in sentencing decisions.

Given these biases, this leads us to ask to what extent are our human rights and fair justice principles really useful in matters regarding the protection of black and minority ethnic people in the court system, but additionally within the criminal justice system as a whole?

There are some, though, who argue that, in more recent times when legal factors are considered, the occurrence of racial bias is actually quite low (Kramer and Steffensmeier, 1993). However, much of the research in this area tells us that racial bias is not only present, but also impacts on court decisions (Abrams et al., 2008; Austin and Allen, 2000; Baldus et al., 1998; Hood. 1992; Mauer and King, 2007; Mitchell et al., 2005; Steffensmeier and Demuth, 2000). Here it has been found that the background of the defendant influences the outcome, especially in matters where sentencing is given. For example, in 81 per cent of the Crown Court cases in 2007, the percentage in which the defendant's ethnicity was recorded, a greater proportion of white defendants (78 per cent) compared with black (75 per cent) or Asian (73 per cent) defendants were found guilty, yet more black defendants (67 per cent) compared with white ones (53 per cent) received custodial sentences (Riley et al., 2009). Although one can say that race does matter in the court system, the degree to which it does is less easy to determine. This is linked to methodological implications (Hood, 1992). The 'black sentences' data is nevertheless though relatively high in comparison to their numbers in the wider population. Although it has been argued that this is because black and minority ethnic people are actually more prone to criminal behaviour, our discussions in previous chapters soundly dispute this, and indicate, for example, that it is more likely to be due to the racialised processes found in society as a whole and the heightened attention that they will receive by other criminal justice institutions before being processed by the courts.

Some studies argue that racial bias occurs especially where cases involve white victims and black and minority ethnic defendants who are perceived to have stereotypical 'black' features (Blair et al., 2004; Eberhardt et al., 2004;

ForsterLee et al., 2006). For example, in their study of death-eligible cases in the USA, Eberhardt et al. (2006: 383) found that the stereotypical physical traits associated with black (African American) people, for example broad nose, thick lips and dark skin, 'function as a significant determinant of deathworthiness' when they appear as defendants in court. Other studies note how additional variables also influence courtroom outcomes. For example, Steffensmeier et al. (1998) argue that age is also a factor in that young black males are more harshly sentenced. Some, such as Agozino (1997; 2008) argue that black women (of African heritage) are seen as 'foreign' others and so are also more readily punished, not only in comparison to their white counterparts, but at an increasingly higher rate than both their numbers in the general population and against the rate of black and minority ethnic men. Doing so means that they are more susceptible to enhanced forms of victimisation and punishment (Agozino, 2000). The suggestion of enhanced victimisation is supported by Scraton and Moore's (2004) recent work on female incarceration in Northern Ireland's Maghaberry prison – a prison that once held the Loyalist prisoner Johnny Adair. Here, Scraton and Moore (2004: 57) found that 'immigration detainees' were also subjected to the same regime as its female prisoners, and in some instances they also reported the existence of negative attitudes by staff towards them as asylum applicants. The enhanced risk of criminalisation of those seeking asylum or considered 'foreign', in Fekete's (2001) 'xeno-racist' sense, is common, not only in the UK, but also in wider Europe, Australia and the USA.

In more recent times, we argue that those who are of South Asian background have experienced harsher punitive measures. For example, of the 58 prosecution cases of the 'rioters' in 7 July 2001 Bradford disturbances, there were massive discrepancies in the sentences given to the Asian youth. For example, consider the cases of Ashraf Hussain, who received a four-year sentence after video evidence showed him throwing several stones, and Alam Zeb Khan, who received a three-year sentence, despite there being no evidence, after he was described by the police as a 'ringleader' in the rioting (Institute of Race Relations, 2002). The particular harshness of these sentences can be better appreciated when they are compared with the lenient sentences given to participants in other UK civil disturbances. For example, Fekete (2003: 1) draws our attention to the case of how:

> Football hooligans and neo-Nazis who terrorised the Asian community in Glodwick, Oldham, in May 2001, leading to two nights of rioting, were cheered as 'heroes' by their supporters, including BNP members, in the public gallery of a Manchester court on 13 June, as they heard that they had been sentenced to a mere nine months imprisonment. Originally the twelve had been charged with riot, violent disorder and racially aggravated criminal damage. But the judge, believing there was insufficient evidence to convict on riot ordered the jury to bring in not guilty verdicts. Half way through the trial, the defendants pleaded guilty to lesser charges of affray and assault.

The argument presented here was that it was not just the individual Asian youths who were being punished, but also their whole communities – including those who had nothing at all to do with the disturbances, apart, that is, from being guilty of being the same race/ethnicity. Following the recent panic emerging around the 'Islamic fundamentalist' and the war on terror, the court's harsher treatment of Asian youth is now more than ever allowed to occur, even within the context of suspended human rights. Smiljanic (2002) refers to the case of the Muslim prisoners, who were held at Belmarsh Prison under anti-terror legislation provisions (namely the Provisions of the Anti Terrorism, Crime and Security Act, 2001), which allowed for their indefinite detention – clearly in contradiction to the right to life, liberty and security articles of the Human Rights Act (1998). Indeed, what is of interest is the way in which Britain's then Home Secretary David Blunkett called for certain rights to be suspended in suspected cases of terrorist activity (Smiljanic, 2002). What emerges from this is the view that, by and large, it is black and minority ethnic groups, especially Asians of the Muslim faith, who are today disproportionately focused on. This was acknowledged in the committee of Law Lords, held in December 2004, who, following the Belmarsh case, ruled that the holding of foreign detainees without trial was not only a clear breach of the European Convention on Human Rights, but also discriminatory.

In recognising the existence of racial bias, best-practice guidance documents, such as the 'Race and the Courts' (Judicial Studies Board, 1999) and the 'Equality Before the Courts' (Judicial Studies Board, 2001), have been produced. Although making a number of practical recommendations, for example the avoidance of making racially based assumptions and the problematising of people of black and minority ethnic background, their practice and effectiveness in reality is poor. In addition, under Section 95 of the Criminal Justice Act (1992), judges were for the first time instructed to avoid use of racist language. This was followed by an announcement by then Lord Chancellor Lord MacKay that a two-year training programme would be launched, its purpose being to train judges in racial awareness, equality and diversity issues, including in oath taking, body language and cross-cultural communication (Skellington, 1996). However, the effectiveness of these initiatives is questionable, not least because of the inability or unwillingness of the judiciary as well as other courtroom personnel to implement them. Thus racism continues to pervade. It can be argued that it is also due to the power of the imagery of the black and minority ethnic individual being more 'crime-prone' (Steffensmeier et al., 1998: 769) and the readiness to believe such an image, even when one has no direct experience of such criminality. This, as discussed in previous chapters, is an image that is validated by urban myths, media messages, political propaganda and, not least, dubious crime statistics. In addition, it is argued (especially in the USA) that even when found guilty, judges are resistant to sending white offenders to prisons whose populations are disproportionately black and minority ethnic, for fear that they will be victimised by black and minority ethnic inmates (Steffensmeier et al., 1998). Hence, even in these instances, the notion of 'white victimhood' at the hands of 'black deviance' exists.

Fair courtroom personnel, fair courtroom justice?

For court staff, black and minority ethnic representation is poor, and certainly disproportionate to their figures in the general population. This is not surprising given the wider barriers that black and minority ethnic people face in securing posts in the criminal justice system. For example, on average a person of black and minority ethnic background makes twice as many applications to solicitors' firms than their white counterparts, and also receives far fewer invitations for interview and offers of employment (King et al., 1990, cited in Skellington, 1996: 154). This finding was supported by the Denman Inquiry (Crown Prosecution Service, 2001), which outlined the under-representation of black and minority ethnic staff in the courts, as well as other serious weaknesses in equality and diversity issues. More recently in a report by Lord Ouseley (2008), it was suggested that the Solicitors Regulation Authority could be charged with being institutionally racist, as there was evidence that they had been discriminating against black and minority ethnic solicitors. What we have therefore is a situation where the numbers of black and minority ethnic court professionals is significantly low. For example, as of 31 March 2009, there were only 57 Recorders (i.e. practising barristers or solicitors), 14 Circuit Judges and 3 High Court Judges of black and minority ethnic background (Ministry of Justice, 2010). Any fair representation that has occurred has been slow; for example, it was only in 2004 that the High Court in England and Wales had its first 'visible' black and minority ethnic judge (Linda Dobbs QC) – this at a time when there was just nine black and minority ethnic circuit judges amongst the 623 (1.4 per cent). Those who do make it into representation often report difficulties of racism (Davis and Vennard, 2006).

In seeking to understand low rates of black and minority ethnic legal staff, it has been argued that the recruitment and retention of black and minority ethnic staff in the legal system is governed by members of white elite, for example representatives of the judiciary, who work with the support of a 'white law' (Gordon, 1993). This is a law that works in the favour of white subjects, largely as a way to maintain its dominance and control, both in legal governance and beyond. The Ouseley Report (2008: 6) supports this view in its finding that black and minority ethnic solicitors and legal staff more often experience a failure to have their complaints of alleged discrimination dealt with appropriately by the Solicitors Regulation Authority. In examining more closely the relationship between discourse, power and racism, van Dijk (1993: 81) argues that racial prejudice 'is strategically ... and persuasively conveyed among dominant majority group members ... it expresses and communicates the shared justifications for discrimination against minority groups'. In the criminal justice system this refers to those in power and authority, and in the court, ultimately this is the judiciary – who may deny or attempt to justify such prejudice (van Dijk, 1992). Within this sub-world exists its own norms, rules, sanctions and behaviour, within which racism is allowed, and because of the power of white elite and their access to publication communication such as media, corporation and education, it is able to reproduce and legitimate racism among white members in lay society (van Dijk, 1992).

In the face of such difficulties, support networks have emerged, which offer internal support (Phillips, 2005). For example, such groups include the Society for Black Lawyers in the UK. Founded in 1973, its primary objectives were to enhance the career of black and minority ethnic lawyers and to create better opportunities for prospective black and minority ethnic lawyers to enter the profession. In her study of the organisation, Britton (2002) found that, for some, membership had a social function, as well as a political one. It allowed members to meet other black and minority ethnic lawyers to 'meet and relax' with, as well as providing support and guidance for each other. However, Britton also found that some black and minority ethnic lawyers chose not to join the organisation or had allowed membership to expire, as they were cautious with its perceived 'left wing' political activity, which they saw as bringing the danger of further 'causing division' in the profession, which Britton argues could be interpreted as a strategy for attempting to just get on and fit in the profession. In many ways, then, this avoidance strategy can be seen as a means for existing within a profession that is already raced, classed and gender biased. However, such a strategy acts to serve as a temporary solution to the problem. Indeed, it can also be argued that the existence of support groups such as the Society for Black Lawyers is limited in its impact. This is a point also made about the presence of black and minority ethnic courtroom staff more generally.

In examining more closely the figures, it is argued that an increase of black and minority ethnic numbers as courtroom personnel in pursuit of fair representation does not necessarily mean a delivery of fair justice. Indeed, it can also be argued that once in appointment black and minority ethnic courtroom staff actually do little to improve the situation. For example in their American study, Steffensmeier and Britt (2001) found that although there were similar overlaps in the sentencing patterns between white and black judges' sentencing decisions, black judges were actually likely to be more harshly punitive. This dislodges from position the view that the presence of black judges alone would automatically lead to equality or a reduction in the high rates of black and minority ethnic over-sentencing. It also disputes the claim that they are necessarily softer on black and minority ethnic defendants who appear before them in court – a claim that has actually been presented as an argument against the increased appointment of black and minority ethnic judges.

There are several possible suggestions as to why black and minority ethnic presence in the judiciary has not led to a reduction in the disproportionate over-sentencing of black and minority ethnic people. First, it could actually be the case that people of black and minority ethnic background commit more crimes, especially those which in accordance to the law warrant harsher sentencing. This is a simple but feasible explanation if we accept the view that we have a neutral and fair justice system in which, black and minority ethnic people are processed. But, as we have discussed in previous chapters, the existence of such a system can be soundly disputed, as we have been able to trace racialised disparities in the criminal justice system as a whole. Next, it can be argued that when in such appointments the power of white law and the institution's culture means that anyone working within them, including those who may be disadvantaged by it such as black and minority ethnic people, is on an individual level highly likely to become 'institutionalised' (Cashmore, 2002), by taking on the racist norms and values of the institution. This may also occur as they would have to wear 'white masks' (Fanon, 1952) as a means to survive and exist in that institution. This is a problem especially given that over-compensation may occur (for example, the harsher treatment of people of a black and minority ethnic background) as a way of proving one's worth and belonging to the culture of that group – a culture that is not only racist and governed by white law, but also is more widely class based, gendered and highly politicised. This is especially so in a culture where black and minority ethnic people would already be viewed with hostility and suspicion, and who would therefore be regularly subjected to 'loyalty tests' (Kanter, 1977: 978) as way of proving their worth to the institution. Although it has been argued that the wearing of 'white masks' is in itself a survival strategy for some black and minority ethnic people, such an analysis must consider the power of white law and ask to what degree can resistance, challenge and correction of an imposed discriminatory white law be achieved in the wearing of this white mask. For example, rather than *wear* the white mask, should we not instead seek to challenge its power, control and authority?

In addition, more black and minority ethnic presence is also problematic for its tendency to 'window dress' (Cashmore, 2002) the courts by placing them in crude 'tokenistic' positions. As such they continue to be defined by their race and perceptions about that race. Such 'tokenism' means that 'they can never be just another member while their category is so rare; they will always be a hyphenated member' (for example, black-judge or black-lawyer) (Kanter, 1977: 968). Tokenism creates a false appearance of fair representation and inclusive practice whereas in reality this is not actually the case. Often tokenistic appointments are hindered by racialised stereotypes or unobtainable expectations (Kanter, 1977), by being driven by the assumption of it bringing stronger black and minority ethnic community links or the input of a black perspective, sufficient enough to adhere to equality requirements. One issue here is that 'such role expectations are not justified where they are different from that of role expectations of white colleagues in similar posts' (Arora, 2005: 141). Also, the burden of achieving equality and neutrality should not solely be placed on the shoulders of black and minority ethnic staff. Their appointment in posts where they may be thought of as token appointments can also be seen as a form of racism in itself, as Comas-Diaz and Greene (in their work on black and minority ethnic career women) note: 'Being hired as a token, or being perceived that way by co-workers is a form of racism because it implies that the woman of colour with professional status is not qualified for her position' (Comas-Diaz and Greene, 1994: 353). In matters relating to race, fairness and the criminal justice system, tokenistic appointments not only present the image of fairness but, more dangerously, but also allow processes of racial bias and unfair justice to thrive. What this means is that the claim, then, that black and minority ethnic presence alone as key courtroom personnel will necessarily bring fair justice is in reality inaccurate, and far more complex than current analysis allows.

This is not to say that the court system would not benefit from black and minority ethnic staff in positions of authority. Neither is it to suggest that increasing their presence in under-represented areas of the criminal justice system should not continue. This is an important aim in its own right. Rather, it is to suggest that their presence and role must be carefully considered so as to ensure that it is not used as a cover to divert our attention from what essentially would remain a racist process. In addition, it must also be ensured that their presence does not occur in isolation from acknowledgement of the wider patterns of racism found in other parts of the criminal justice system, and within wider society more generally. To do this, we need to move beyond a simple conception of justice as being something that is personified and delivered in court-system justice. By this we mean that we must recognise that the court system is not a separate and neutral domain, but rather it is a crystallisation of the wider power relations found in a racially biased society.

Beyond the docks

Box (1983: 201–202) notes how, if given the luxury of time and length when writing *Power, Crime and Mystification*, his book 'would also have documented further the positive relationship between power and crime by exposing the enormous amount of criminal victimization carried out by members of the Home Office and the Prison Service against those supposedly in 'their protective custody'. Such corruption and abuse of power occurs on a regular basis, carried out often by democratic societies such as the UK and the USA, ironically in the name of democracy and security. Individuals working within these agencies also legitimate their abusive actions in the name of a supposed pursuit of state security, and are often supported in doing so by state bodies. For example, consider the charging in 2004 of American soldier Lyndie England, who had served at the Abu Ghraib camp in Iraq, with the abuse of detainees and prisoners. Amongst other things, Lyndie England had forced them to lay naked in a human pyramid. At other times they had also been forced to perform simulated and sexual acts. Despite the inhumanity of such abuse, it has been alleged their practice is now taken as a routine feature of such camps and often seen as 'part of a wider pattern stemming from a White House attitude that "anything goes" in the war against terrorism, even if it crosses the line of illegality' (Senator Patrick Leahy, quoted in *Guardian*, 23 June 2004). Such cases include those of Moazzam Begg (2006), and Binyam Mohamed. The latter, in February 2010, won his case in the UK Court of Appeal to have published a summary of what Washington had told London about his treatment in Pakistan. Here Mohamed claimed that the British government and MI5 knew about his mistreatment and torture whilst in secret detention in Pakistan for suspected terrorism charges – charges which were all dropped in October 2008. The British government and MI5 both deny the claim.

The victims of such abuse are often those who already exist on the margins of society or who provide agencies of the state with convenient scape-goating opportunities, not least to hide a variety of other evils, or to act as a useful public-relations exercise, or even to gather support for what would otherwise be unfavourable policies. Put simply, the abuse of such individuals is interlinked with wider abuses of power, themselves driven by financial and political gain. The threat to these groups' civil liberties is presented by the state, and readily accepted by many in lay society, as a mere point of 'collateral damage' to wider security issues (Roach and Trotter, 2004). However, when the 'threat' to civil liberties becomes a suspension of human rights, we enter as new phase of danger.

These sites of abuse are located, quite literally, in distant locations; they are 'out of sight' and, so the logic goes, 'out of mind'. Thus, as Scraton and Moore (2004: 3) note, due to their 'closed nature', 'people held in detention, whether in prison or otherwise, are particularly vulnerable to breaches of their human rights'. The lack of access to these sites for lay members of the public, the media, investigative journalists and local MPs, means that its prisoners ('detainees') are very conveniently forgotten (Brittain, 2007). Moreover, when their existence is finally raised in our consciousness, it is met with the insistence of the wider public that they were unaware of such abuses in these locations, or worse that they are somehow justified. This is worrying and a key way in which such state abuse and corruption is allowed to continue. As Brittain (2007: 60) notes of American policy in Guantanamo, of which we have seen UK compliance:

> On the President's orders the Geneva Convention did not apply; half a century of humanitarian law has been written off, just like that. These were not prisoners of war; they were something completely different invented by the Pentagon and called 'enemy combatants'. So, as a result, hundreds of men ... have been held ... without knowing what they are accused of, having no contact with their families ... and with little access to lawyers. Worst of all, they have no idea if they will ever, ever be freed.

The attempts to ensure access to justice, when hindered by positions of relative powerlessness, in societies and countries which lay claim to democracy and fair justice is very difficult, but not impossible. Often these processes are lengthy and difficult, but some fight to highlight experiences of abuse and miscarriages of justice; for example, consider cases such as the Birmingham Six, the Guildford Four, Judith Ward, Stefan Kiszko, the Bridgewater Four and the Cardiff Three, amongst some of the many cases that later had convictions overturned following revelations of miscarriages, which included falsification of evidence, police use of threat, force and abuse to obtain (false) confessions, and the withholding or fabrication of evidence. All these miscarriages were rooted in the biased and discriminatory nature of the courtroom, and its partnering criminal justice agencies. In matters relating to racial bias, the case of Satpal Ram is held up as a case in point, not only of biases within the criminal justice system and the courtroom, but also the persistence of such bias at appeals stages.

In 1987 Ram was jailed for stabbing a white man, Clarke Pearce, in an Indian restaurant in Birmingham. It has been claimed by Ram's campaigners that the Pearce family had been well known in the local area for their racism and violent behaviour. On this occasion, Ram, who was 20 years old at the time, had been attacked in the restaurant whilst out for a meal with two friends, by a group of six white people. It was claimed that the group became aggressive and racially abusive to Ram's table and other restaurant guests. An argument followed, where Ram claims Pearce smashed a glass and twice stabbed him. In defence, Ram stabbed Pearce with a knife (used at his workplace). Both were taken to hospital for their wounds. Pearce, however, refused medical treatment and pulled out his drips. He later died of blood loss in the operating theatre. A week later Ram handed himself into the police. At all stages, Ram had argued that he was innocent and had actually acted in self-defence after what he claimed was a racist attack on him. Hence he refused to admit guilt of the charge. However, a number of problems hindered fair trial. For example, Ram's barrister, who had only met with Ram 40 minutes before his trial, had misread the pathologist's report (which listed that of Pearce's six wounds, only two of them were the result of the blade; the rest were superficial and caused when Pearce had fallen onto the broken glass); as a result, he told Ram that his plea of self-defence was unstable, changing this instead to provocation, and then went on to advise him not to give evidence. In addition; the context of the attack was not discussed, yet Pearce's friends were allowed to give character references which depicted Pearce as an innocent victim. In comparison, the main independent witnesses, who were Bengali-speaking waiters, had not been provided with any formal interpretation. Instead, the police had written statements on their behalf (which the waiters later went on to disown) and the (white) trial judge (who could not speak Bengali) had said that he would interpret for the waiters. It is not surprising therefore that an all-white jury convicted Ram of murder after 20 minutes of deliberation. Therefore, it is argued that a combination of police bias in the gathering of evidence, the discriminatory nature of courtroom processes and the incompetence of Ram's legal representation ultimately led to his conviction for Pearce's murder. As a black and minority ethnic prisoner, convicted for the murder of a white man, Ram was destined to experience racism whilst incarcerated. This was further intensified when Ram had begun his appeals process.

Of particular concern, though, are the ways in which during his appeals campaign Ram experienced an additional form of victimisation by the Home Office, who refused to acknowledge that serious flaws, underpinned by the racially discriminatory nature of the courtroom and the criminal justice system as a whole, had influenced the case. In June 2002, Ram was released on a life licence – meaning that the Home Office authorities are able to revoke his freedom at any time. Indeed, as Ram's lawyer had said at the time of his release: 'It does not mean they accept he is innocent and he is still challenging his wrongful conviction. This is a victory but not complete vindication' (Daniel Guedallla, 2002, quoted in *Guardian*, 15 June 2002). Many argue that the criminal justice agencies involved were excessive in their treatment of Ram, as he had refused to admit guilt and instead claimed that he had been a victim of a miscarriage of justice. Ram also claimed that he had experienced racism at all levels of the criminal justice system:

> I had 74 transfers [from one prison to another], I had over six years of solitary confinement, I had countless indignities, psychological abuse, constant intimidation, physical abuse and mental trauma ... Following my conviction the lawyers who represented me at my trial told me I had no grounds for appeal. I thought that was unbelievable, but I was determined to pursue an appeal. I've had two appeals, in 1989 and 1995, and each time the courts have been very hostile to me. I believe that racism exists at every level of the criminal justice system. I've experienced overt racism, right from my initial arrest at the hands of the police. The police presented the evidence in reverse. They made me out to be the instigator when in fact I was the victim of an unprovoked attack. I should never have been convicted. Then there was my treatment in prison. There was overt racism at the hands of prison officers. I was the victim of numerous assaults, thrown in strip cells, put in body belts. It was constant. Lastly there was the endorsement of my treatment by the judiciary and the Home Office. They changed the goalposts to suit themselves. But I had loyal people – family, friends, campaigns, organisations and activists – who gave me the strength to carry on. The criminal justice system has always been a class system. If you're working class and a person of colour then you are going to be discriminated against at every level as you are processed by that system. The justice system is a means of social control. I've been targeted over the years because I maintained I acted in self defence. (Satpal Ram, 2002, quoted in *Socialist Worker*, 6 July 2002)

Ram's treatment by the police, courts, prison and British government, who still today refuse to acknowledge his claims of racism, his plea of innocence and any failure on their part, during arrest, trial, incarceration and release, is very telling. It is a clear illustration of a criminal justice system which not only fails to deliver fair justice, but also when it is challenged on the basis of perceived miscarriages, and racist miscarriages at that, then does all it can to silence its victims. Thus, despite the number of measures in existence which are designed to re-address miscarriages of justice, such as the Criminal Cases Review Commission, in reality it can be argued that their potential to re-address wrongs and to highlight limitations of the criminal justice system are somewhat limited. It is here that some argue that the value of campaign groups lies not only in their 'action' element to correct injustices, but also in their ability to expose truth and the failure of agencies (Savage et al., 2007).

REVISION QUESTIONS

1 Does everyone experience the right to a fair trial?
2 What does the evidence say about the existence of racial bias in the court?
3 Given that it is one part of a wider criminal justice system, can racism ever be eradicated in the court system?
4 Will the appointment of black and minority ethnic court personnel and judges mean fairness in court practices and sentencing decisions?
5 How and why was Satpal Ram a victim of unfair justice?

FURTHER READING

Agozino, Biko (1997) *Black Women and the Criminal Justice System*. Aldershot: Ashgate.

Alexander, Claire (2005) 'Embodying Violence: 'Riots', Dis/order and the Private Lives of the Asian Gang', in Claire Alexander and Caroline Knowles (eds), *Making Race Matter: Bodies, Space and Identity*. Hampshire: Palgrave Macmillan. pp. 199–217.

Eberhardt, Jennifer L., Goff, Phillip A., Purdie, Valerie J., and, Davies, Paul G. (2004) 'Seeing Black: Race, Crime and Visual Processing', *Journal of Personality and Social Psychology*, 87: 876–893.

6

Proportionate Punishment?

In Chapter 3 we emphasised biopolitical questions to effect a shift beyond decontextualised analyses of hate as exceptionalised racism towards an understanding of how racism's apparently exceptional incidents – racist attacks, for instance – are better understood as being central to the regulation of racial boundaries that organise society. In other words, what might appear to be the exceptions of racism are actually bound up with the government of subjects. We now expand our analysis by considering punishment. We suggest that it can be more helpful to think of punishment regimes in terms of the condensation of racialised power than simply getting caught in a positivist trap of measuring disproportionality at the expense of understanding power. We also hope to sign-post some of the more recent contributions to work on biopolitics which have responded to the intensification of state power by re-emphasising sovereignty (Agamben, 1998, 2005; Edkins et al., 2004). Therefore, in this chapter we are not seeking to offer a micro-level account of, say, the experiences of black and minority ethnic prisoners, but rather we intend to sketch out some dimensions of the topographies of power which bind punishment and detention regimes to broader exercises of biopolitical racism.

Situating disciplinary racism

In this chapter we wish to extend our analysis by considering how we can situate punishment regimes within the context of race and power. In so doing, we want to make a shift from traditional empirical criminological approaches to looking at punishment regimes, and instead consider them in relation to conceptual questions about power. Our rationale for this is that although it took a comparatively long time for race to enter the agenda of academic criminologists (Fitzgerald, 1998), when it did so it tended to be associated with a series of debates played out in largely empiricist terms. These debates have often been problematic, and they can sometimes leave us balancing competing and contradictory empirical claims in the context of 'race and crime' debates. Discussing the challenges these pose to criminological research, Phillips and Bowling

(2003: 269) cite as an example the disjuncture between official statistics showing links between ethnicity and those arrested and imprisoned for particular crimes, on the one hand, and self-report studies which challenge these empirical claims, on the other. A natural parallel to this can be found in the way in which race and detention are presented in debates. For example, as we will see in a succeeding chapter, although Asian community activists and their supporters claimed that Asian participants in the 2001 Bradford disorders were subjected to disproportionate and discriminatory sentencing (Allen, 2003), other researchers have rejected these claims (Carling et al., 2004).

Phillips and Bowling respond to the challenges of race and crime approaches with an important defence of empirical criminology, noting the ways in which empirical work can be informed by minority perspectives (Phillips and Bowling, 2003: 268). Given the value of this important defence of empirical criminology, in this chapter we proceed with a slightly different approach, by emphasising recent theoretical debates about power and how these relate to debates about punishment. Our reason for doing this is partly because we acknowledge that criminological approaches to issues around race have attained considerable empirical sophistication, but recognise also that as an empirical discipline theoretical approaches to race within criminology have sometimes received less attention. In this chapter, we are therefore avoiding offering a 'traditional' exploration of experiences of punishment – indeed, there is a plethora of material on this which is already available – but instead begin by problematising the emphasis on dis/proportionality as an entry point into a series of theoretical debates illustrated by contemporary case studies from the war on terror.

We begin by noting that dominant approaches emphasising dis/proportionality have an obvious general usefulness in identifying patterns of potential and actual discrimination within the criminal justice system, and that for this reason they emerged as an important focus of concerns about sentencing regimes. However, we suggest that dis/proportionality approaches are problematic for a number of reasons. First, to focus attention solely on measuring whether (and how) minorities can be disproportionately affected by sentencing practices obscures important analytical questions about power. This lies at the centre of our approach in this chapter. It is particularly important because the attempt to measure disproportionate impacts on black and minority ethnic groups can have the normative effect of centering white people's experiences as natural and normal. Second, questions about proportionality do not reveal all that there is to know about how race works within practices. For example, a particular police officer might stop and search white working-class individuals and black and minority ethnic individuals in perfect proportion to the available population. However, the assumptions made by the officer may be race specific. Race and racism do not simply operate where there is evidence that one group receives more attention than another, but can be manifested in the assumptions made about different groups. Finally, we are concerned about the emphasis on dis/proportionality because of the ways in which public clamour for ever more proportionate punishments to fit crimes has in fact taken the form of a clamour for harsher punishments, and has been mobilised by media moral panics. Classic works on race and the state have highlighted how race was used to inscribe notions of urban crisis during the 1970s and 1980s (Hall et al., 1978), and shown how the moral panics about black criminality mobilised to this end were central to the emergence of different modes of white governmentality which link state actors with racist incidents on the street (Hesse, 1997). This helps illustrate a further problem with debates about what is a proportionate response to crime, since there is never any absolute measure for what can be considered proportionate. In the case of whether the sentences handed to black and minority ethnic people convicted of crimes are in proper proportion to those handed to white people, the arbiter is the normalcy of white sentencing. In the case of attempts to measure whether or not sentencing regimes are proportionate to the nature of the crime, the attempt to determine what is proportionate is a hegemonic exercise too often expressed through the registers of 'threat' and 'fear' of the other on the pages of the tabloids.

To shift our focus away from an emphasis on dis/proportionality and towards a more nuanced analysis of power we begin by noting that prisons may appear to be a distinct domain, but that they clearly reproduce wider racialised divisions and the relations of power which are expressed through these. For example, the findings of a prison inspection report (HM Inspectorate of Prisons, 2005) highlighted problems such as verbal racist abuse by white staff and prisoners, and the subjection of ethnicised minority prisoners to additional forms of control and discipline not meted out to white inmates. The National Offender Management Service (2008) has highlighted fears that victimisation will ensue if racism is reported. Such findings demonstrate that wider forms of biopolitical racism – that is, the use of race in regulating human life – have a position at the heart of the state's disciplinary apparatus. Such realisation necessitates a conceptual shift away from the focus on disproportionality and towards analysis of the institutional interplay at work in reproducing racialised divisions.

We seek to explore this interplay in this chapter by moving beyond the exceptionalised location of the prison, and placing its biopolitical functions in the context of wider attempts to regulate racialised boundaries. However, that is not to say that we think experiences in these carceral spaces are irrelevant to contemporary racism. Experiences of 'traditional' forms of incarceration do reveal much about the condensation of power to which minorities are subjected as do control orders. For example, on 21 March 2000, 19-year-old Zahid Mubarek was beaten to death in Feltham Young Offenders Institution by his cellmate Robert Stewart. Stewart was reported to have been a known racist who idolised the racist murderers of Stephen Lawrence (Kelso, 2000). In the aftermath of the murder a number of allegations surfaced which purported to shed light on the experiences of black and minority ethnic inmates. These included the unsubstantiated claim that prison officers had invented a game called 'coliseum', which involved placing incompatible cellmates together and betting on the (violent) outcomes. The Commission for Racial Equality (2003) produced a report on the case, highlighting systematic failings and systemic racism. It was not until 2004 that the campaigning of Mubarek's family finally led the Home Secretary to announce a full inquiry. When the Zahid Mubarek Inquiry did report, it contained an indictment of the experiences of black and minority ethnic internees and staff, highlighting extremely troubling perceptions among black and minority ethnic prisoners about the unequal treatment they face, and the complexities and contradictions of racism, for example with Asian prisoners more likely than their black counterparts to feel respected by staff, but less likely to feel safe (Zahid Mubarek Inquiry, 2006: 537). If racism persists within the prison system, this has been well documented; what we are concerned with is not a micro level consideration of life within the prison but the relationships between different institutions across a broader topography of power.

Reproducing racial boundaries

Since we are primarily concerned with tracing out conceptual questions relating to how racialised boundaries are regulated across dispersed sites including the prison, we begin by noting that an interesting range of literature has emerged from the US to explore these questions through a combination of empirical rigour and theoretical sophistication. Of the numerous approaches which have emerged, the example upon which we wish to focus is provided by the work of Wacquant (2001), who has written about the construction of a carceral continuum based on functional and structural continuities between prison and hyperghetto. We select this as an example to illustrate our discussion because of its theoretical and empirical strength. Wacquant suggests that the over-representation of African Americans in prison requires us to move away from a crime and punishment paradigm (2001: 97) and instead understand the ways in which African Americans are defined and controlled by a sequence of 'peculiar institutions' which have played the role of defining, confining and controlling African Americans (2001: 98). Within this reading, the ghetto and prison converge to produce continuous spaces for control (Wacquant, 2005). One of the strengths of Wacquant's work is its combination of empirical rigour and theoretical clarity. This is reflected in the complex and multi-layered analysis he offers of the structural convergence of prison and ghetto and their increasingly complementary functions. For example, Wacquant notes a fusing of prison and ghetto culture through which the ethnic and racialised gangs of the street are reproduced in prison, and the culture of the prison is reproduced in street culture (2001: 116). Thus, Wacquant's analysis also takes into account the important cultural dimensions which illustrate and infuse the arrangement he seeks to theorise. In other words, Wacquant's analysis is not simply confined to the analysis of statistics, but poses broader questions about power, dominant meanings and how a cultural logic of racism can emerge which works through the complementary institutions of ghetto and prison.

In the context of a global war on terror, Wacquant's work has opened spaces for a wider critical engagement with the relationship of the carceral regime to wider processes through which minorities are managed. For example, Khoury (2009) draws from Wacquant's account to develop her own conceptual account of racial profiling and social control. This is particularly interesting because it begins to interface Wacquant's work with more Foucaultian analyses of power. In another theoretical piece, Daulatzi (2007) offers interesting parallels to Wacquant's notion of a shift from plantation to prison by exploring the cartographies of power which connect different parts of the global US carceral enterprise. According to Daulatzi, the 'movements of empire' (2007: 134) which blur the distinction between the domestic and the foreign have enabled the emergence of a transnational carceral imaginary which links carceral practices in the USA with a broader range of state practices associated with the war on terror in a wider global field, such as extraordinary rendition, secret detention, and so on. In Daulatzi's reading, the construction of African American Muslims as posing a threat to democracy (2007: 136) and the conflation of 'terror' with fears of black criminality (2007: 136) help connect national and global practices as the carceral regime is exported during the war on terror. To Daulatzi, the links between the domestic and global carceral archipelago are underwritten by the global expansion of private prisons, and he cites one head of state correctional facilities as having said of the now notorious Abu Ghraib prison in Iraq that it was 'the only place that we agreed as a team was truly closest to an American prison' (Daulatzi, 2007: 139).

In the context of a war on terror, works such as these help to illustrate the close connections between different disciplinary spaces and processes. For example, a growing literature has pointed towards the close links between the USA carceral regime, police, security services, tax and immigration enforcement in the construction of a suspect Arab population in the wake of 9/11. Drawing attention to this, Murray (2004: 31) has noted that immediately following 9/11, practices such as secret detentions and immigration enforcement converged when over a thousand innocent people were arrested and questioned in the search for terrorists. Mathur (2006) summarises this context in stark terms:

> ... [Arab Americans] found themselves literally under siege and were subjected to popular hostility and racist attacks. The neighbourhoods were in a state of virtual lockdown, with women afraid to venture out to the grocery store or to send their children to school ... Sweeping arrests left families separated and terrified and streets deserted. In a manner reminiscent of the Palmer raids and McCarthyism, domestic repression, carried out in the name of national security, targeted selected groups as the 'enemy within'. In addition to the arrests, the FBI began randomly interviewing thousands of men with Muslim names, creating further panic ... law enforcement officials began picking up South Asian and Middle Eastern men off the

streets, from their homes and from their workplaces. Arrests were made on the basis of tips, reports of 'suspicious activity', which apparently consisted of having a South Asian or Middle Eastern appearance. These reports came largely from neighbours, disgruntled colleagues, employees, ex-girlfriends or landlords. Most of the arrests took place between 2 and 6am and the 'midnight knock' came to be dreaded. Men were taken away from their homes in handcuffs, while their wives and children were held off at gunpoint. (Mathur, 2006: 34)

The war on terror illustrates what can happen when popular clamour for ever more 'proportionate' punishments to match the threat posed to the security of the nation is invoked to drive a racialised punitive regime. In Chapter 3 we pointed to the hegemonic logic which frames both 'street'-level hate politics and state racism. But to discuss a logic of biopolitical racism we must also signpost the wider shifts and processes which frame its emergence. Our conception of control racism drew from Deleuze's (1992) reconsideration of a shift from discipline to control. But this position (including the subsequent literature it has informed) emphasises the radical dispersal of power across civil society as accompanying a crisis in the 'traditional' disciplinary institutions in the wake of flexibilisation and the increasing focus of disciplinary institutions on risk management. But can we reconcile this position with the continued importance of disciplinary enclosures? In the analysis of contemporary control racisms, the emphasis needs to shift away from methodological essentialism and instead address contested terrains of power. In the discussion which follows, we begin this by briefly acknowledging the processes which have framed the emergence of control racism before developing our reading of the multiple modalities which are played out in the exercise of contemporary biopolitical (control) racism by drawing on the case studies of control orders and the detention of asylum seekers.

Control racism and punishment

The studies cited above illustrate the ways in which carceral regimes relate to the exercise of racialised power across broader social fields and institutions. This convergence in the expression of biopolitical racism thus also marks its diffusion across dispersed nodes. It is therefore worth noting that the intensification of state power which has occurred under the guise of pursuing the war on terror has witnessed a number of developments which pose questions about the place of disciplinary enclosures and their relationship to wider processes and institutions in the context of this radical dispersal of power. For example, extraordinary rendition, the extra-judicial transportation of terror suspects, has effectively acted as a means of subcontracting punishment and interrogation work to other countries, often in the face of claims that the countries to which suspects are secretly transported do not adhere to the same guarantees of rights and may practise torture. In 2009

Robert Lady, former head of the CIA in Milan, was sentenced in absentia by an Italian court to eight years' imprisonment for the kidnapping of an Egyptian suspect in Italy and his rendition to Egypt, where the suspect is alleged to have suffered mistreatment. Also convicted were over 20 other CIA officers, although two others were acquitted on the grounds that they enjoyed diplomatic immunity (Hooper, 2009).

This intensification of state power has entailed a range of practices – for instance, nationwide anti-terror sweeps and the mass incarceration of Arab Americans in the USA (Meeropol, 2005) – which also reflect a radical diffusion of state power. In the UK, the intensification of power during the war on terror involved attempts to employ high-security detention without trial. When this practice was ruled discriminatory in December 2004 it was replaced with new provisions under the Prevention of Terrorism Act 2005 (Amnesty International, 2006) which introduced civil 'control orders' which deprive suspects of their liberty without recourse to trial, and the breaching of which was criminalised (Bates, 2009: 100). The Prevention of Terrorism Act 2005 created two types of control orders: derogating control orders, which could be imposed on an individual believed to be, or to have been, involved in terrorism-related activities based on application to a judge; and non-derogating control orders, which could be issued in emergency cases in which the Home Secretary had reasonable grounds to believe that members of the public needed protection from an individual currently or previously involved in terrorism-related activities (Amnesty International, 2006). Control orders were able to restrict a suspect's liberty to conditions which resemble house arrest. Since this breached the European Convention on Human Rights, they required derogation from article five. Control orders seriously restricted the liberty of individuals, often on the basis of secret intelligent without access to which suspects could struggle to challenge the state's evidence (Amnesty International, 2006; Bates, 2009), in a process summarised by Amnesty International (2006: 26) as 'stripping of a person's right to a fair trial'. In January 2010 the High Court ruled that control orders placed on two terrorism suspects were unlawful. The suspects had not received trials, but had been placed on control orders in 2006 following a hearing of a panel of the Special Immigration and Appeals Commission at which 'closed evidence' was presented by the security services (Gardham, 2010). The suspects' orders involved 16-hour-a-day house arrest, bans on using the internet or mobile phones, monitoring of all movements and vetting of visitors (Travis, 2010a). These orders were retrospectively quashed because they had been based on secret intelligence kept from the suspects, and a further ruling by three appeal court judges in July 2010 enabled the suspects to claim damages (Travis, 2010b). In January 2011, home secretary Theresa May of the Conservative–Liberal Democrat coalition government proposed that the existing control order regime would stay in place until December 2011 after which it would be replaced by a 'watered down' version. Key differences in the proposed new regime include the removal of the home secretary's authority to determine that an individual suspect be placed under conditions of virtual house arrest or to order that they be forced to move (Travis, 2011). However, in the face of criticism that the new regime amounts to little more than a 'rebranding' and that the same underlying logic remains (Ryder, 2011), we find it instructive to consider the original control order model.

These rulings were significant because control orders were central to the UK government's counter-terrorism strategy, as was indicated when Lord Carlile, an independent reviewer of UK anti-terrorist laws, suggested that the wholesale removal of the orders would be detrimental to national security (Kennedy, 2010). Control orders are thus significant because of their place in anti-terror strategy, and for the purposes of this chapter because they reflect both the intensification of power and its dispersal in contemporary biopolitical regimes. In this respect, control orders have parallels with other ways of dealing with suspect populations based on risk, for example through the use of Anti-Social Behaviour Orders (Lynch, 2008; MacDonald, 2007). If control orders reflect a biopolitical shift associated with the radical dispersal of the power to regulate life away from the traditional disciplinary enclosures, how can we account for the carceral regime? To put it another way: if the control order is to control racism what the prison (as a disciplinary enclosure) is to disciplinary racism, should we assume that the prison has had its day? Our brief discussion earlier suggested that prisons remain important sites for the detention and management of ethnicised minorities who fall foul of the criminal justice system, and indicates that the shift from discipline to control outlined in the Deleuzean literature is not once-and-for-all, for control supplements discipline, but does not replace it. Control and discipline are co-terminous. However, as we now seek to demonstrate, it is important to grasp how practices such as detention fit into a wider context of power. In the following discussion we seek to consider, in the context of a convergence between wars against asylum and terrorism (Sivanandan, 2006), how we can analyse distinctive contemporary modes of regulating the life of ethnically marked individuals through processes such as immigrant detention.

Conceptualisations of the shift from discipline to control are framed by recognition of global processes which occurred from the 1970s, including flexibilisation; the post-Fordism which underpins the radical diffusion of biopolitical functions across the private sector and civil society; and the increased importance of risk (Clough, 2003). It is also worth noting the post-industrial condition implied by this thesis, which has simultaneously created a socially excluded post-industrial sub-proletariat (Gorz, 1982) pathologised by the neo-liberal state as the site for the commission of exceptionalised racism, as we noted in Chapter 3. These wider processes connect with the global shifts in capitalist accumulation which have shaped the processes of migration which have brought new migrants to Britain in search of security: asylum seekers. Finally, they are bound up with the shifts in the exercise of state power which are reflected in the emergence of contemporary control racism. It is beyond the scope of our book to offer more than the most briefly sketched-out detail of these broad processes, but we note that they assume particular forms in racialising the social in those specific settings, and therefore set out the material context of our analysis, relating it to some of the wider concerns traced out in our book. They also frame the emergence of a particular penal logic which is aimed at regulating life by focusing on these dregs of abandoned life (Selmeczi, 2009).

The process through which the treatment of established minority groups within Britain and new migrants and asylum seekers have converged, across geographically dispersed sites, at borders and in asylum detention centres, on the one hand, and in post-industrial towns and cities in the north of England, on the other, is framed by economic change which has taken shape around deindustrialisation and flexibilisation since the 1970s. These processes, built upon by post-industrial decline throughout the 1980s and early 1990s, coincided with wider neoliberal retrenchment as the welfare state was reduced. In the towns and cities such as Oldham and Burnley these processes were structurally bound up in the emergence of patterns of residential segregation and concentration of different ethnic groups into different economic opportunities and forms of housing. Thus, the rolling back of the welfare state, shift to a service economy and loss of employment combine to shape both patterns of residential segregation and peripheralisation within Britain, and globally; and they collide around the policing of racialised boundaries around both established minority groups and asylum seekers. Central to this is the way in which the biopolitics of border policing is played out 'in different and often unexpected ways at a number of sites in contemporary political life' (Vaughan-Williams, 2009: 110). These sites include border policing within communities racialised by the government as threatening and interrupting the closure of the nation due to their excess, pathological, ethnic social capital and border policing within the penal regime itself. This process shifts our attention away from understandings of race and crime in hegemonic terms and instead challenges us to consider how racialised minorities are subject to control by specific state practices. In this context, we are interested in how the detention of asylum seekers reflects these processes, as particular logics of control emerge as nodes within a wider discourse of control racism and as different modalities of power. Having considered such questions in relation to the politics of hate, we now consider them in relation to asylum detention.

The New Labour government's *Fairer, Faster, Firmer* white paper (Home Office, 1998) marked the starting point of a process through which the government would increasingly frame asylum and immigration in terms of the need for swift and firm responses to a problem viewed in terms of security and crime. This was supported by developments which criminalised asylum seekers, and by a shift in emphasis towards control which included the introduction of a controversial voucher system, mandatory dispersal, which was itself linked to processes of spiralling control and racist abuse against asylum seekers and their demonisation in the media (Kundnani, 2001; Lynn and Lea, 2003), and detentions and deportation. The debates which framed the 2002 Immigration and Asylum Act sought to redefine the terms of the debate by linking control of asylum seekers to national interest amid a further shift in emphasis towards the notion of the threatening asylum seeker. Processes of spatial confinement and regulation, along with criminalisation, were linked to fears of organised crime and terrorism under the terms of legislation such as the 2000 Terrorism Act, and the Asylum and Immigration Act 2004, which further criminalised asylum seekers (including children). The campaign against asylum and the war on terror thus converged (Sivanandan, 2006), with the racist construction of asylum seekers being linked with the state's normative politics of community cohesion which pathologises established diasporic communities (Worley, 2005), and its counter-terrorism strategies in a wider project concerned with governing populations.

It is thus significant that the attempt to abolish habeas corpus for foreign nationals and introduce detention without trial for them under the Anti-Terrorism Crime and Security Act 2001 (later replaced with control orders under the Prevention of Terrorism Act 2005) symbolically link the war on terror, the punishment and criminalisation of Britain's Asian Muslim communities and the deviantisation of asylum seekers in the context of the securitisation of immigration and border control (Fekete, 2004; Yuval-Davis et al., 2005). Within this process, similar arguments were used by the government on the excessive alterity (Grillo, 2007) of black and minority ethnic communities to be normalised through the conservative politics of community cohesion, and the excessive difference of asylum seekers. At the same time, the criminalisation of asylum seekers was framed by a wider hegemonic move towards more punitive treatment for asylum seekers. The language of this discourse emphasised the 'fairness' of dealing with asylum seekers more swiftly and summarily, and was punctuated with appeals to prevent the asylum seekers from exploiting the country's resources. The moral panics which were central to this repeatedly emphasised the crossing of symbolic boundaries and taboos, amid scare stories such as the eating of the monarch's swans by culturally alien asylum seekers (Brook, 2007). Thus, as asylum seekers were progressively criminalised as posing a crossnational threat of criminality and cultural difference over and above simply a transnational flow of humans, detention became couched as a proportionate response to the dangers they posed. The state response to this came to rely upon the increasing use of Immigration Removal Centres.

Sovereignty and asylum detention

Having introduced questions around the exercise of racialised governmentality, in this chapter we expand our analysis of the exercise of power over black and minority ethnic people who come into contact with the Criminal Justice System by focusing on the question of punishment. This chapter thus enables us to think through some of the more recent challenges to the established literature on governmentality, in which 'traditional' conceptions are critiques as displaying a zero-sum conception of power which theorises the state *out* of its analysis, dissolving it into a web of micro-power relations. This case study helps us to restore the centrality of the state by considering the usefulness of recent contributions informed by the work of Giorgio Agamben (1998, 2005), who has extended Foucault's analysis by re-inserting an emphasis on sovereign power (Edkins et al., 2004). This particularly relates to the power of the state to suspend the normal juridical order (Agamben, 2005) and reduce human subjects to *homo sacer*, or a life stripped of political value (Agamben, 1998), through an arrangement which is spatialised through the metaphor of the camp. The case studies deployed in this chapter relate directly to this conception, and illustrate it clearly: the suspension of basic rights through the imposition of control orders on terrorism suspects; the detention of asylum seekers; and the violences to which racialised minorities can be subjected in prison all present an ideal case study for the consideration of this notion of camp and the stripping away of the political value of certain forms of human life, although the emphasis in the literature is to emphasise asylum as an issue (Diken and Laustsen, 2005; Garner, 2010; Gregory and Pred, 2007).

During the war on terror, the racialisation of asylum seekers securitised them (Sivanandan, 2006), constructing them as a threat to Britishness in ways which made them limit figures who signified established racial boundaries. This racism links asylum seekers to established minorities, and in turn to terrorism suspects, or those felt to resemble them, ensuring that all are linked within a shared racial logic. But asylum seekers function differently as limit figures, for they are subject to different logics of containment and control than are ethnicised minority Britons. This is a result of the logic of detention which works to ritualise and formalise the process of marking as racially different the threatening other. The asylum seeker thus becomes a liminal figure, because the asylum seeker marks a threshold between different states in the process of gaining access to Britishness. The limit figure also represents a terrifying life: like the convicted criminal or the terrorism suspect, s/he can be dealt with punitively in the absence of either a crime or a trial; has no legal status of citizen; and constitutes a form of life which seems particularly likely to experience forms of abuse and violence (even, self-immolation), or even death. For instance, in August 2001, Firsat Dag, a Kurdish asylum seeker was stabbed to death. While his murderer was only sentenced to a minimum of 14 years' imprisonment, Dag's family had their compensation halved because he had applied for asylum under a false name (Athwal and Bourne, 2007: 108). Such processes implicitly place a value of life. The work of Giorgio Agamben has come to be associated in particular with studies of asylum as a result of the ways in which asylum seekers come to act as limit figures. This reflects three key concepts in Agamben's work: bare life, state of exception and camp.

Within the discourse on immigration, asylum seekers shift from subjects deserving of protection to beings who can no longer be protected amid a media clamour to strip them of rights and benefits. This distinction emerges from the ways in which asylum seekers represent a life stripped of its political value (Gordon, 2004: 16). To Agamben (2000: 22) the asylum seeker comes to fill an ambiguous position, as a non-citizen who 'cannot either be naturalized or repatriated ... in a condition of de facto statelessness'. This condition of statelessness is spatialised through detention in detention centres which imprison asylum seekers outside the normal rule of criminal law, and without proper judicial oversight, and is defined around the exclusion of asylum seekers from a sense of belonging or the formal category of citizenship. Yet the nature of seeking asylum means that it is not necessarily possible to return 'home', since to do so can result in persecution, repression, death, or imprisonment for many people. Thus, asylum seekers literally become without formal political status as citizens, and their detention reflects this. As Steve Garner (2010: 156) notes, asylum seekers are barred from accessing the 'good life' accessible to citizens and are primarily designated in terms of what they are not legally permitted to do – a status illustrated by the ease with which they can be interned without trial or crime. The same applies to those subjected to control orders; while the main point of exit from control orders is deportation (Bates, 2009), the likelihood of facing torture following such an exit remains high.

Asylum seekers are reduced to 'bare life' (Agamben, 2000: 22) because of their lack of access to citizenship (Ong, 2006: 22). Thus, bare life, in this case, the asylum seeker, although it could easily also be the terrorism suspect or the victim of racism inside a prison, comes to occupy an ambiguous position, as a manifestation of a form of life which has been made worthless both in order to demonstrate the threshold between the political and the animal (McNamee, 2007: 497), and because this distinction takes the fundamental form of distinguishing between citizens and those who are stripped of citizenship. Bare life (the asylum seeker) becomes the locus of struggles over boundaries. But bare life is not simply a question of being denied access to citizenship, but the inscription of sovereignty through this. This power is exercised through the suspension of a stable juridical order, or, in Agamben's (2005) terms, the creation of a 'state of exception'. The creation of a state of exception plays an important role in determining the shape of asylum seekers experiences. Asylum seekers' ambiguous legal status is reflected by the legal vacuum in which they can find themselves, with the state able to treat them in ways which would not normally be legal, principally, by imprisoning them without trial or crime into detention centres (Garner, 2010: 156). But the suspension of a stable legal order has other manifestations, entailing a shift away from reliance upon force of law to the invocation instead of 'rules' which are discretionary and arbitrary (Watters, 2008: 181). This reflects the situation in which asylum seekers find themselves; detention is not subject to proper judicial oversight, but instead represents a regime held together by bureaucratic procedure. This bureaucratic procedure is enacted by a startling array of actors, in a range of positions: not only those located within the state, but also private contractors operating on behalf of the state. As Garner (2010: 157) notes, people can even apply for asylum in one state only to have their application processed by bureaucrats in an entirely different state. The implications of this are significant, for they ensure that the lack of proper legal status for asylum seekers is subject to arbitrary bureaucratic exercise of power. It also reduces the status of the abuses to which asylum seekers are subjected. For instance, the report by the Prisons and Probation Ombudsman for England and Wales (2005) on allegations of racism at Oakington tends to emphasise questions relating to the use of hand-cuffs to restrain prisoners as being fundamentally questions of proper procedure. Thus the use of restraint itself is framed as a technical, or a quasi-bureaucratic practice, bounded by specific procedural requirements (including a form to be completed before use).

Routinised surveillance and the dividualisation and digitisation of the bare life bodies (through scanning, fingerprinting, etc.) become necessary to protect the well-being of the society protected by their exclusion (Zylinska, 2005: 86), though these processes themselves follow an arbitrary bureaucratic rationality. These practices are centrally involved in the regulation of borders, and the situation in which asylum seekers and refugees find themselves 'spells out the demise of the hold of legal categories over people' (Soguk, 2007: 304), and this occurs within the context of the normalisation of biopolitical practices by constructing them as simply bureaucratic. This logic extends more widely to support the privatisation of biopolitical control of asylum seekers. For example, Birnberg Peirce and Partners, Medical Justice and NCADC (2008) have highlighted the ways in which private companies contracted the state to detain and remove asylum seekers are allegedly bound up in abusive practices within the detention regime. Thus, the role of the private sector in the detention centres is cemented, while carriers also become a further link in extension of an extra-judicial tier of control bound to their confinement within the centres, as a result of the threat of £2000 fines for each undocumented person found to be brought in by official carriers.

Agamben's 'homo sacer' (1998) is a figure who occupies an ambiguous legal position, since s/he 'exists as the exception, included by exclusion, made present by being banned, illustrating the limit condition of worthless life on the threshold between the political and the animal' (McNamee, 2007: 497). This stripping of worth is effected through the demonising of asylum seekers as a threat. This has been particularly important, because the emergence of the asylum detention regime has coincided with increasing convergence between representations of the immigrant threat and representations of the terror threat. As Tsoukala (2008: 66–67) notes, in the wake of the 9/11 attacks, senior members of the British government linked asylum with terrorism, suggesting that had the hijackers passed through London they could have been able to escape extradition by claiming asylum. This cynical conflation of terrorism and asylum helped reframe the idea that asylum seekers pose a threat to safety and security. The distinction between citizen and foreigner which is the basis of all western multi-racist states

(Sayyid, 2004) thus becomes central to the state of exception (Guild, 2005: 110). Agamben's work has increasingly been applied to the study of the exercise of state power over asylum seekers, and the concept of 'homo sacer' or 'bare life' illustrates why. The discourse through which asylum seekers are constructed as bogus is one which denies them legitimacy, but moreover which denies their completeness as subjects. The asylum seeker is thus subject to forms of ban and containment which prevent their entry into the community, in the name of protecting the country and preserving the integrity of its boundaries.

The ban acts as a simultaneous attraction and repulsion (Agamben, 1998: 110), since it draws the asylum seeker close through detention under sovereign power while simultaneously exiling the asylum seeker. That is to say, the asylum seeker is contained in a site over which the state has unremitting control, even through its subcontractors, but at the same time is removed from society. The fundamental distinction which makes this possible is the drawing of a sovereign distinction between the life of the citizen on the one hand, and a life lacking any political value on the other (Agamben, 1998: 124). That life which lacks any political value is bare life (homo sacer) and is defined in particular by the creation of 'a human victim who may be killed but not sacrificed' (Agamben, 1998: 83). That is, the ambiguous legal status of the asylum seeker, stripped of rights, basically opens the possibility that the asylum seeker can be subjected to violence without it being considered to be a murder or a sacrifice.

The possibility for subjecting asylum seekers to violence and abuse is particularly noted on the street (Athwal and Bourne, 2007). But within the detention regime itself there have been repeated allegations of abuse. The high levels of reporting by detained asylum seekers of feeling unsafe in their environment reflect perceptions of a normalisation of violence, or its possibility, which illustrate the practical value placed on bare life. The report by the Prisons and Probation Ombudsman for England and Wales (2005: 105) into allegations of racism in Oakington Immigration Reception Centre condemned the presence of a xenophobic subculture based around 'a casual acceptance of violence and abuse'. Thus, continued high levels of asylum deaths in the UK (Athwal and Bourne, 2007) illustrate a wider process through which value is placed on the life of asylum seekers, and which is also manifested in detention practices. Many of the experiences of detention remain contested. For example, HM Inspectorate of Prisons (2007) found no evidence to support allegations that officers in Colnbrook routinely carried staves and also concluded that routine strip searches were not carried out. Nevertheless, allegations of mistreatment persist: a report by Birnberg Peirce and Partners, Medical Justice, and the National Council of Anti-Deportation Campaigns (2008) claimed to highlight a troubling range of abuses of power in the detention and removal of asylum seekers. More recently, it was reported that women on hunger strike at Yarl's Wood detention centre had been beaten by staff (Townsend, 2010). Meanwhile, detained asylum seekers continue to mobilise in response to what they claim are systematic attempts to reduce their human value. Wood (2009) cites a statement issued by hunger striking asylum seekers which said:

> We are going on hunger strike until they release us. We have been in detention centres for months and years and our cases have not been handled professionally. Most of us are being falsely removed to countries like Afghanistan and Iraq, which are clearly war zones. Most of us have families in the UK. What are we supposed to do? Leave them behind or take them with us right into the middle of a war zone to be killed? The immigration laws and policies are clearly not fair and the only way you will find this out is by visiting us here in detention. (Wood, 2009)

Agamben's concern about the construction of a form of life which lacks political value is played out in the debates over the politicking of asylum seekers and its role in regulating the boundaries between citizens and enemies. This takes the form of a suspension of a stable juridical order. This suspension is, according to Agamben (2005: 2) the dominant paradigm of contemporary politics, and it works by producing in contemporary practice 'a legally unnameable and unclassifiable being' (Agamben, 2005: 3). Asylum seekers effectively exist in such a limbo, lacking the rights of citizenship, and often being confined into the camp-like structure of detention centres. Thus, the camp becomes paradigmatic of contemporary bio-politics (Edkins, 2003: 196), partly through the ways in which detention works, but also as a result of how the detention of asylum seekers is complemented by practices which disperse them across 'ghetto formations' (Diken and Laustsen, 2005: 87). Gregory and Pred (2007: 79) note that the criminalisation of migrants enables the passing of more restrictive anti-asylum measures, while creating 'stateless spaces in extra-territorial locales where states hold migrants in legal ambiguity as a mechanism of control'. Such spaces include Sangatte, but also include the immigrant reception centres, in which the violence, threat of violence and risk of self-harm are dispositifs of power which work to cleanse the country of the stain placed upon it by the presence of the threatening other. The detention centres thus reflect an intensification of control, and manifest the logic of Agamben's conception of the camp. In this context, we find a series of links established: a link between the new popular racism on the street (which we considered in Chapter 3), and the behaviour of officers (and sub-contractors) of the state in constructing the asylum seeker as being outside of law.

We began this section by noting Sivanandan's observation that contemporary racisms slip between different 'others': from Muslim to terrorist to asylum seeker. This is because all are linked within the conception of a new popular racism (Kundnani, 2001) which conflates the securitisation of integration in post-industrial north with the securitisation of borders, contesting each of these on the bodies of those it marks as racialised. The literally human cost of the system is illustrated by the legal framework, which ensures that anti-asylum laws prevent legal entry, restrict right to work and benefits, and ultimately even deny failed asylum seekers access to all but the most emergency health care

(Athwal and Bourne, 2007). The treatment of asylum seekers centrally illustrates Agamben's work: the sovereign power to step outside the normal rules – to suspend a stable juridical order – is both paradigmatic of the treatment of asylum seekers and the spaces into which they are concentrated, and serves the function both of regulating access to the nation and consolidating state power. Agamben (1998: 131) notes that 'one of the essential characteristics of modern biopolitics … is its constant need to redefine the threshold in life that distinguishes and separates what is inside from what is outside'. In this way, the emergence of the state of exception 'as the dominant paradigm of government in contemporary politics' (Agamben 2005: 2) is inescapably bound up in the regulation of the life of asylum seekers and the intensification of state power.

To conclude, in the context of proliferating racisms which constitute the other as existentially threatening within a zero-sum game of bioracist power, what it means to demand proportionate punishment is subject only to the limits placed on sovereign power itself. In such a context, an over-emphasis upon disproportionality risks missing individual tragedies which might not in themselves be sufficient in number to comprise a disproportional pattern. The key to understanding contemporary racisms lies in attuning our analysis to the shifting contours of state power, particularly given the ways in which exceptional measures have become central to the policing of suspect populations in the wars on terror and asylum. The treatment of asylum seekers in the contests over sovereign borders and racialised boundaries comes to reflect the state's attempt to reassert its sovereignty, what happens all too often is that the sovereign privilege of suspending the normal juridical order is all too often exercised. This occurs both in those cases in which the denizens of our global economic order can be denied life, and in the routine construction of them as a form of life with no political value and stripped of any legal status. As this happens, those in detention centres are subject to violence, abuse and bare power which acts on them in the most routinised, banalised forms through the simple logic of bureaucratic exercise. Thus, the official reports on claims of force in Immigration Reception Centres time and again view coercive practices such as use of handcuffs not in terms of violence but rather in relation to administrative procedure. In the same way, the subjection of terrorist subjects to control orders which are civil in nature renders them controlled by administrative procedure. Within the racism which links asylum seekers, presenting a threat to 'us', to diasporic Asian Muslim communities, the control racist state embeds its normative politics not only in the exercise of power over racialised minorities but also does so through bureaucratic rationalities. This is significant, for the retreat into bureaucratic rationalities is at the same time a retreat from proper legal status (citizenship). Thus the procedural-bureaucratic racism which 'engages' minorities through a normative politics of community cohesion based on essentialist pathologies of black and minority ethnic social capital exists in the context of the biopolitical practices which organise and regulate life in prisons, in immigration reception centres, and wherever racialised moral panics surface to organise formal and informal responses against the racialised.

REVISION QUESTIONS

1   Does a punitive practice have to be disproportional to be racialised?
2   What do control orders tell us about the intensification of state power?
3   What is the relationship between exceptional measures used to police the war on terror and those used to detain asylum seekers?
4   How does the racism experienced by asylum seekers problematise the role of the state?

FURTHER READING

Amin, Ash (2003) 'Unruly Strangers? The 2001 Urban Riots in Britain', *International Journal of Urban and Regional Research*, 27(2): 460–463.

Athwal, Harmit and Bourne, Jenny (2007) 'Driven to Despair: Asylum Deaths in the UK', *Race and Class*, 48(4): 106–114.

Gordon, Paul (1993) *White Law: Racism in the Police, Courts and Prisons*. London: Pluto Press.

Moeckli, Daniel (2007) 'Stop and Search Under the Terrorism Act 2000: A Comment on R (Gillan) v Commissioner of Police for the Metropolis', Modern Law Review, 70(4): 659–670.

Tyler, Imogen (2006) 'Welcome to Britain: The Cultural Politics of Asylum', *European Journal of Cultural Studies*, 9(2): 185–202.

Zembylas, Michalinos (2010) 'Agamben's Theory of Biopower and Immigrants/Asylum Seekers Discourses of Citizenship and the Implications For Curriculum Theorizing', *Journal of Curriculum Theorizing*, 26(2): 31–45.

7

Victims' Rights and the Challenge of Discrimination

Before we consider how resistance to racism can focus on a politics of identity, we now turn to forms of collective mobilisation to consider their importance in engaging with institutionalised racisms and promoting change. When we consider resistance in Chapter 8, we will emphasise the importance of anti-essentialist approaches to resistance. In this chapter we consider the ways in which an anti-essentialist conceptualisation of identities can impact upon our analysis of the ways in which group-based resistances articulate resistance to racism. In particular, we are interested in the ways in which campaigns and activisms which focus on particular material ends also entail a complex politics of contesting racialised boundaries. As such, we build upon the arguments we have begun developing in Chapters 3 and 6, and lead into our discussion in Chapter 8.

Resistance and collective mobilisation

In Chapter 3 we emphasised a shift away from conceptions of hate as sporadic, exceptional, individual instances, and towards a notion of a politics of hate which we noted was centrally governmental in its rationalities and effects. This conception was important, for racism is articulated very differently, and by a diverse array of actors. In order to grasp the fragile and contradictory unity of these many different events vis-à-vis racism, we need to move beyond the nominal notion that they bear similarity as 'racism', and consider the ways in which hegemonic practice imparts a sense of stability and unity to diverse articulations of racism across different nodes. Of particular importance is the way in which the hegemony of whiteness organises and structures these activities as modes of white governmentality. In Chapter 3 we noted that the apparent paradox of an expansion of white far-right activities and an intensification of the policing of minorities during the war on terror occurred paradoxically in the context of significant progress by the state in recognising and dealing with institutionalised racism. One benefit of introducing the notion of white governmentality is that it enables us to consider how informal racialised rule can be maintained in spite of its formal questioning (though not abandonment) (Nabi, 2009; Winant, 2001: 99). In other words, a conception of white governmentality can help us to consider the ways in which a racialised social order is patrolled and policed by a range of actors in a range of different and often contradictory ways. A conception of white governmentality was also important because of the ways in which it introduces a spatial element into the analysis of race and power. Governmentality entails the organisation of bodies and spaces in relation to each other in the management of subjects and populations, as we saw in our considerations of the case of asylum detentions and the politics of far-right hate.

Consequently, it is interesting to note that the forms of resistance engendered by the exercise of white governmentality entail mobilisations against a broad range of actors which are perceived as being loosely aligned in defence of the racial order. It is also important to acknowledge the extent to which spatial concerns come to the fore in collective mobilisations. A good illustration of this can be found in the context of the urban disorders which occurred in a number of northern English towns during 2001. This case illustrates the breadth of adversaries engaged by local black and minority 'rioters' and, later, by community activists, who variously took on far-right groups from outside the area; the local far-right support base; local whites who had no particular ideological commitment to the far right but were drawn in at the fringes; sections of the media; and the criminal justice system. Spatial questions were central both to the disorders and to the campaigns which followed as activists criticised state responses and attempted to promote calm. The disorders took the form of a series of struggles over racial boundaries which were played out in a spatial mode through constructions (by the media and, in some cases, the state) of neighbourhood space in racial terms, with space marked 'Asian' and 'Muslim' constructed in terms of deviance and threat. As Kundnani's discussion shows, the construction of ethnicised areas as 'no-go' areas for whites ignored the structural factors which had caused racial spatialisation in these towns (Kundnani, 2007). The trope of the 'no-go' areas also worked as a 'discursive knot' – a point at which a number of discourses articulate with each other (Jäger and Maier, 2009: 47) – and saw the convergence of concerns about racialised criminality, urban decay and white victimhood.

The scandal of the 'no-go' (for whites) areas became the hegemonic way of representing certain areas which were felt to resist white encroachment. Given that this mode of representing these areas implicitly fell back upon the assumed race of their inhabitants, the problem of areas resistant to white encroachment works to symbolically inscribe ideas of black and minority ethnic resistance to enwhitement more generally. Ralph Grillo has explored how in these terms the hegemonic conception of minorities as having an excess of alterity emerged, linking ideas about residential and social segregation ('parallel lives') with polemical claims that multiculturalism had fed this surfeit of ungovernable difference, in order to assert a politics of integrationism couched in terms of community cohesion (Grillo, 2007). The scandal of no-go areas thus led to the emergence of a loosely articulated response which involved a range of agents purporting to be struggling over the raciality of this deviant space: on the one hand, as McGhee notes, the state's community cohesion policy has been widely criticised for constructing 'segregation' largely in terms of the failure of ethnicised minorities to integrate with whites, thus ignoring problems such as white flight, racism and underlying structural causes (McGhee, 2009: 46–47); at the same time, far-right mobilisations have also come to focus on the problem of areas claimed to be 'no-go' to whites as a result of similar notions of 'self-segregation' or simply because of the presence of large numbers of ethnicised minorities, as was evident in Nick Griffin's claims that London is no longer British (Hazelton, 2009). We noted earlier that the hegemonic nature of whiteness works to unify expressions of racialised governmentality across dispersed sites and articulants, and this case study provides an interesting illustration of how this can occur. No project can become hegemonic unless it is able to overcome the particularity of its architects and obtain a wider moral and intellectual authority by incorporating some of the claims and interests of other groups (Hunt, 1990: 311). Struggles to enwhiten the 'ethnic enclaves' of the northern towns might otherwise have remained localised at the level of the racist far right but were instead consolidated by the incorporation of a broader popular demand to bring them into a state of order.

The state's response to the disorders focused upon re-inscribing the racial boundaries which the participants had been contesting. The Home Secretary, David Blunkett, scolded the Asian participants by arguing that 'we have norms of acceptability and those who come into our home – for that is what it is – should accept those norms just as we would have to if we went elsewhere' (Alexander et al., 2007: 784). This response conflated the struggle over racialised boundaries in the northern towns with the regulation of national borders. In turn this constructed the South Asian participants as being outsiders, even though there is no doubt that many of them were British-born, and it valorised the attempts to struggles over the enwhitenment of their neighbourhoods. As local South Asians were cast as an internal enemy (Dwyer et al., 2008), they were represented as being typical of a generation of criminalised ethnic minority youth. This contrasted with the representation of white rioters, who were exceptionalised as being unlike most whites (Burnett, 2004: 6–7) in a way which worked to recuperate a legitimate project of enwhitenment from the disparate expressions of racialised governmentality taking place. This state legitimated project of enwhitenment was on which which gender and race intersected in responses to the uprisings, as the 'problem' of Asian criminality was emphasised as a problem of pathological masculinities (Amin, 2002: 10; Dwyer et al., 2008). This gendering of the riots was reflected by the ways in which the central tropes of Asian territorialism and threat to whites (Webster, 2003) were linked to notions of dangerous masculinities. But it was also reflected by the ways in which problematic notions of family and motherhood were linked to stereotypes about Asian inassimilability:

> Women are often constructed as symbolic border guards of ethnic and national collectivities and the lack of knowledge of English of some of the mothers or grandmothers of the rioters in the north ... has come to be associated ... with the root causes of the riots. (Yuval-Davis et al., 2005: 527)

The state's response was variegated, and involved promoting a discourse which constructed Asian and Muslim minorities as having a surfeit of alterity which interrupted closure of the nation (Grillo, 2007), thus necessitating a broader critique of multiculturalism and a promotion of 'community cohesion', and a blunt response from the criminal justice system. This latter part of the state's response led to claims that young Asian Muslim males involved in the 2001 disorders were subject to over-sentencing in the ensuing trials. The response to these perceptions of racially gendered injustice was one of outrage, and some of the most organised activism to challenge the sentencing came from Asian women who mobilised to protest against the sentences handed out. Asian women from Bradford launched a particularly effective campaign, producing a leaflet demanding 'Fair Justice for All'. This spawned a coordinated campaign to highlight the length of the sentences handed out to Asians involved in the disturbances and draw attention to the claims that they were disproportionate. The campaign culminated in a report, produced by Allen for the Forum Against Islamophobia and Racism (2003), which highlighted the severity of the sentences handed out to Asian participants in the disorders and raised concerns about institutionalised racism. It also drew further attention to the campaign against the sentences which had been led by Asian women, and which sought to raise awareness of the alleged disproportionate sentencing; to have the sentences reduced through proper legal process; to highlight the root causes of the disturbances; and to educate young people to pursue their problems through democratic process, demonstrations and promote a young, energetic community leadership (Allen, 2003: 13). A subsequent report (Carling et al., 2004) challenged some of the central assertions and aims of the Fair Justice for All campaigners, suggesting that the sentencing had been less indiscriminate than in previous similar situations, and moreover that the allegation of inequality in the sentencing of Asian participants compared with their white counterparts was not sustainable.

The extent of the debate which followed the sentencing stands as testament to the success of the Asian women campaigners who had forced open spaces for engaging with the state on the severity and wider impacts of its treatment of the rioters. In fact, the campaign had its precursors. Some 20 years previously, in July 1981, a dozen young Asian men were arrested and charged after having manufactured Molotov cocktails in an attempt to defend their community against racist attacks by skinheads (Howe, 2000). The 12 were activists who had been involved in campaigning on immigration cases such as that of Nasira Begum (Brah, 2006: 58), and their case was itself to become the focus for intensive campaigning for the right to self-defence against racist violence (Westwood, 1991: 107). Among those who actively campaigned for the so-called Bradford 12 were South Asian women activists, including Amrit Wilson, who wrote a powerful piece at the time summarising what she saw as the situation:

> The black community in Bradford also believe that the nature of the charges [against the twelve] also show that the police aim to crush and discredit black self-defence: that behind the charges the real issue is not petrol bombs at all but the right of the community to defend itself when police protection is not available. Most weekends Bradford is invaded by the National Front. Homes, businesses and places of worship in and around Bradford have been firebombed. Attacks on the street are commonplace. In the last few weeks there have been several such attacks. For example, on July 24 two Asian owned houses were gutted in a vicious arson attack; two white men were charged but released on bail. On July 14 an Asian schoolboy was attacked by a gang of about 40 white youths with a petrol bomb shouting racist slogans and giving the Nazi salute; only two were charged and that too only with assault and stealing petrol for their bomb. (Wilson, 1981: 1527)

Another precursor to the mobilisation of Asian women following the 2001 riots occurred following an earlier disorder which took place in Bradford over three days during June 1995. The case involved confrontations between young Asian males and the police (Waddington, 2010), and has some significance as having been one of a series of episodes which were represented by the media in ways which marked a shift in racialised representations towards notions of Asian criminality (Goodey, 2001; Webster, 1997). The disorder was sparked when police attempted to arrest two Asian youths who were playing football in the street (Burlet and Reid, 1998), although the underlying causes of the ensuing disturbances were found by the Bradford Commission Report to be related to deprivation (Bradford Commission Report, 1995, cited in Valentine, 2006: 7). Burlet and Reid (1998) have drawn attention to the voices and experiences of Asian women, highlighting the ways in which Asian women in Bradford intervened during the riot, between lines of rioters and police, and the ways in which their subsequent activism highlighted the fallacy of the idea that women's interests were being represented through existing systems of community leadership. In particular, Burlet and Reid highlight the ways in which Muslim women in Bradford challenged the local state's responses to the riot, by highlighting the ways in which it involved consolidating male access to mechanisms of power and community representation.

What unites these various collective mobilisations against racism is the idea that all were concerned with resisting not one external antagonist, but multiple antagonists, whose racisms constituted dispersed nodes loosely articulated together by a wider hegemonic politics of whiteness. As such, it was significant that the activisms witnessed in Britain over the past decade take numerous forms, but frequently draw attention to the specific ways in which a complex politics of whiteness is expressed across dispersed nodes and agents in particular contexts. As such they have tended to challenge practices of racialised governmentality at the level of institutions of local and central state, and mobilise to defend 'community' space against the far right. These mobilisations also illustrate the extent to which spatial concerns are as bound up in resistance as they are in white governmentality. Finally, just as white governmentality finds its technologies used across multiple points of action, resistance is also expressed across a range of different social locations by a diverse range of actors, including those – women in particular – who might stereotypically be missing from discussions about black and minority collective mobilisation. This therefore poses important challenges in terms of how we understand the emergence of political subjectivities, and how we can account for the role of gender in forms of collective action. In the succeeding sections of this chapter we consider these questions.

Rethinking political identities

One of the key challenges posed by race is the need to recognise that there are no essential racial identities. But once we recognise that racial identities are socially constructed, then we are also forced to accept that there can similarly be no privileged essential political identities for black and minority ethnic people. In other words, just as any discussion about race includes understanding the ways in which its boundaries are being inscribed and struggled over, so too does any consideration of political identities which are articulated around appeals to a racial grammar. Our way of dealing with this question is to acknowledge that the inscription of racial boundaries is itself political. We established this argument in Chapter 3, drawing from Laclau and Mouffe's (1985) notion of the political in relation to the possibility of antagonism. Thus, in contrast to essentialist assumptions characterising racial politics to be guided by essential characteristics internal to minorities, as is the case in accounts of 'Muslim extremism' espoused by far-right groups such as the English Defence League and British National Party, the ways in which black and minority ethnic people mobilise collectively around racialised political identities is both a reflection of the ways in which they are racialised as different (through racist discourse) and an expression of their struggles to claim agency over their own identities. The point is therefore that we cannot conceive of a form of racism which does not meet with politicised response, as we witness processes through which identities are constructed and realised, fought over and transformed (Sayyid, 2004), as they are differently positioned and repositioned in relation to other discursive elements and identities. The various attempts to stabilise what those shifting meanings convey are themselves hegemonic operations, contingent on the one hand on the success (or otherwise) of different kinds of attempts to hegemonise particular constructions of what it means to be a racialised or ethnicised minority political actor. Black and minority ethnic activism against racism takes place in the context of a politics through which identities are constructed and realised, fought over and transformed, as they are differently positioned in relation to other discursive elements and identities at any point in time. But once we recognise that there can be no privileged political identity, and that to claim otherwise is essentialist, we are a step closer to being able to account for the emergence and significance of forms of collective mobilisation against racism. An anti-essentialist approach would entail focusing upon the ways in which identities are constructed and acquired, foregrounding the contingency which informs their articulation, and the agency central to their expression (Howarth, 2000).

To begin with an anti-essentialist account of the ways in which black and minority ethnic people mobilise around particular collective political identities is therefore contingent upon rendering visible the struggles over the political agency of minorities. To illustrate this, we find it helpful to consider the question of involvement in 'mainstream' politics. This is, of course, a major problem. Contemporary discourse on trying to engender the emergence of 'moderate' Muslim political identities is all too often based upon the mistaken assumption that 'mainstream' politics presents a neutral terrain which lacks any obstacles to minority participation. But this is not necessarily the case. For example, of the major established parties, it is commonly assumed that the Labour Party is most likely to represent the needs and opinions of black and minority ethnic people. This reflects a number of factors including the traditional class-based politics of old Labour, as well as the traditional racial politics of a Conservative Party which has been seen, for example, as having played a significant role in the emergence of new racism (Barker, 1981). But the relationship between Muslims and the New Labour party has been complicated by a number of factors. First, it is worth noting that even today, political parties actively engage in a politics of race. We considered an example of this in Chapter 3, when we discussed the relationship of New Labour's 'third way' politics to the emergence of an expanding politics of hate in the context of the wars against asylum and terror. Indeed, the party has been repeatedly accused of pandering to right-wing opinion and 'middle England' thinking of race and immigration issues in recent years (Younge, 2009a). Second, it has been claimed in recent years that among more socially conservative Muslims, support for the Conservative Party was increasing on account of its historical emphasis upon 'traditional' family forms, for example, the heterosexual marital family. Third, Muslim support for New Labour has further been complicated by its foreign policy over the past decade, and in particular by unpopular decisions such as the pursuit of a war against terrorism which has been associated with increased surveillance and suspicion of Muslims, and an unpopular war in Iraq.

While the Labour government invested significant effort in promoting 'moderate' political identities among Muslims, its own conception of what 'moderacy' means has been contested. For instance, although Ken Livingstone, Labour's former Mayor of London, has defended the Islamic theologian Yusuf al Qaradawi as a moderate (Hari, 2008), Qaradawi has been regularly accused of homophobia and anti-Semitism and the Home Office has banned him from entering the country. This case appears relatively straightforward, for Qaradawi has a long history of homophobic and anti-Israeli rhetoric. This also illustrates the contestedness of the kind of Muslim political identities it has sought to promote. For example, the Muslim Council of Britain was courted as a key ally against extremism and provided with considerable amounts of funding, only for the Labour government to suspend its relations with the organisation in 2009, before making moves to reinstate them in 2010.

It is also worth noting that Muslim relations with organised centre-left politics have never been entirely unproblematic. In the case of student politics during the 1990s, justifiable concerns about the activities undertaken by tiny fringe groups such as al Muhajiroun often fed into a wider demonisation of Muslim students such that on one occasion the election of a student with a Muslim name as Students Union President resulted in a media furore over a 'fundamentalist' takeover of the union, despite the fact that the student concerned had stood on a pro-sports ticket and was derided by some students for his apolitical stance (Bright, 1995). Cases such as this illustrate some of the ways in which wider stereotypes about black and minority ethnic people can impact upon political representation. For example, noting that the racialisation of politics has historically entailed the stereotyping of black and minority ethnic politics in terms of corruption (Solomos and Back, 1995), Kingsley Purdham has starkly highlighted the continued difficulties encountered by some members of black and minority ethnic groups in gaining access to 'mainstream' political parties:

> At both the local and parliamentary levels Muslim Labour party members have been accused of: illegally recruiting or inventing members in order to secure the selection of a Muslim candidate in Manchester (Gorton), Preston (Central), Oldham (Central), London (Tower Hamlets), (Bethnal Green), (Stepney), Nottingham (East), Rotherham (Central Ward), Bradford (University and Toller) and Glasgow (Govan); and of using council funds to bribe Labour party members to secure support for a particular Muslim Labour candidate in Birmingham (Sparkbrook, Ladywood, Small Heath) and Bradford (University ward). Muslims have, in turn, variously accused the local and national party of discrimination, prejudice in candidature selection, delays in the acceptance of membership applications and exclusion from meetings. (Purdham, 2001: 149)

One consequence of the complication of Muslim–Labour Party relations since 1997 has been the increasing role of Muslim organisations seeking to lobby the government and the large parties into taking more notice of Muslim community grievances. While Muslim representation in senior positions in the main political parties is increasing, a particularly important channel for mobilisation has been the Respect Party, largely because of its willingness to provide space for Muslim opposition to the war in Iraq. Muslims' experiences with party politics reflect a range of factors which have impacted upon community members. However, they also illustrate a general problem which black and minority ethnic political actors may encounter when seeking to engage in established channels for political activity. This problematic has been most marked in the case of class-based politics which for a long time dominated the political landscape. Even participation in the trade-union movement occurred in the face of institutionalised racism, as was illustrated when industrial action occurred among sections of the labour movement in support of Enoch Powell following his sacking in the wake of the notorious 'rivers of blood' speech. In their work on Birmingham, John Rex and Sally Tomlinson (1979) noted that whereas white working-class politics had an industrial locus, black and minority ethnic mobilisation could be far more complex, taking into account such factors as histories of colonial domination and slavery, structural positions as workers and in relation to housing, and the shape of relations with the state as exemplified in policing and the educational system. But while this meant that the political activism of African Caribbean communities was not focused on 'traditional' leftist structures, South Asian workers' associations were able to bridge this gap more effectively, simultaneously engaging in community politics while carrying out 'elite' negotiations with the left and unions. Indeed, Phizacklea and Miles (1980: 93) note that for a considerable length of time, general acknowledgement by the Trades Union Congress of the need to challenge racism was undermined by its refusal to acknowledge the real extent of racism in Britain, and by its resolve that the true cause of the problems facing minorities was not racial discrimination but their own refusal to integrate. Consequently, the stance of the Trades Union Congress in relation to key issues around race and racism was ambiguous to say the least; while it opposed racist immigration legislation in principle, in practice it did not oppose the Commonwealth Immigrants Act (1962) and only retrospectively opposed the Immigration Act (1971) through a Congress motion passed two years later (Phizacklea and Miles, 1980). As Virdee (2000) has noted, the historical organisation of trade unions around difference, including different skills, led to forms of action which were also sectionalist.

It fell particularly to black and minority ethnic people to organise collectively, not only to place pressure on the state, but also to exert leverage on other agents of change. The emergence of a number of modes of labour organisation among black and minority ethnic communities along the lines of workers' associations was particularly important. These associations developed links with trade unions and laid the ideological ground both for the greater incorporation of black and minority ethnic workers' needs by the trade-union movement, and for the subsequent development of a more radical youth politics, as would manifest in the Asian Youth Movements (Ramamurthy, 2006). By the time of the Grunwick dispute in 1976, the support from mainstream trade unions came both from white union leaders and rank and file workers, who raised donations to support the strikers (Virdee, 2000: 142). Rex and Tomlinson (1979: 125) describe this starkly: 'an industry with low profit-margins employs Asian labour and where some workers are prepared to accept a non-union shop, while others protesting against pay and conditions, strike and form a union'. Even though the Grunwick dispute indicated the progress that had been made in challenging racism within the trade-union movement, it also highlighted the distinctive position of black and minority ethnic workers within a racially gendered labour market, as they were forced to mobilise even in order to receive the same basic level of unionisation.

If the collective mobilisation of black and minority ethnic groups has involved contesting racist practices across dispersed points of engagement by a radically differentiated range of antagonising actors, each of whom represent a contradictory array of interests, from the state to the far right, then the political identities around which black and minority ethnic activists can mobilise also defies simplistic, monolithic description. Political identities are struggled over every bit as much as ascribed racial classifications. This requires an awareness of the ways in which, in the face of obstacles to participation through 'mainstream' political structures and cultures, members of ethnicised and racialised minorities have engaged in counter-hegemonic practice to stabilise the contested meanings of collective political identities.

We saw in Chapter 3 that the logic of identities as negatively relational is both central to anti-essentialist conceptions of race and identities, and necessary for a proper understanding of the political. As such, we emphasised the potential for antagonisms in our conceptualisation of a politics of hate, as opposed to a sporadic, exceptionalised and seemingly random rash of individual hate incidents. In this discussion we drew attention to the ways in which Muslims have been constructed as threatening, by linking them to ideas of criminality, terrorism and alienness. This discursively fixes representation of the other in terms of a slippery and undifferentiated notion of Muslim external antagonism that is threatening to white Britishness. Central to this mode of constructing Muslim alterity is the establishment of equivalency between British Asian youth and external threats to Britishness. Although the war on terror intensified this manner of discursively representing Muslims, the process predated this period.

In response to white on black racism, a unified black political identity was hegemonised by anti-racist campaigners as the locus for collective political action resisting racism. Articulated in a range of ways in differing contexts, this unified diverse members of different communities with different histories around the idea of shared experiences of racism. But the challenges posed by this black political identification were felt overtly challenging by the state, which responded with particular vigour following the urban disorders of the early 1980s to attack the anti-racist projects which had been so important in hegemonising this embracing notion of blackness. In place of antiracism, the state promoted a narrow mode multiculturalism concerned largely with controlling minorities. The new project entailed a sanitisation and fetishisation of differences which concentrated power and funding in the hands of largely male, and often socially conservative, community leaders, thus accelerating the fragmentation of notions of political blackness by playing on the differences it had unified and taking the sting out of black youth protest politics. This strategy interrupted the ways in which anti-racism attempted to draw equivalency across a range of interest groups and ethnicised and racialised communities, and worked to emphasise their innate cultural difference. In so doing, it reified the hold of race while revealing it in new forms which were articulated against the new racist imaginary which had emerged during the 1980s.

These forms of racism reflected, and reinforced, the different ways in which racial frontiers were being drawn, but also shaped the ways in which these were contested. For instance, if it is the case that anti-Muslim racism emerged in this context, and was to become important to biopolitical racism during the war on terror (Tyrer, 2011), then it is also the case that the ways in which Muslims expressed their identities actively involved contesting these frontiers, as we have seen. A reconsideration of the ways in which different forms of direct action were expressed in these different contexts also reveals the different ways in which these frontiers were constructed and contested. Even though the 'uprisings' of the early 1980s frequently took the form of alliances between youth from a range of racialised and ethnicised communities, including white young people, they were characterised in hegemonic discourse as being indicative of the 'black problem' facing the country. In contrast, the urban disorders which occurred in the north of England during 2001 became popularly characterised as illustrating the problem of a supposedly inassimilable Muslim community, in spite of the provocative role played by the far right, and in spite of the fact that the Bradford disorder was not only preceded by organised far right mobilisation, but was also succeeded by white youth disorders in white working-class areas. The language used to fix these different cases reflects the ways in which, in different contexts, different kinds of modes of collective organisation have come to the fore, and the ways in which these have illustrated both the ways in which the hegemonic racist discourse has shaped the labels applied to minority groups, and the ways in which collective actions have contested these. For example, while it is the case that a shift away from appeals to a unifying 'black' political identification was hastened by the state's promotion of a depoliticised multiculturalism which fragmented sites of mobilisation across multiple ethnic identifications, it is ironically also the case that resistance also contributed to the decline of a unifying black collective identity. This is because, as mobilisation around notions of blackness progressed during the 1970s, the subversion of state and popular racist ascriptions of blackness this entailed led to a de-essentialisation of what blackness was felt to mean. In turn, this entailed a number of wider shifts for alternative modes of resistance.

Unsettling traditional modes of politics

Forms of collective mobilisation and resistance by black and minority ethnic people have tended to unsettle traditional modes of politics because they have often entailed stepping outside the established expectations governing political behaviour. These challenges have been felt not only by the state and white racist antagonists, but also by 'mainstream' progressive movements which have often failed to adequately reflect the needs of black and minority ethnic people. The obvious example of this is the labour movement, which experienced significant difficulties in taking into account the significance of race in the post-war period. But this problem was not simply the result of institutionalised racism, but also problems over the analytical status of race. Rather than rehearse old debates concerning the analytical status of race in relation to social class, we now turn to a consideration of mobilisation by black and minority ethnic women. This illustrates the recognition that we are not talking about the primacy of one discourse over others – race, class or gender – but, rather, it illustrates the importance of conceiving of 'an articulated ensemble of social relations structured in dominance' (Gilroy, 2002: 26). Exploring this through a consideration of gender also relates back to our earlier consideration of South Asian women's resistance in Bradford, and provides some conceptual glue to help understand the nature of the resistance politics in which they engaged.

Black and minority ethnic women have histories of activism and mobilisation which have frequently been overlooked. For example, the legacy left by Claudia Jones included both black and minority ethnic media and the Notting Hill Carnival, an annual event of immense significance particularly given the context of racism within which it was created. The best-known organisations through which black and minority ethnic women have mobilised include groups such as Southall Black Sisters, although there are numerous others, from the Muslim Women's Helpline to Newham Asian Women's Project. The significance of black and minority ethnic women's organisation has emerged from their unique position in simultaneously challenging gendered and racialised oppressions through a recognition of their intersections (Sen, 1999: 182), and by simultaneously highlighting black and minority ethnic women's experiences of sexism and racism (Gill and Rehman, 2004: 76). Black and minority ethnic women's groups have engaged with family, community and state, as a result of which they have been able to recognise the particular oppressions experienced by black and minority ethnic women without retreating into cultural essentialist explanations, and work to support women within their own families and communities, advocate and lobby for them in individual cases as they encounter racially gendered state practices, and campaign for wider policy and legal changes (Sen, 1999: 182–3).

Newham Asian Women's Project was founded in 1985 to work with South Asian women experiencing violence, and to 'challenge the impact of imperialist concepts of Western feminism and institutional racism on the delivery of appropriate and effective services to South Asian women' (Gill and Rehman, 2004: 76). This work particularly involved raising awareness of the state's failure to deal adequately with South Asian women's experiences of violence (Gill and Rehman, 2004: 77), coordinating and leading protests, and developing partnerships with other organisations in order to challenge practices in police and courts which denied Asian women adequate protection from violence. A good example of the ways in which black and minority ethnic women mobilised was campaigning against virginity testing of Asian women by immigration officers at Heathrow airport (Siddiqui, 2000). Siddiqui also cites the example of the protracted, and ultimately successful, campaign to free Kiranjit Ahluwalia, a South Asian woman who was imprisoned for killing her extremely violent husband.

Such campaigns were particularly important because of the ways in which liberal multiculturalism has often served to valorise misogynistic practices through the faulty rubric of 'cultural difference' (Cameron, 1993: 742). Such attitudes created particular barriers for black and minority ethnic women seeking justice in the face of domestic violence; the liberal multicultural response was simultaneously sexist and racist, since it retreated into cultural essentialisms which specifically disadvantaged black and minority ethnic women. The grassroots movements which emerged included particularly important interventions which challenged the state's response to the domestic violence experienced by minority women. For example, Amina Mama's seminal study of responses to domestic violence against black and minority ethnic women was starkly titled 'The Hidden Struggle' (Mama, 1989).

As a result of the pressing problem of racism, black and minority ethnic women's mobilisations often began life in wider anti-racist campaigns and struggles, with the more clearly definable feminist agenda having arisen through the need to respond to the oft-overlooked problem of domestic violence against minority women (Siddiqui, 2000: 83–84). Bryan et al. (1985: 132) note that during the 1950s and 1960s, the increasingly vicious racist violence to which minorities were subjected, with women particularly vulnerable, proved an important catalyst in mobilising black and minority ethnic people who had not previously prioritised political organisation. These processes were accelerated with the resurgence of racism during the 1970s, and Avtar Brah has highlighted the context within which such mobilisations came to the forefront, noting that the late 1970s were a period marked by racist murders, such as those of Gurdip Singh Chagger, Altab Ali, Kennith Singh, Blair Peach and the organised racism of the National Front (Brah, 1999: 16–18). But while dominant accounts of black and minority ethnic people's collective mobilisation have largely privileged male experiences questions of gender (Werbner and Anwar, 1991), the mobilisation of black and minority ethnic women proved an extremely significant, not only in providing important services, such as advocacy, helplines, hostels and refuges, but also in contesting the silence and complicity of both male-dominated community leaderships and the state, while developing partnerships and alliances with a broad range of groups.

The mobilisation of black and minority ethnic women in Britain has been extremely important in highlighting and challenging racially gendered state practices, particularly in the face of the threat of violence. The most important feature of these forms of activism has been the extent to which they have illustrated the complex relationship between race and gender. In spite of this, the political activism of black and minority ethnic women in Britain often goes under-explored and under-acknowledged in accounts of minority ethnic mobilisation. Acknowledging its significance poses us with a series of significant challenges:

> Conjure up a picture of an Asian woman: what comes in your mind's eye? Reflect on it a moment: write it down: draw it. Have the words 'passive, submissive', been a part of your portrayal? Have you imagined a woman beaten down and subjugated by the arranged marriage system – a woman ruled by the wishes of her family – a woman not able to assert her own ambitions and desires – let alone fight against poverty, degradation, repression? If so – this portrayal of an Asian woman is a figment of your imaginings. Racist imaginings which have taken strands from oppressive Hindu practices, imperialist ventures, capitalist projections, and welded these into an inhumane whole which shackles us down. Your task is to un-learn and re-learn. Our task is to create new imaginings. (Trivedi, 1984: 38)

This quote illustrates the inescapably gendered nature of racism. The stereotype of black youth criminality is a stereotype largely figured in gendered terms, moored to problematic notions of the uncontrollable masculinities of the racialised. Likewise, racist stereotypes of Muslims which emphasise extremism or political violence are references to forms of male violence; in contrast to these, Muslim women have tended to be stereotyped in terms of silences and absences, as shrouded figures lacking in agency whose presence works only as a symptom of the presence of the masculinised forms of political agency which are felt to have denied them their agency. Within the racist imaginary, there is no refuge from the centrally gendered terms of racism, and there are likewise no forms of racist violence which are not in turn equally gendered.

Black and minority ethnic women's mobilisations emerged to challenge the Eurocentric conceptions held by those who adhered to forms of 'white feminism' as defined by the attempt to universalise as natural and authoritative 'white' women's experiences (Scraton et al., 2005). In contrast, the emergence of black feminisms emerged as part of a broader struggle which tended to focus upon empowering both men and women (Collins, 1990) while emphasising the importance of black women's experiences and the salience of race. The critique of white feminisms which opened up during the 1970s was not limited solely to challenging the absence of discussions about black women and their experiences by white feminists, but rather by the terms on which white feminism accounted for their identities. Particular sources of frustration involved the idea that white feminism emphasised a fundamental gender difference which was often rooted in the idea of an essential sexual difference between women and men. This homogeneous representation of women ignored the different structural positions of white and black and minority ethnic women, it was argued, and in turn marginalised black women within the women's movement, rendering race and racism relatively invisible. Such accounts ignored white women's own problematic relationships to racism, the different positions of white and black men, in which white women could racially oppress black men, and obscured black women's experiences of racism.

In this context, the growth of forms of collective resistance within Britain's black and minority ethnic communities highlighted the ways in which struggles over race came to entail parallel struggles with white-dominated progressive movements. Hazel Carby's seminal paper 'White woman listen! Black feminism and the boundaries of sisterhood' (Carby, 1982) illustrated this, and drew attention to the fallacy of a universal feminism in the context of a world in which white women and black women had differing experiences of family and work, and different historical relationships to racism. Consequently, 'White woman listen!' echoed an earlier cry by Sojourner Truth, which bell hooks would later rehearse: 'Ain't I a woman?'

The idea of a black feminism met with a range of critiques (Knowles and Mercer, 1992), but as Young (2000) noted, blackness was not invoked in this context as a reference to an essential, ontic black female subject, but rather as a way of recognising the forms of oppression and resistance which had become central to minority women's lives against the essentialist notions of blackness to which they were subjected. But the most influential notion to emerge from these struggles, which linked grassroots struggles by black and minority ethnic women with academic writings, was the concept of intersectionality. Intersectionality was premised on a rejection of the idea of an 'additive' form of oppression, since 'there is no such thing as suffering from oppression "as Black", "as a woman", "as a working class person"' (Yuval-Davis, 2006: 195). Thus, intersectionality rejected approaches which had simply sought to add one essential oppression to another into double and triple oppressions. As such, the notion of intersectionality built upon black feminists' critiques of white feminism, but differed in that it managed to escape the essentialisms of both white and black feminisms of the time. As such, it provided a way of moving beyond undifferentiated, essentialist conceptions of gender, class and race which reduced the status of race to simply being a surface effect of class or peripheral to gender (Anthias, 2001). A closely associated problem with the dominant essentialist model was that it tended to fragment notions of oppression and therefore the identities of the oppressed (Yuval-Davis, 2006). Thus, intersectionality enabled an understanding of the intersections of race, class, and gender:

> Gender, race/ethnicity and class are central elements structuring resource allocation ...
> [and] modes for classifying populations ... This does not construct them as separate
> sets of social relations or systems of domination as Walby (1990) suggests ... Although
> it is true that they each specify a particular object of reference for making the

category: this does not imply any essential ontological inevitability around any of the categories. None the less they are all linked to sociality: Class: in terms of the production and reproduction of economic life; gender: the production and reproduction of sexual difference and reproduction; and ethnicity: the production and reproduction of collective and solidary bonds relating to origin or cultural difference. Whilst not constituting them as autonomous systems this denotes a specificity to the forms of subordination that characterize them. (Anthias, 2001: 377)

The ways in which black and minority ethnic people have mobilised together illustrate a number of ways in which they have unsettled established racial orders. It is certainly the case that most of the gains made against racism have emerged from struggle, as the campaigns led by Doreen Lawrence following the murder of her son, Stephen, demonstrate. But even gaining access to political opportunities has been problematic for black and minority ethnic people. Emerging black and minority ethnic political cultures brought together strategies for material resistance with cultural significance and played a key role in hegemonising powerful anti-racist political subject positions. Later, in the wake of the state's assault against these, alternative forms of collective mobilisation emerged to contest the depoliticising multiculturalism model which had been devised to contain minority populations within monolithic notions of 'community' and 'culture' without offering any alternative means of political expression. The struggles in which black and minority ethnic people have engaged have reflected the particular positions of minorities within articulated ensembles of oppressions. Contemporary reflections of this continue to upset racialised and gendered assumptions about minorities. For instance, recent writings about Muslim women challenge the ways in which Eurocentric scholarship pathologises them as being voiceless and oppressed, instead highlighting the complex ways in which they demonstrate agency. Bano, for example, has written that the liberal discourse which frames the law and public debates about Muslim women and family law effectively 'frames out' recognition of Muslim women's agency in spite of the complex ways in which Muslim women negotiate agency (Bano, 2011: 156). Similarly, Afshar et al. (2005) explore how, in a context in which Muslims face increasing hostility, Muslim women express political agency in sophisticated ways, creating feminist political identities of their own as the basis for a new range of political alliances which could mark 'the first steps towards a new multicultural national identity and cohesion' (Afshar et al., 2005: 279). Such works are extremely important, for they not only illustrate the complex ways in which Muslim minorities challenge the exclusionary rhetoric which problematises minorities as inassimilable, but also challenge the hegemonic rhetoric which renders Muslim women voiceless and without agency.

Finally, we need to emphasise the ways in which these struggles over racial meanings are contested in relation to the organisation of disciplinary spaces in very specific ways. Brah (2006) notes that the Asian Youth Movements of the 1970s were incredibly important in witnessing the articulation of a new BrAsian discourse which involved expressing claims to the localities they called 'home' while challenging the ways in which they were constructed as other. The same has been true of all collective mobilisations by black and minority ethnic people, as they have contested essentialist conceptions of 'ethnic space' and 'our land' in the face of white governmentality which regulates racial boundaries across multiple nodes.

REVISION QUESTIONS

1 What kind of obstacles have black and minority ethnic groups faced in 'mainstream' political organisation?
2 How do forms of autonomous resistance by black and minority ethnic people reflect challenges to, and redrawing of, racialised boundaries?
3 How has resistance to racism by black and minority ethnic women's groups unsettled traditional conceptions of racial politics?
4 What is the significance of the concept of 'intersectionality' in explaining the relationship of class, race and gender?

FURTHER READING

Brittain, Victoria (2007) 'Racism, Liberty and the War of Terror: Guantanamo', *Race and Class*, 48(4): 60–63.

Hesse, Barnor (1997) 'White Governmentality: Urbanism, Nationalism, Racism', in S. Westwood and J.M. Williams (eds), *Imagining Cities: Scripts, Signs, Memory*. London: Routledge. pp. 85–102.

Yuval-Davis, Nira (2006) 'Intersectionality and Feminist Politics', *European Journal of Women's Studies*, 13: 193–209.

8

Forms of Resistance

Within apartheid South Africa; among slaves in antebellum southern states of America; under colonial occupation; in the face of Holocaust: in even the most oppressive of racialised social orders, wherever there has been racism, it has been met with resistance. No discussion of racism would be complete without considering resistance to racism, for not only does racism emerge in diverse iterations as a global phenomenon (Bonnett, 2000: 25) to be as ubiquitous as is racism, but in doing so it both transforms the lives of those who experience racism and leads to changes in the racism to which they are subjected. In the context of the war on terror and the demonisation of Muslims as a deviant, criminalised other posing an existential threat to 'us', questions of resistance are particularly important because they reflect the extent to which the actions of the state following miscarriages of justice visited upon minorities pose particular obstacles to receiving justice. The case of the war on terror also illustrates the difficulties of resisting and contesting the demonisation of racialised minorities in the context of zero-sum investment in tropes concerning the murderous, threatening other. In this chapter, we develop this theme to explore the uses of contemporary anti-essentialist perspectives in the analysis of resistance to racism in the context of the demonisation of Muslims.

Contextualising race and resistance

Every system for governing social subjects meets with resistance, and the interplay between attempts to regulate the lives of racialised minorities and resistance shapes the ways in which members of different racial groups experience society. To consider black and minority ethnic people solely in terms of their subjection to white governmentality without emphasising their responses would entail a reductionist reading of identities and fail to account for the agency of racialised minorities. The resistances which emerge in response to racism are therefore central to our understanding racism experiences. In the face of the complex strategies and political rationalities which underpin modern racism, resistance emerges with particular sophistication to contest the values, norms, practices and institutions involved in the commission of racism; offer alternative politics for inclusion; and develop and deploy a broad range of resources and technologies to contest particular forms of racism (Goldberg, 1993: 224). In the context of a racialised social order, even the most seemingly mundane activities can become politicised as acts of resistance, and the most basic networks can become important resources for resistance. bell hooks (2008: 148) notes, for instance, that in the face of white racism and the dehumanising gaze of white surveillance, even the domestic space of the front porch can become a focus for the emergence of resistance communities.

In a similar vein, recent social sciences work has drawn from the coming into vogue of work on social capital following the publication of Putnam's 'Bowling Alone' (2000), by focusing on the role of social capital in resisting racism. Thus, despite criticism of the methodological inadequacies of social capital concepts (Harriss, 2002), its serious conceptual shortcomings and often conservative ideological baggage (Adkins, 2005), and the fact that social capital remains ill-defined, particularly in relation to race and ethnicity (Goulbourne and Solomos, 2003), social scientists have increasingly grappled with whether or not the concept can be rehabilitated for work on race and ethnicity (Cheong et al., 2007). Social-capital approaches are often accused of confusing cause for effect in conceiving of racism (Bhavnani et al., 2005: 115), pathologising minorities as suffering from 'cultures of poverty' (Bonilla-Silva and Baiocchi, 2001: 123) and reinscribing essentialist conceptions of urban crisis which originated in problematic conceptions of underclass (Byrne, 2000). Moreover, the New Labour government's return to assimilationism and community cohesion (Worley, 2005) was influenced by problematic assumptions rooted in Putnamian conceptions of social capital. While it is beyond the scope of this chapter to explore this contested concept, we invoke it here to illustrate the extent to which contested academic conceptions closely reflect the complexities which surround the question of resistance to racism. Even though on some level, social-capital approaches appear to shed light on how relationships can be mobilised as resources relating to classed (and raced) distinctions, they offer approaches which are far from being unproblematic. Thus, even though it would be essentialist to assume certain forms of networks are inherently 'good' or 'bad', to consider the ways in which black and minority ethnic people draw upon particular relationships and networks to resist racism and its effects in relation to a range of forms of experiences of racism and exclusion *can* run counter to the historical tendency to pathologise black and minority ethnic family structures as inadequate, so long as care is taken to avoid reproducing essentialist assumptions. For instance, Alleyne's work (2002) has shown how membership of loosely articulated networks can be important in responding to forms of racist exclusion.

The example of social capital is interesting, because although we believe its problems are sufficiently serious to dissuade us from drawing from such approaches in this book, it does emphasise the importance of recognising the forms taken by collective relations in response to racism. The approach we use instead emphasises the political nature of these relations, by highlighting the ways in which they are expressed through a logic of difference. This is a point to which we shall come presently, although first we establish that resistance to racism thus takes multiple forms, drawing from a range of material practices:

> Social oppression affects every major aspect of the lives of those targeted by it, whether its form is slavery, legal segregation, or contemporary racism. This totalizing reality is too often forgotten in current public and scholarly discussions of historical or contemporary oppression. Resistance under such circumstances often has to be subtle, covert, and enshrouded in requisite fear and necessary caution. Nonetheless, those who are the targets of omnipresent oppression are almost always more than 'victims', for they fight back as best they can; and they and their families most often survive or thrive under the most difficult conditions. Dialectically over time, their resistance frequently shapes how whites react and buttress the system of racism – in an ongoing process of response and counter response. (Feagin, 2006: 276)

But racism and resistance, when understood in anti-essentialist terms, are far more fluid and complex than this; power is not linear and neither are race and its resistance (Walker, 2002: 92). Race and resistance are instead processes of ebbs and flows, when even what one side understands to be a 'move' can be denied or contested, and subverted, and when the moves might not even be alternate:

> I want to stress that resisting racist exclusions in the wide array of their manifestations is akin to a guerilla war. It will involve, and often unpopularly, hit-and-run sorts of skirmishes against specific targets, identified practices, and their rhetoric of rationalization; against prejudices and institutional rules; and against pregnant silences and unforeseen outbursts. It is a guerilla war that is often ceaseless, though there may be the equivalent of cease-fires. In this war, positional strategies and tactics of maneuver need to be as fluid as the content of the racialized discursive formation and exclusionary expressions they oppose. (Goldberg, 1993: 224–225).

Discourse, racism, essentialism and anti-essentialism

To progress our consideration of anti-essentialist approaches to resistance, we emphasise the role of meaning and signification in constructing ideas about race and racial difference (Miles, 1989). This emphasis is developed well in anti-essentialist accounts, which acknowledge race as discursive (Goldberg, 1993; Omi and Winant, 1994). To recognise that race is discursive does not mean ignoring the material dimensions of race and racism, but acknowledging Stuart Hall's (2002: 453) point that race 'is a discursive system, which has "real" social, economic, and political conditions of existence and "real" material and symbolic effects'. Thus, resistance is not merely a question of the resources which are mobilised to *cope* with the *effects* of discrimination and disadvantage, but the terms on which racial meanings are themselves constructed. As Root (2001: 358) points out, 'to resist means that one does not accept the belief system, the data as they are presented, or the rationalizations used to perpetuate the status quo around race relations'. Thus, resistance is as much discursive as it is concerned with mobilising certain resources, as critical theorists of race centrally acknowledge (Essed and Goldberg, 2002). In this reading, resistance also involves contesting values, norms and institutions, and because the discursive exists in 'real' material conditions, 'dissolving a racist discursive formation ... requires struggles ... corresponding to the ... broad constitutive elements of any discursive formation ... And it will involve taking apart the mechanisms by which social subjects come to identify themselves racially and discriminate against those deemed racially other' (Goldberg, 1993: 225).

Our consideration of resistance begins from the premise that anti-essentialism forms a necessary tool for the understanding of race and resistance. Essentialism refers to a belief in an 'ultimate essence that transcends historical and cultural boundaries' (Brah, 2000: 341), and which explains the behaviour and belief of subjects through spurious recourse to the essential properties putatively ascribed to those subjects (Burr, 1995: 19). Essentialism encourages us to oversimplify the social world by reducing our understanding of the subjects inhabiting it, to a simple causal logic rooted in problematic taxonomies. Moreover, essentialism is the central conceptual strategy of all forms of racism. Racist essentialisms take numerous forms: appeals to science as a basis for the construction of fixed notions of phenotypical difference involve essentialism, as do appeals to culture in order to construct cultural stereotypes, such as in the logic of new racisms (Barker, 1981) that emphasise the cultural difference and alienness of ethnicised minorities. A final form of essentialism which often affects writings on race is the uncritical reproduction of contested racial categories. This 'methodological essentialism' (Stone, 2004: 137) takes a category of analysis which is socially constructed in context-specific ways, such as 'race', and reproduces it as a generally valid category of analysis without being aware that the category itself only comes into being through its specific social construction and operationalisation.

The drive for anti-essentialism thus forms an important means of challenging racist ideas, offers a necessary corrective to essentialist social sciences texts which have constructed problematic conceptions of racial difference and responds to concerns about the essentialist conceptions of blackness around which anti-racism emerged. Anti-essentialism focuses on the social construction of categories, the fluidity and contested of identities, and the role of power, language and discourse in constructing identities. The essentialist belief in transhistorical essences which define objects of study and their behaviours is unpicked through the adoption of an anti-essentialism which enables social scientists to recognise that:

> The 'whatness' of any given entity is socially constructed. In adopting an anti-essentialist perspective, discourse theory is concerned with the construction of meaning and identities, and rejects claims about the 'necessary' character of historical and political phenomena ... If, for example, race, gender, or colour are significant factors in

understanding specific phenomena, it is only because they have been constructed as such in that specific context ... discourse theorists see political processes in terms of the social construction of both the elements of a process and the concepts deployed to analyse that process. (Sayyid and Zac, 1998: 251)

For example, 'the things that make up human identities, such as masculinity/ femininity, hetero-/homosexual, sane/insane, black/white, working-middle-class and so on ... may be seen as socially bestowed identities rather than essences of the person, and this is why the term "identity" is often found in social construc- tionist writing' (Burr, 1995: 30). The central attraction of anti-essentialism is straightforward: it enables us to analyse the complexity and contestedness of identities without resorting to simplistic stereotypes. In the case of race, it is particularly important, for race thinking always follows essentialist logics. In this chapter we foreground anti-essentialist approaches to resistance, since doing so enables us to shift our attention away from the idea that the racialised identities which populate the social somehow exist in stasis outside the context of the ways in which the racialised categories themselves are brought into being through complex series of struggles (Sayyid, 2004). This encapsulates the difference between essentialist and anti-essentialist approaches: while essentialist approaches reproduce essential categories, anti-essentialist approaches examine the ways in which they are brought into being.

For instance, despite its emphasis on the performance of identities, Goffman's work on stigma (1968) was consciously distinguished from social constructionism (Treviño, 2003: 11), and has often been accused of essentialism (Berger, 2008: 16–17) because of its emphases upon 'abominations of the body', blemishes and 'the tribal stigma of race, nation and religion' (Goffman, 1963: 14) as being inter- nal to the body of those onto whom the stigma is placed. To Goffman, while the stigma is created by society, the source of the stigma is essential to the stigmatised person. In contrast, anti-essentialist approaches emphasise the ways in which sources of stigma are themselves socially (discursively) constructed. For example, anti-essentialists accept that race has no scientific basis, and that its discursive construction is central to the ways in which subjects are racialised and subjectified as belonging to particular conceptions of racial groups.

To illustrate this, it is worth returning to the notion of racial formation developed by Omi and Winant (1994), who refer to the structural settings within which racist discourse constructed particular racial categories and dominant ideas of the subjects associated with them. Exemplifying this, they note that those taken into slavery would have accounted for their identities in terms which made sense to them on tribal, rather than colour, lines. But the same people were constituted as 'black' through their insertion into an economic order based on the colonial power, the slave trade, and a colour line which justified their barbaric treatment by constructing them as 'black' (and as inferior because of their constructed blackness) (Omi and Winant, 1994: 66).

But in turn, African Americans mobilised to challenge these conceptions of blackness, subverting the racial order by using familiar signifiers of difference (for example, 'black') in unfamiliar combination with other symbols to hegemonise a new sense of what that identity meant as a focus for resistance to racism, rather than subjection by it. For instance, when Dr Martin Luther King Jr spoke of the emergence of a 'new Negro', he was simultaneously subverting a category brought into being by white racism and attempting to construct a political identity based on resistance and the idea of radically alternative notions of African American identities, which themselves built on popular cultural representations of autonomous African American self representation (Gates and Jarrett, 2007). Yet these constructions were themselves challenged by more radical activists who, influenced by pan-Africanism, attempted to construct black political identities in other ways. For instance, this often involved the move from the terminology 'negro' to a unifying notion of blackness, distinguished as being radical rather than reformist, and consciously appealing to the signifier 'black'.

In much the same way, Sayyid (2004) reminds us that the ethnoscape of Britain is populated not by identities which somehow pre-existed in essential terms, but by identities which have been constituted through complex processes of racism and its resistance to racism. What it means to resist is central to how we understand racialised identities, for which reason it is necessary to move beyond essentialist ideas about culturally fixed identities mobilising fixed networks or removing culturally bounded stigmas, to anti-essentialist interrogation of the categories themselves and the complex processes through which black and minority ethnic people have contested their meanings. To illustrate this, the case studies in this chapter focus on forms of resistance during the war on terror, and forms of resistance against anti-Muslim racism.

The war on terror provides considerable evidence of the complexity of material forms of resistance to racism, and the challenges entailed. To illustrate this, it is worth considering the case of miscarriages of justice which have occurred based on mistaken identities. The war on terror has been accompanied by a process through which Muslim minorities have been subject to a generalised representation as posing an existential threat to 'us'. This emergence of a Muslim 'suspect community' (Pantazis and Pemberton, 2009) constructed through the mobilisation of racialised moral panics has been cynically invoked by the racist far right in the commission of an unfolding politics of hate, as we saw in Chapter 3, as well as increasingly defining the shape of relations between the state and Muslim minorities. The spillover effect of this has been huge; between January 2003 and December 2004, there was a 300 per cent increase in the number of South Asians stopped and searched under section 44 of the Terrorism Act (2000). Although section 44 was ruled unlawful by the European Court of Human Rights in January 2010, it was central to a wider concentration of power which was brought to bear on minority groups during the war on terror.

In March 2005 Home Office minister Hazel Blears declared it was a 'fact of life' that Asians and Muslims would be targeted more under anti-terrorism stop and search powers (Kundnani, 2006). A month after the shooting of Menezes, Blears distanced herself from Ian Johnston, Chief Constable of British Transport Police, after he expressed similar views (Lippert-Rasmussen, 2007: 385). Speaking to the House of Commons Home Affairs Committee in 2005, Lord Hope repeated the suggestion that terrorist suspects would be linked to particular communities (Moeckli, 2007: 667). But the negligible rates of terrorist conviction resulting from stop and search practices could suggest that a more concrete achievement was to cement the conflation of the war on terror with racialised miscarriages. Certainly, miscarriages born of mistaken identity have been a global feature of the war on terror. Such cases included the American arrest and deportation (to face torture) of Maher Arar, an innocent Canadian businessman (MacPherson Watt, 2005), and the shooting in London of Jean Charles de Menezes in July 2005 by armed police who mistakenly believed him to be a terrorist on the run in London. Prolonged campaigns have followed such cases; Arar's attempted lawsuit against the Bush administration was rejected on grounds of national security in 2006, leading to a lengthy struggle for justice, while it took four years of highly public campaigning for the relatives of de Menezes to receive settlement from the authorities, with no charges ever pressed against the officers involved in his death. A lengthy campaign for justice also followed a major anti-terror raid in Forest Gate during 2006 which had resulted in the shooting of an innocent householder, who faced the additional indignity of being falsely slurred as a paedophile in leaks to the media. In 2008 University of Nottingham postgraduate student Hicham Yezza was arrested after downloading (for research purposes) an al Qaeda document from the website of the USA Department of Justice. Despite a lengthy public campaign of support, Yezza was eventually sentenced to imprisonment and deportation on the grounds of having attempted to evade immigration enforcement. A wave of arrests in the North West of England in 2009, allegedly launched when emails discussing a potential wedding were intercepted and interpreted by the state as coded discussions about possible terrorism (*Evening Standard*, 2009), failed to result in anti-terrorism charges, but did lead to the deportation of a number of those concerned, again restricting their chances of contesting the grounds of their treatment.

The secrecy surrounding counter-terrorism operations and the restrictions placed on rights of those suspected of terrorism have also created serious problems for those wrongly identified as terrorists. This was evident in the case of Lotfi Raissi, an Algerian-born pilot arrested in London on 21 September 2001 at the request of the United States Federal Bureau of Investigation, who claimed to have evidence of his involvement in the 9/11 attacks. The case against Raissi was so weak that an extradition request was reputedly based entirely on claims that he had lied on his pilot's licence application, and was ultimately dropped after the suspect had spent five months in high-security imprisonment. The victim of this miscarriage was not released from all charges until 2003, after which he was forced to engage in a lengthy and obstacle-ridden legal battle for compensation against the UK and American governments, while his career was completely destroyed by the groundless allegations made against him by prosecutors.

Resistance to such incidents has entailed lengthy and obstacle ridden campaigns seeking justice for the victims of these miscarriages, often in the face of state secrecy and media coverage which has frequently enhanced the sense of suspicion. The victims in such cases have often faced serious obstacles in taking their cases to the law and their campaigns belong to a lengthy history of struggle by victims of racist injustices. This history has included important mobilisations which effected the shift from grassroots campaign to national cause. The 'Free Satpal Ram' campaign is an example of this, but in many ways contrasts with the experiences of many of the victims of the war on terror, who have often found their reputations tainted beyond repair by the experience, and faced additional problems such as deportation.

Wider forms of mobilisation are also problematised by the war on terror. Birt (2005, 2006) has shown the growing visibility of Muslim political expression while also considering normative aspects of state dealings with Muslim communities. For instance, the Muslim Council of Britain was initially viewed as a key 'moderate' Muslim ally by the government, before being placed under pressure to bring its politics into line with those of the government (Kundnani, 2009). The state has also provided funds to support the work of moderate Muslim groups such as the Quilliam Foundation. Such work may have the effect of developing capacity within Muslim communities, and could contribute to the political strategies they employ, opening out a range of new political identities for Muslim minorities. This could obviously have positive effects in challenging militancy. However, debates about the use of the terms 'moderate' and 'extremist' underline the need to approach superficially stable political categories with care, and to be aware of the subtle ways in which seemingly benign labels can racialise groups. Some view the state emphasis on 'moderate' Muslims as having the opposite effect of actually blurring the distinction between 'moderacy' and 'extremism' (Youmans, 2004: 120–121). This is partly because the term 'moderate' only gains its meanings when deployed in opposition to the term 'extremist', so any invocation of one term becomes a means of inscribing the other. Indeed, Baroness Warsi, Britain's first Muslim woman Cabinet member, noted in a speech on Islamophobia in January 2011 that the tendency to divide Muslims into either 'moderate' or 'extremist' is unhelpful (Batty, 2011). Such debates illustrate the complexities surrounding the ways in which we speak of political identities, and underline the importance of ensuring that when we employ terms such as 'moderacy' we take care not to use them in ways which reaffirm stereotypes about Muslim otherness and extremism by presupposing a natural link between Muslims and extremism. After all, in spite of the recent rise of the far right and a number of recent far right terrorist plots, it would seem unimaginable to reduce representations of white people's political identities to the extent to which they are extremist or moderate, and to do so could actually risk narrowing the range of political identities they express through democratic practice.

Despite the state's attempts to encourage the emergence of range of moderate Muslim organisations, it is worth bearing in mind that forms of Muslim community activism and mobilisation often remain problematised as disruptive or even extremist. This is partly a result of the legacy of the 2001 disorders discussed earlier, which included a state discourse that overtly problematised the excessive alterity of Asian Muslim communities and questioned the value of multiculturalism. It is also partly a consequence of the wider war on terror, which witnessed an authoritarian turn by the state in its dealings with Muslims and frequently intense media scrutiny of Muslims, fuelling increased suspicion. This context of suspicion further politicises the networks and relationships which are mobilised to resist racism, but also highlights a key feature of racism. Once we accept that racism is about racist meanings as well as material inequalities justified by these meanings, it follows that resistance to racism is not simply a case of mobilising material resources to resist racism, but also about the strategies employed to challenge the discursive systems which underpin racism itself.

Cases such as these illustrate the challenges faced by members of racialised and ethnicised minorities in resisting racism in a context in which to resist can often pit individuals against an array of actors articulating different nodes of a discourse of anti-Muslim racism which constructs the racialised as posing an existential threat to 'us'. Central to our understanding of resistance to racism is a recognition that it entails discursive, as well as material, strategies. This is based on a recognition that racism works both discursively and structurally. Acknowledging this, Omi and Winant (1994: 55–55) note that racial formation is 'the sociohistorical process by which racial categories are created, inhabited, transformed, and destroyed ... race is a matter of both social structure and cultural representation. Too often, the attempt is made to understand race simply or primarily in terms of only one of these two analytical dimensions.' What we have not yet considered is the discursive nature of resistance to racism. This is the focus of our consideration in the following section of this chapter, as we begin to draw out the importance of taking into account anti-essentialist approaches to resistance.

Muslim resistance: from Rushdie to the Danish cartoon protests

To help illustrate the complexities of resistance against racism, and the extent to which forms of counter-hegemonic practice are bound up with challenges to the racial order, we now wish to consider the case of Muslim mobilisation in response to a series of cartoons of the prophet Muhammad which were published by the Danish *Jyllands-Posten* newspaper on 30 September 2005.

This case study helps illustrate the importance of looking beyond superficial assumptions about the political behaviour and identities at stake when black and minority ethnic people mobilise.

The first Muslim response to the publication of the cartoons was a protest outside the newspaper's offices, although after the cartoons were reprinted by a Christian magazine in Norway in early 2006, an international campaign of some ferocity ensued. The globalised nature of the response by Muslims was fuelled by coverage of the affair on the Al Jazeera and Al Arabiya television channels (Müller et al., 2009: 30) but also reflected the transnational identifications made by many Muslims. As the issue escalated, a number of horrifying incidents took place, including a plot to murder the cartoonist Kurt Westergaard in Denmark and an attempted terrorist attack in Germany (Müller et al., 2009: 30). A series of demonstrations took place during February 2006, and during one such gathering outside the Danish Embassy in London, a number of protesters held up banners which called for the execution of those who commit blasphemy. In July 2007 three British Muslim men were handed six-year prison sentences for soliciting to murder in the demonstration, while a fourth was sentenced to four years for stirring up racial hatred. Media reports of the shocking and violent responses to the cartoons helped cement the idea that the whole affair simply concerned a collision between the demands of an overly religious minority and a liberal democracy. As a result, the cartoons were reprinted in a number of European countries in defence of the right of free speech (Harding and Wilsher, 2006) which was increasingly taken for granted as being the key issue at stake in the affair.

Although media portrayals of the affair emphasised the idea that the protesters were centrally motivated by extreme religious belief, the protests were far more complex than this. Coverage of the extremist nature of the protesters tended to obscure the spectrum of Muslim political identities on display in the protests and the array of demands they were making. Although extremists were eager to capitalise on anger about the cartoons and cynically used the protests as a platform for expressing their own views, there were in fact a number of splits among protesters. The most obvious split was between those in Muslim countries who tended to view the cartoon affair in a theological context and European Muslims who tended to understand the cartoons in very different terms as a reflection of the social problems experienced by Muslim minorities (Müller et al., 2009: 33). Among European Muslims, those who viewed the cartoons as being fundamentally about social, rather than theological, issues were also quick to distance themselves from the militants who had attempted to hijack the platform for their own ends. In Britain, Muslims angered by the activities of radical protesters in the February 2006 demonstration swiftly organised a follow-up demonstration which they intended would be a peaceful alternative, and which would clearly distinguish their aims and protest repertoire from those of the radicals who had attracted negative media publicity. Muslim community leaders, activists and intellectuals also began disseminating their own readings of the cartoon affair, through the internet and the Muslim press. What was most significant about these responses was that many of them tended to emphasise the idea that the central problem with the cartoons was racism. Within such accounts, blasphemy was often underplayed. Summarising the issues played out in Muslim grievances, Professor Tariq Modood, a leading theorist of multicultural citizenship, wrote:

> From the Muslim side, the underlying causes of their current anger are a deep sense that they are not respected, that they and their most cherished feelings are 'fair game'. Inferior protective legislation, socio-economic marginality, cultural disdain, draconian security surveillance, the occupation of Palestine, the international 'war on terror' all converge on this point. The cartoons cannot be compared to some of these situations, but they do distil the experience of inferiority and of being bossed around. A handful of humiliating images become a focal point for something much bigger than themselves. (Modood, 2006: 5)

Accounts such as this help take us from the superficial analysis that the cartoon affair simply centred on the refusal of some Muslims to accept criticism of their religion, and places the cartoons into a wider context. The idea that the cartoons came to symbolise the wider treatment of Muslims is extremely important, for it relies on our ability to recognise that the cartoons themselves bear broader cultural and social meanings. Variously described as 'satirical' and 'ironic', the cartoons were never intended to bear straightforward meanings and cannot therefore be assumed to transmit the straightforward meanings attributed to them in media commentaries. In fact, while some of the 12 cartoons appear mundane and harmless, others were extremely problematic: one depicted Muslims in an identity parade, another appeared to show a scimitar-wielding prophet jealously guarding two burka-clad women, while a third depicted the prophet Muhammad wearing a turban loosely wrapped around a bomb with a burning fuse. Even within their own terms as an attempt to test free speech, the cartoons had been intended to provoke a Muslim response, although to effect this through images which conveyed a mixture of traditional orientalist images and contemporary stereotypes of Muslims as terrorists and criminals would always cause offence. The cartoons did not simply poke humour at a religious prophet, but validated the stereotypes they employed in the course of this and, in so doing, made a comment about Muslims more generally (Modood, 2006: 4). In fact, the cartoons deliberately played on notions of Muslim alterity, and the attempt to 'test' free speech was expressed around the representation of Muslims as a threat to democracy and Danish culture (Jensen, 2009: 68). As Ridanpää has noted, the cartoons 'were aimed to operate more or less destructively, attacking the Muslim world in a way which cannot be considered "innocent laughter" within any discursive community' (2009: 736).

When the cartoons are placed into context, it is not difficult to see how they caused offence to Muslims. Media reports of the protests demonstrate the inadequacy of essentialist accounts of the affair, which involve representing the protesters as a monolithic group, obscuring the diversity of political identities on display and the breadth of issues they contested. Such essentialist accounts also seek to fix the meanings of the affair in the essentialist terms of a straightforward collision between essentially Muslim and essentially democratic European worldviews, but fail to take into account the contested nature of the identities at play in the protests. Since no account of the protest would be complete without taking this into account, we now place the protests into context in order to explore this dimension of the affair.

Outlining the issues about racism and multicultural citizenship at stake in the affair, Tariq Modood has noted that:

> Two factors are critical to the lack of sympathy for Muslims in Europe. First, there is a lack of recognition that the way that Muslims are treated is a form of racism – after all it is less than 15 years ago that Britain's Commission for Racial Equality and most British anti-racists denied that the vilification of Muslims was a form of racism. ... The second reason is the idea – prevalent among anti-racists, the progressive intelligentsia, and beyond – that religious people are not worthy of protection; more than that, they should be subject to not just intellectual criticism but mockery and ridicule. (Modood 2006: 5–6)

This places the cartoons affair into the wider context of struggles over Islamophobia which have been played out over the past two decades. Since these struggles have had the effect of contesting the stability of the racial order and the nature of racialised identities, it is necessary to consider them. Islamophobia, as it is widely termed, emerged during the 1990s although there was a widespread reluctance to recognise its existence prior to the terrorist attacks of 11 September 2001, which were followed by increased anti-Muslim racism. In spite of this, Muslims still found themselves engaged in struggles over the ways in which their identities were essentialised in order to deny anti-Muslim racism the same legal status as other forms of racism (Tyrer, 2011). We can only understand this if we situate Muslim resistance to the unfolding politics of hate we discussed in Chapter 3 within the context of struggles by Muslims to unsettle the external ascription of essentialist racial categories, in the face of attempts to defend that racialised order.

For much of the post-war period, Muslims were largely rendered invisible in state policy which tended to essentialise groups of South Asian heritage through the use of the single appellation 'Asian', despite it referring to ethnicities linked to a region considerably larger than the size of the European Union and encompassing a huge range of diversity. Commonalities between South Asian Muslims and Muslims from other ethnic backgrounds tended to be ignored within the terms of this approach. Muslim attempts to describe themselves primarily as Muslim unsettled expressions of racialised governmentality for two reasons. First, the shift towards expressions of Muslimness occurred in the context of a series of struggles for rights to be recognised. These included politicisation during the first Gulf War (Werbner, 1994), and a struggle for educational provision which met their faith needs at a time when the state was committed to compulsory

Christian worship in schools. The most important of these struggles occurred during the Rushdie affair. The Rushdie affair appears in many ways to fore-shadow the later cartoon affair we discussed earlier, not least because of the way in which reporting of the affair focused largely on the participation of extremist elements, rendering moderate supporters invisible, and obscured the complex range of issues at stake in the protests to solely highlight theological motives. The affair became used as a 'stick with which to beat the immigrants' (Asad, 1993: 303) and was widely characterised in the media and by politicians in terms of the murderous rage of the racialised other seeking the death of an author. In reality, militant voices were in a tiny minority during the protests of the Rushdie affair, and what had swelled the size of the protests was the way in which they were viewed by Muslims as a symbolic flashpoint in a wider mobilisation for rights and recognition.

This under-acknowledged aspect of the protests was reflected, on the one hand, by the close association with campaigns about education (Troyna and Carrington, 1990: 103) and, on the other hand, in demands for coverage under blasphemy legislation which were significant in so far as they reflected a demand for legisla-tive protection. The Rushdie affair was a key stimulus to political organisation among Muslims (Werbner 1994: 114), but also presented serious challenges to state race-relations strategies for categorising and managing minorities (Khan, 2006: 183). Second, the expression of Muslim identities interrupted processes of racialised governmentality because it involved a large-scale movement comprising members of a racialised minority exercising agency to determine the terms on which their identities were categorised. This naturally unsettled the processes through which ideas of race were constructed. Muslim attempts to describe them-selves primarily as Muslim reflect an attempt to step outside the terms of a gram-mar for speaking about difference which collapsed an impossibly broad range of differences into a comparatively narrow range monolithic, essential categories by the state.

Expressions of Muslim identities unsettled processes of racialised governmental-ity because the lack of a single representative organisation to mediate between the state and Muslim communities posed additional challenges to the state in trying to manage its relations with Muslim communities. Later on, when the government began intensifying its attempts to manage the Muslim community in the wake of the 9/11 terrorist attacks, this led to a complex politics through which the state attempted to develop its relations with the Muslim Council of Britain (MCB) as a potential representative body (Birt, 2005). When these relations became strained by policy differences between the MCB and the New Labour government and by the realisation that the organisation was not able to unify all Muslims, government policy began increasingly focusing upon promoting a range of alternative 'moder-ate' Muslim groups, some of which were completely synthetic, as part of its Prevent counter-radicalisation strategy. The absence of a representative body has been viewed as a weakness by the state and by many Muslims, but has in fact been a further irritant in relations with the state by interrupting attempts to manage Muslim communities and complicating racialisation processes.

The first phase of campaigning by Muslims focused on gaining formal recognition through such demands as a claim for inclusion of a category of 'Muslim' in the 2001 national census. As Muslims became more organised and confident in their mobilisations, they became increasingly focused upon winning rights and recognition. A major campaign for inclusion of a question on religious identities in the UK national census was seen by Muslim community activists as an important step towards recognition by the state, and one which could lead to greater legal protections against discrimination and harassment. But since the mobilisation by Muslims of a specifically Muslim identity asserted agency in stepping outside the established rules of ethnic and racial classification, it posed a challenge to a social order based on race and mobilised identities as a means of collective resistance (Modood, 1992). This interrupted attempts to fix in essentialist terms what is meant by 'race' and 'ethnicity'. Muslims undermined biological notions of race (Khan, 2006), as a result of which the forms of racism they experienced as Muslims were not recognised as racism, since the state's definitions continued to privilege biological conceptions of both race and ethnicity (Meer, 2007).

Opposition to the recognition of Muslims thus gave way to an opposition to recognising anti-Muslim racism. In this context, hostility to legal protection against anti-Muslim racism qua racism came to be an important component of Islamophobia (Khan, 2006), and was based on two faulty logics. First, it was based upon an essentialist distinction between 'race' and 'religion' (Khan, 2006: 185). But, as Hall (2000) points out, race works in two modes: it has its biological logics, in terms of how people are racialised as having immutable phenotypical characteristics which constitute them as a race, and its cultural logics in terms of how people are racialised as possessing essential cultural characteristics which mark them as an ethnic group. In this sense, Islamophobia is clearly a racialised discourse, in so far as it constructs a particular social group as being bounded and homogeneous, sharing a range of essential characteristics. Islamophobia overlapped with, and organised, other racist expressions. Second, opposition to recognising Islamophobia increasingly took the form of a problematic defence of the idea of race as immutable. This was expressed around the idea that Muslims do not constitute a phenotypical racial group, and therefore anti-Muslim racism should not be considered as a form of racism (Khan, 2006; Meer, 2007). This response was problematic; race is socially constructed and no groups exist in those terms in any case (Tyrer, 2011); rather, race as a 'civilisational' discourse constructs people into races (Hesse, 2004). This response was more than simply a repudiation of the idea of Islamophobia; in fact, it represented a defence of a particular racial grammar in the face of the challenges which had been posed by the agency exercised by Muslims over their own self-identification (Sayyid and Vakil, 2011).

As such, anti-Muslim racism took the basic form of a struggle to maintain the shape of a particular racial order, and an ideological rearguard which was mobilised in defence of the idea of the immutability of racial identities and their external ascription to minority groups (Sayyid and Vakil, 2011). This defence of the racial order occurred in the face of Muslim resistances to racism and the agency displayed by Muslims in stepping outside the organising grammar of the racialised social order. And the emergence of anti-Muslim racism to defend the terms of the existing racial order took the form of an anti-Muslim racism which emerged as a new popular racist expression (Kundnani, 2001), which came to construct Muslims as threatening and alien, and which was articulated across different discursive nodes and structural positions to unite a range of institutional actors, as we discussed in out consideration of the contemporary politics of hate in Chapter 3. This is important, for it illustrates the ways in which the contemporary discourse of anti-Muslim racism which has been so central to the war on terror has not simply emerged as a backlash response to the attacks of 9/11 and 7/7, but rather has been framed over a longer period of time, largely as a response to the ways in which Muslim mobilisation to resist policies they felt excluded them also entailed an attempt to step outside, and resist, the terms of ascribed racialised categories, and to resist by selecting their own modes of identification. But this itself had a dislocationary effect: that is, it could not easily be explained within the terms of the hegemonic discourse (Howarth and Stavrakakis, 2000) through which the racialised are denied agency or the right to determine their own terms for identification. The hegemonic response to restabilise the racial order took the form of a retreat into the logics of 'race', by attempting to overtly buttress as 'real' and binging the very idea of 'race' itself. While this defence of the racial order involved denying Muslims protection against racism based on the spurious assumption that race is real and biological rather than socially constructed, it also witnessed the racialisation of Muslims as a culturally alien, criminalised community.

The hegemonic redescription of Islamophobia as merely religious rather than racist worked to marginalise Islamophobia within progressive equalities discourse (Modood, 2006). One effect of this has been that Muslim resistance to Islamophobia has ended up finding expression in a range of channels and contexts which differ markedly from those used in the pursuit of broader anti-racist politics. Liberal reticence towards recognising Islamophobia as a form of racialised discourse was in some cases bound up with a reluctance to promote religious identification. However, the marginalisation of Islamophobia within progressive rights projects had a contradictory effect to that intended, and meant that Muslims were frequently denied access to 'progressive' registers for the expression of the rights claims, and were instead forced to campaign through religious registers. The Danish cartoon affair illustrates this: because the cartoons recycled popular contemporary stereotypes about Muslims, the affair cannot be understood outside the context of contemporary manifestations of anti-Muslim racism. However, the hegemonic construction of Muslims as anti-liberal, anti-progressive and anti-democratic denied them space within the dominant discourse of rights when responding to the cartoons. The result was that British Muslim anger at the stereotypes circulated in the cartoons found expression through theological registers. Liberal objections to Muslim mobilisation against Islamophobia on the grounds that it radicalises and Islamicises were myopic and contradictory, and in fact were bound up with the expression of resistance through religious registers by foreclosing access to the profane.

In conclusion, we began this chapter by acknowledging that wherever there is racism there can be found resistance, and that the nature of the resistance met by racism helps to shape the racist response. In the context of the war on terror it is easy to assume that 9/11 really did set in train the emergence of an Islamophobia which has become the defining form of today's politics of hate, as we saw in Chapter 3. But, as we have seen, contemporary anti-Muslim racism has been a long time in the making. Indeed, the criminalisation of Muslim youth as posing an existential threat preceded 9/11; the chief difference was that whilst in the wake of 9/11 it was possible for the state to seek to coopt institutions of civil society, such as universities, in policing this suspect community by surveilling Muslim youth, it was ironically in the wake of the atrocities which occurred in September 2001 that Islamophobia became increasingly difficult to ignore (as the resistance and opposition to the criminalisation of Muslim students since that date demonstrates). Anti-Muslim racism emerged principally in response to the ways in which Muslims challenged the racial order by stepping outside the racist grammar to identify themselves on their own terms. In doing so, it illustrates the ways in which the shape of racism is influenced by the forms of resistance with which it meets. The case of Islamophobia during the war on terror reveals the extent to which opposition to racism contributes to the shape that racism takes in response. It also illustrates our central contention in this chapter: namely, that in order to consider the ways in which racialised minorities resist racism, there needs to be sufficient space in the criminological imagination to take into account the view that resistance to racism is shaped in particular structural circumstances, and that it is also always as discursive as it is material.

REVISION QUESTIONS

1 Given the extent of the state power brought to bear on terrorism suspects, what are the problems of thinking through the resistance of victims of miscarriages of justice during the war on terror?
2 What do the experiences of Maher Arar, Lotfi Raissi and Hicham Yezza tell us about the problems of resisting racism?
3 How have Muslim young people been stereotyped as extremists?
4 What is the significance of the anti-essentialism to our understanding of the complexities of the identity work which goes into resisting ascribed racial labels and racialised markers of deviance?

████████████████████████ FURTHER READING ████████████████████

Delgado, Richard and Stefancic, Jean (2001) *Critical Race Theory – An Introduction.* New York: New York University Press.

Kundnani, Arun (2008) 'Islamism and the Roots of Liberal Rage', *Race and Class*, 50: 40–68.

Phillips, Coretta and Bowling, Benjamin (2003) 'Racism, Ethnicity and Criminology: Developing Minority Perspectives', *British Journal of Criminology*, 43: 269–290.

Sayyid, Salman and Vakil, AbdoolKarim (eds) (2011) *Thinking Through Islamophobia: Global Perspectives.* London: C. Hurst & Co.

9

Researching the Agenda

Doing criminological research into race and crime matters has always been problematic. This is especially so when researching criminal justice institutions. Here, there are a series of key methodological concerns bound up in political ties. These are related to issues of access, truth, power and control. The existence of corruption, abuse and violence are just a few of the problems that are commonly associated with *the dark side of the law*. How, then, do such institutions respond to the requests of criminologists, especially critical criminologists,[1] to undertake research within that institution, especially when that research 'challenges official discourses and the power, authority and legitimacy of state institutions' (Scraton and Chadwick 2001: 73). Furthermore, what is to be done when the research uncovers some 'unwelcome truths' (Sapsford 1996: 60)? In such instances, as Scraton notes, researchers are often accused of 'idealising' the 'view from below', of distorting the analysis in pursuit of political agendas ... (and) to build academic reputation' (Scraton 2007: 17).

This chapter begins with a consideration of how criminological knowledge about race and crime issues has been constructed and utilised. Drawing on our own research into racially motivated crimes, racism in the police force, and black and minority ethnic excluded youth and pathways into crime, this chapter gives a critical coverage of some of the issues entailed in undertaking research into race and crime, including issues around gate-keeping, power and authority, accessing a marginalised group, undertaking research with over-researched groups and, negotiating disclosure of findings, especially those that are critical of practice. It considers some very important dilemmas that occur when research enters dark territory, such as investigation into attitudes about race and racism that are held by agents of the criminal justice system or research which involves scrutinising those institutions whose history and culture has evidenced corruption or particularly problematic cultural norms. This is evident with the Police Service of Northern Ireland (PSNI) whose own past service history was rife with discrimination, corruption and 'secretive policing arrangements' (Patten 1999: 25), and embedded in a 'defensive, secretive and sometimes obstructive culture' (Power 2003: 199). How, then, do criminologists researching such an institution gain access to *true* data? In addition, how can the researcher make meaningful use of that information, without being perceived as embarking on an axe-grinding attack of that institution? Whether or not such an attack is warranted, it is argued that all criminological research should also set out with the goal of providing solutions to problems that it uncovers, and to do this jointly through a considerate, but firm, negotiation process, with any individuals within that institution who also seek genuine accountability and fairness within their institution. In light of these questions, a series of guidelines are being offered on how problems can be more productively addressed.

Generating knowledge on race and crime

Historically, social science, including sociological and criminological, presentation of black and minority ethnic groups has been reflective of their treatment in wider society: blaming, ignoring or misrepresenting. Even when it has sought to analyse and champion resistance, its consideration has not been problem free (Murji, 2007). Wider criminological research has largely been detrimental to their interests and has seldom taken account the depressing reality of their experiences. Early criminological understanding of race and crime highlighted links between race and crime, for instance by suggesting disproportionate rates of 'black criminality', and sought to do this with reference to biology – see, for example, the work of Lombroso (1876). Links were also made to heredity, intelligence and IQ (Dugdale, 1877), which derived largely from an unquestioned acceptance of Darwin's theories of evolution (1859). These argued that there was a category of people whose biologically inherited laziness, immorality, deviousness and poor intelligence levels would not only make them prone to more criminal and deviant behaviour, but would also slow down the advancement of the nation (Herrnstein and Murray, 1994; Williams, 2008). These people, it was argued, should be removed from society and eventually eliminated, through such means as long-term imprisonment and sterilisation programmes. To varying degrees, many countries embarked on this strategy. For example, in the USA between 1911 and 1930 a variety of laws were also passed which allowed sterilisation – which continued right up until the 1970s, and in Britain too between 1900 and 1930 sterilisation was practised (Williams, 2008). At its most extreme, we saw the extermination of the Jews in Nazi Germany.

The problem here is that it is often the same groups of people, for example black and minority ethnic groups, especially those populated within the newer immigrant communities, who are viewed as having faults in biology and intelligence and thus disproportionately prone to criminal behaviour. This was supported by the IQ studies of Jenson (1969), Gordon (1976) and Herrnstein and Murray (1994). Later, criminology soundly criticised these arguments. This included the questioning of the status of intelligence (Jones, 2001), as is it suggested that IQ testing is actually a measurement of the privileges emerging from class-biases and, in terms of race, is unfairly determined by the dominant culture (Mercer, 1972). It is something that is determined by environment and access (as illustrated in the studies of Gillborn and Mirza, 2000; Loehlin et al., 1975; Simons, 1978; all cited in Jones, 2001: 380). And, because black and minority ethnic groups populated within newer immigrant communities tend to be located in poorer areas, where wider experiences of poverty and deprivation are common-place (in health, education, housing, employment), it is argued that social stress levels are high, which then explains high crime rates (Williams, 2008). Hence, rather than biology or intelligence being a cause of criminal behaviour, it is more likely to be due the poor 'social conditions and treatment of these groups since their arrival in Britain' (Williams, 2008: 276). Race aside, if low intelligence was to explain one's proneness to criminal behaviour, how can we explain criminal activity that is more likely to occur amongst the middle classes and affluent mem-bers of society, for example embezzlement, fraud, corporate crime, white-collar crime, homicide?

In a rejection of genetic theories of race and criminal behaviour, W.E.B. DuBois in 'The Philadelphia Negro' (1899) and 'The Relations of Negroes to Whites in the South' (1901) argued that history, politics and economics, as well as other social phenomena, placed the 'American black' in a particular 'social condition' (DuBois, 1899: 8) which put upon them increased social stress. This could then explain high crime rates amongst the black population. DuBois argued that high rates of criminal behaviour amongst the black population in America existed, but that they must be viewed within context. This context emerges out of the linger-ing impact of slavery and relatively sudden emancipation which placed them in a transient stage, experiencing segregation and residence in slum areas. This, along with the state's demand for young convict labour, class inequality and institutional racism, as well as the daily experiences of racism, and the gross racialised injustice faced by blacks in comparison to whites, when being dealt with by law and order agencies, led to the breeding of crime. However, although it was not so different from those crimes committed by whites, 'black crimes', argued DuBois, were pre-sented, regulated and punitively responded to by much more extreme and harsh measures, all underpinned by the deep-rooted racism that existed in the South: 'All these faults are real and important causes of Negro crime. They are not racial traits but due to perfectly evident historic causes' (DuBois, 1904: 56).

Following criminological critique of the biological trend, there then emerged other support for the view that black and minority ethnic groups were socially and culturally deprived, not so much in the sense that DuBois (1899, 1901, 1904) noted, but instead largely as a result of a deficient black culture. Here problematic parenting and unstable kinship systems, itself located in poverty, deprivation and immorality, were seen to be not only to blame for criminal behaviour, but also indicative of black culture as a whole. Such views gained popularity following publications of official reports, such as the Moynihan Report (1965). It was argued that being raised in such environments acted as an obstruction to full and healthy participation in wider society, especially for young black men, who experienced a particular type of emasculation as a result of being raised by a single-parent mother and in the absence of a father figure (see Lawrence, 1982a). Such a view is still popular today (Haskins, 2009), and has impacted on how black and minority ethnic people are treated on an everyday basis in wider public, and more specifically in relation to social welfare policy, such as immigration, health care, education and employment, presenting the view that all black and minority ethnic people are 'contaminated by the alien predisposition to crime which is reproduced in their distinctive cultures' (Gilroy, 1982: 52). Such patterns of racial criminalisation apply to all black and minority ethnic people, including more recently newer immigrant communities from Eastern Europe and those presented as lower hierarchical white 'others', such as the Irish. All of these have been viewed as being either biologically or culturally delinquent (Tonry, 1997, cited in Jones, 2001: 381). Labelling these groups in this way serves a purpose for a white majority society whose history and privileged position has emerged from (and relies on) its racist exploitation and discriminatory practices.

In terms of criminology, it was only recently that some sections of the discipline began to raise questions about the actual data which claimed to show that black and minority ethnic people committed more crimes. Following problematic claims made by police officials, some criminologists in the UK became concerned with the inaccurate presentation of black and minority ethnic criminality and the misuse of 'official data' to support such dubious claims. For example, consider Hall et al.'s (1978) analysis of the response to the muggings panic, where statements such as the following were made: 'many of the perpetrators of muggings are very young black people' (Metropolitan Police Commissioner, Sir Paul Condon, 1995, cited in The Runneymede Trust, 1995: 1). Criminologists highlighted the problematic data-set used by Condon, for instance an internally conducted study of crime victims' descriptions of attackers, in which about 80 per cent stated that the attacker was a black male in his late teens or early twenties (Holdaway, 1997). This raises methodological concerns about use of statistical data from one's own organisation and the reliability on victim's perceptions about the crime and the attacker (Holdaway, 1997), and the use of such data in an emotionally and politically driven era of white bias.

Critique utilised sociological race theories, such as Critical Race Theory. Having been influenced by some European philosophers, such as Antonio Gramsci and Jacques Derrida, and some American radical figures and movements, for example Frederick Douglas, W.E.B. DuBois, Cesar Chavez, Martin Luther King, the Black Panthers and the Chicago works of the 1960s and early 1970s (Delgado and Stefancic, 2001: 4), Critical Race Theory highlighted the inaccuracy of analysis on race and crime. It also noted the marginalisation of black and minority ethnic academics (such as DuBois), and emerged first in the USA, then in the UK and other countries, as a way of counteracting black academic marginalisation, and the problematic theorisation of 'black criminality', as well as a means of making black and minority ethnic voices visible (Collins, 1998; hooks, 2003). Its key contributors include Derrick Bell, Alan Freeman, Kimberle Crenshaw, Angela Harris and Patricia Williams.

Russell (1992: 667) argues that we need to develop more precisely a 'black criminology'. This is because race and racism are still very much influential on the lives of black and minority ethnic people and the criminal justice 'service' that they encounter. This is despite a recent body of literature emerging from the USA which insists that these links are not as strong as they once were. For example, Dilulio (2005) argues for social science research to:

> ... tell the truth, as the data disclose it, about the reality of black crime and black punishment. The bottom line of most of the best research is that America's justice system is not racist, not anymore ... if blacks are overrepresented in the ranks of the imprisoned, it is because they are overrepresented in the criminal ranks – and the violent criminal ranks, at that. (Dilulio, 2005: 76)

Dilulio (2005) then calls for further analysis into black victimisation, especially within the context of black-on-black crime. This is supported by the work of DeLisi and Regoli (2005), who in their secondary analysis of criminological data on race and crime, argue that there is little evidence to support the view that the American criminal justice system is racially discriminatory against blacks. They therefore argue from this that there is a 'declining importance of skin colour' (page 87) in matters relating to race, crime and discrimination, and as such criminologists need to study and report on black criminality without fear of being labelled as racist when they do find higher rates of offending amongst black and minority ethnic people. This is highlighted by Walsh's (2008) study of black serial killers in the USA. Walsh (2008) argued that despite the common criminological and public perception of most serial killers being white, itself developed largely from biased media portrayals and news reporting, there is actually an over-representation of African American serial killers, and as such this must be reported on truthfully. However, we argue that black-on-black crime does not occur in such huge numbers as some would have you believe, and in claiming that it actually is a very common occurrence actually serves to mask black and minority ethnic victimisation at the hands of white offenders. It does this via attention diversion strategies, as well as failing to raise questions about the criminal justice system who not only fail to respond to the needs of black and minority ethnic victims, but who also serve black and minority ethnic victims an additional portion of oppression and victimisation.

However, some criminologists (Braithwaite, 1989; D'Alessio and Stolzenberg, 2008; Dilulio, 2005; Lea and Young, 1984; Walsh, 2008) argue that a significant number of studies and reports still show high rates of offending behaviour amongst some black and minority ethnic groups, and this must be examined. To do this, though, a call is made for criminologists to move towards a 'multidimensional approach to understanding minorities' experiences' (Phillips and Bowling, 2003: 270).

This includes first recognising the diversity of black and minority ethnic experiences. This would benefit from a replacement of the term 'black' and 'black and minority ethnic' in criminology, in favour of one that moves beyond a simplistic and essentialised black–white dualism, which explains their use of the term 'minorities' and their call for a 'minority perspective' in criminology (2003: 272) as opposed to Russell's use of 'black criminology' (1992). This is supported by Garland et al. (2006), who argue that such generic terms can often obscure the visibility and of groups and the diversity of their experiences. Similarly, there needs to be much more work done within black feminist criminology (Huey and Lynch, 2005), or, in line with Phillips and Bowling's (2003) arguments above, a minority feminist perspective, not least because black and minority ethnic women's experiences are not generalisable to the experiences of white women, whose struggles and matters of concern over history have undergone different transformations, and who have themselves acted in the role of oppressor to the black and minority ethnic woman.

In addition, it is also necessary for us as criminologists to locate our own racial biases and the impact of this on our work. Phillips and Bowling (2003: 270) argue that criminology must embark on 'a critical deconstruction of the processes of knowledge production *about* minorities, which in its current state means squaring up to the discipline of criminology itself', going so far as to ask if it is in itself institutionally racist (page 284). Given that current criminology itself is, like other key disciplines and organisations in the UK, developed within a racist context, evident not least in early criminological writings (for example, consider Cesare Lombroso's *The Criminal Type*, published in 1876), to what degree is it now completely free from its racist roots?

Barriers in researching race matters

When researching powerful state institutions, politicised issues of access, power, control and conflict are some of the key methodological concerns. This is especially true when undertaking research into race matters within criminal justice institutions, such as the police. Researching any police force or its officers, especially when studies seek to gather an insight into attitudes about race, is extremely difficult. Often researchers are met with suspicion and hostility, and prior to gaining actual research access it would be naïve to ignore that they may be subject to an informal vetting operation by the police (Power 2003; Sapsford 1996). Scraton highlights how for critical social researchers with an 'oppositional agenda ... [that] seeks out, records and champions the "view from below", ensuring the voices and experiences of those marginalised by institutional state practices are heard and represented' (Scraton 2007: 10), such as in areas of racism, it is extremely difficult, if not impossible, for the researcher to remain neutral and objective. This is, Scraton argues, how it should be: 'rather than claiming some mythical "value-neutrality", or sanitised, controlled environment, critical social researchers position their work, identify themselves and define "relevance"' (Scraton 2007: 11). It is important to realise, though, that even when researchers are 'cleared' in the vetting process, or if they declare openly their position and their willingness to fairly and/or positively represent the institution or agent under study, it is not always easy to penetrate official representations of views, particularly when issues of power come into play. Here, Punch (1979), in his later reflections on his observational study of police corruption in Amsterdam, highlighted the need for researchers therefore to be aware that sometimes it is vital to be able to 'read between the lines' by not accepting presented representations at face value. We argue though that in all cases, it is vital that criminologists and researchers are able to *read between* the lines, as this is where true representation lies.

Although access for the criminological researcher to these sites is extremely difficult to obtain, it is not impossible, as seen in the studies of Holdaway (1983) and Punch (1993). Often sources are surrounded by both physical and non-physical barriers, each guarded by its own set of gate keepers. These are individuals or processes, which can be both formal and informal, which control the access of the researcher to the research site. Consideration of how we manoeuvre gate keeping is vital, given that 'because of its "closed" nature, the criminal justice system is littered with gate keepers' (Jupp, 1989: 134). As researchers we need to ask ourselves, to what degree can one navigate such gate keeping, not only to access research sites, but furthermore in order to gain access to true accounts once in the site? In particular, how can one be sure that what they are accessing goes beyond official representations of views? After all, even if access is granted, there can be additional sub-layers of gate keepers who each have their own set of 'interests they want to protect, and aims and goals they wish to promote' (Jupp, 1989: 148–149). In the case of policing, for example, police officers' use of informal policing methods is well known and has been well documented (Holdaway, 1983). Officers view these informal methods as essential in undertaking *real* police work, and are often the types of activities that, for a variety of reasons, they want to hide from public view. So, when confronted with a researcher, given the 'mutual secrecy and trust' (Cain, 1973: 190) elements of a police culture, it is not uncommon for suspicious and defensive police officers to block research, erect barriers or to present more favourable (false) images (Manning, 1974, cited in Jupp, 1989: 150; Power, 2003; Punch, 1993). Despite some of the methodological issues associated with politicised difficulties, hostility and resistance when researching criminal justice institutions, there are a number of criminological studies which have overcome these and gone on to produce valuable findings. These include the works of Graef (1989), Holdaway (1983), Keith (1993), Kemp et al. (1992), Mawby (1979), Muir (1977), O'Neil (2005), Punch (1993), Reiner (1978) and Smith (1983). This indicates that although such research can be difficult, it is not impossible.

Such hostility and access issues not only exist when researching institutions and state agents, but are often present when undertaking research into the experiences of black and minority ethnic groups. This is not surprising given the biological roots of criminology, and the use of officialdom to legitimate notions of black and minority ethnic deviance. There is also the problem of research fatigue (Clark, 2008), which often occurs when certain groups are over researched. This is often a claim made about black and minority ethnic groups (Afshar et al., 2002; Butt and O'Neil, 2004). This is often linked to a frustration emerging from high levels of research participation, and little evidence of delivering change to the researched group; for example, these are claims often made about research projects looking into the criminalisation of black African Caribbean youth in Toxteth, and more recently of South Asian Muslim youth following the 2001 disturbances in some of the town and cities in Northern England. When research fatigue occurs, not only are we as researchers and criminologists risking the validity of research data and the risk of losing access to the field in further studies, but more significantly, we are causing harm to participants. This is especially so when, other than having an academic interest, the researcher does not have any other direct link with the research group. It is not surprising then that the black and minority ethnic community have been cautious of research proposals, often viewing them as a form of abuse in itself, where academic interest lies solely in securing large grants or in making career moves (Gordon, 1973).

Given that criminology is largely a white-dominated discipline, black and minority ethnic groups may also have hostility to the criminologist, feeling that they are yet another form of racial oppression. Russell (1992) argues that having more black criminologists may help address such mistrust, resentment and hostility. This parallels the development of feminist criminology. However, Phillips and Bowling (2003: 273) contest this, arguing that 'all criminologists, regardless of their ethnic identity, can contribute to minority perspectives ... our notion of minority perspective is an inclusive one'. Indeed, we argue that all criminologists, regardless of race and ethnicity, *should* seek to contribute to the development of such perspectives. This could be done, for example, through consideration of Critical Race Theory, especially in terms of its methodological approach, which seeks to 'honor research participants' who have suffered from the 'white lie' (Vaught, 2008: 566). This theory acknowledges that often marginalised and disempowered groups, such as those of a black and minority ethnic background, 'mask' their true selves/identity in order to manoeuvre through structural inequalities, racist institutions and to survive in a society where whiteness equals privilege; for example, African American slaves did this as a tactical survival strategy (Rodriguez, 2006: 1068). Black and minority ethnic people often internalise racially discriminatory attitudes, meaning that their 'mask' is 'often steeped with self-hatred and other internalized oppressions' (Rodriguez, 2006: 1068). Rodriguez (2006) and other Critical Race Theorists argue that black and minority ethnic groups need to develop a critical consciousness of residence in a racist and white supremacist society, and then seek to break through the 'white masks', empower oneself and seek justice (Anzaldua, 1998; hooks, 2003; Rodriguez, 2006).

The question criminological researchers must consider is the degree to which such masking also occurs in the research field. From a Critical Race Theory methodological approach, it is argued that research methods such as narrative, especially in the form of storytelling and counter-storytelling (Delgado, 1989), for example poems, biographies, memoirs and songs, could be used as a means of removing the mask and accessing 'truthful' data, whilst also facilitating empowerment as the narrator is challenging and correcting a white supremacist (hi)story[2] (Rodriguez, 2006). For example, consider the sociological and criminological studies[3] of Weedon (2004) into Aboriginal women; Wright et al.'s study into school exclusions and deviant behaviour (Wright et al., 2009); and Weis's (1998) study into race and violence in the USA.

In seeking to overcome such barriers, it is useful to take direction from Phillips and Bowling (2003) who argue that to undertake 'good' research into race and crime matters a number of principles, in line with 'anti-racist' research, must be followed. These are as follows:

1 Acknowledge that the research relationship is one that is underwritten and structured by a variety of power relations between the researcher and the researched.
2 The pursuit of multiple truths, as opposed to one definite claim to truth.
3 Inclusionary research participation in the production of knowledge, for example research field and data interpretation.
4 The development of rapport and trust between the researcher and research participant. Sometimes this can be best facilitated by the matching of certain factors, such as race, age and gender, and is likely to bring the benefit of increased divulging of data.
5 Non-exploitative research, so as to minimise harm to an already vulnerable group. This can be supported by always seeking to be accountable to those being studied (Phillips and Bowling, 2003: 273–276).

To this we add the need for the criminological researcher to acknowledge the racial biases of their discipline, both in terms of its historical roots and some of its contemporary works. Doing this allows criminology to be honest about its own position of power and authority, and to recognise that it too can quite legitimately be seen as a source of harm.

Presenting accurate and meaningful data

In overcoming issues of access, though, for the criminological researcher such research problems do not end once they have left the field. Indeed, in many cases the real battle begins in the data presentation and dissemination stages. In particular, how does one go about publishing any disturbing truths that may have been uncovered? Often findings which critique any areas of criminal justice institutions or the practices of its agents are often confined to being disseminated within the supportive environment of academic circles, such as criminological conferences, subject journals, and so on.

When they are disseminated more widely in policy and criminal justice administration areas, often they are not well received, and may even be subject to the threat of libel action (Punch, 1989). Therefore ethical responsibility to the organisation under study must be upheld, not only for moral reasons, but for legal ones too (Punch, 1989). It may be the case that in response to such critiques, institutions may also seek to silence the research via suddenly restricting access to the field; halting any other planned work; or by critiquing its scientific basis. This leaves the threat of other repercussions, such as academic discreditation and stigma, or even personal injury and death (Marks, 2004; Thomas and Marquart, 1987). It is true that in recent years criminal justice institutions have opened up more to criminological research, largely as a result of a desire of wanting to be seen as being concerned with legitimacy (Sapsford 1996: 67). The degree to which institutions actually acknowledge academic findings and recommendations remains, though, debatable. Therefore it can be argued that there is still a lack of trust and open hostility between some criminal justice institutions and some criminological researchers, especially those of a critical criminological background. Such feelings are justified on both parts. The critical criminological researcher is considered as being on the 'side' of the powerless and those pushed to the margins of society. They seek to question the taken-for-granted, by deconstructing and critiquing structures of power and authority, and the processes of which such power is exhibited and maintained. They not only unearth their existence, but call and make recommendations, and often campaign for their elimination. On the other side, criminal justice institutions and their agents may want to keep secret the reality of their practices, and so any participation in research may simply be used as a form of lip service or a public-relations exercise, as Brewer and Magee (1991) recognised in their research of the then police force in Northern Ireland, the Royal Ulster Constabulary (RUC), and how such research access *looked* favourable for the RUC by demonstrating that it was open to criminological analysis, regardless of whether this was in reality actually the case.

That is not to say, though, that research barriers cannot be overcome. Some research that Patel undertook into the PSNI and the policing of racist incidents in Northern Ireland can be used here to consider the ways in which, although research barriers existed, they could also be overcome in order to present data that is accurate and meaningful (Patel, 2011). In this research, a member within the PSNI senior management team, as well as the officer of supervisory status within the PSNI Community Safety Branch, who was Patel's primary contact, had both requested that they have sight on the some of the key findings and conclusions drawn from the research. This had been negotiated as part of Patel's access to the PSNI, for example its officers and internal documents. It is assumed that this was of particular interest to the PSNI given that they were aware that the first site of dissemination was to be at an international police symposium, at which they would not themselves be present, and whose audience consisted of several senior figures and high-ranking officers within the international policing community. For matters relating to image, representation and reputation, this concern is of course understandable, especially in light of past problems that have plagued Northern Ireland's police service (see Patten, 1999). As a result of providing a draft copy of the presentation to the PSNI, Patel was requested to remove some sections of narratives and their criminological commentary. As one would expect, these sections were those which especially contained comments which could be considered at the very least highly problematic, and even suggestive of racism having an impact on operational level attitudes and police practice.

The PSNI's request for the removal of some sections of police narratives and criminological commentary was responded to in several ways. Before this is discussed, it is important to remind ourselves that despite some concerns around the 'hijacking' and control of data, sight on a draft copy of the findings and the key recommendations had previously been granted as part of the negotiated access to the PSNI. Indeed, it would be the researcher's duty to produce a true representation of all findings, especially those dark uncomfortable truths which highlight the experiences of the relatively powerless and oppressed, at the hands of those powerful institutions. In terms of the research focus of the study discussed here, it is the researcher's particular duty to highlight findings that illustrate problems which may hinder the successful policing of racist incidents. However, it is also vital that the research contract, whether formalised or not, is adhered to. This helps to ensure that research harm is minimised, for example, for the reputation of the researcher, their affiliated institution, the research project's funding body, the research participants and all those who are likely to be affected by the findings of the research, particularly victims pursuing justice who would benefit most from policy and practice changes. It also helps to maintain good, or at the very least amicable, research relations, which are vital for research access and reputation.

In this case, the response to the PSNI's request for omitting and removing some data from the international police conference presentation was considered in some depth and discussed carefully with the PSNI research contacts. Guidance and advice was also sought from several criminologists who had similar research experience on other projects. As a result, Patel agreed to the requests. Doing so was seen as a necessity for the maintenance of research access; the importance of safeguarding such research access has also been noted by Reiner and Newburn, 2000; Marks, 2004; Van Maanen, 1988. In fairness, it also means that all the hard work that the PSNI were doing to successfully police racist incidents and implement the recommendations of Patten (1999) would not be overshadowed by what they would maybe consider to be the non-representational views of some, at best naïve, officers in need of more diversity training, and at worst 'a few rotten apples'. This was important, not only to the PSNI, but also to Patel, who had clearly discovered during the study that the PSNI's active efforts to improve their policing of racist incidents were in the main positive and being spearheaded by some officers with a genuine desire for progressive change, and who were working very hard to make changes that allowed a meaningful move away from the problematic policing that had plagued Northern Ireland's police service in the past. Indeed, one would go so far as to say that in the short space of time that the PSNI have been addressing their policing strategy in this area, it seems that they have introduced more policy and practice changes than other UK police forces since the release of Macpherson's recommendations in 1999.[4] Agreeing to the requests in this way and at this time, for example for the purpose of this particular dissemination site, was therefore viewed as acceptable. This is because it did not detract from the main key findings and conclusions of the research, or the arguments presented.

However, without doubt, although a research relationship between the researcher and that police force had been maintained, there nevertheless remained some feeling of injustice at having essentially sacrificed data, 'sold out', and in many ways having reinforced the power and authority of the very institution under study, in its ability to hide from view some of their dark truths. But, to say that the sense of injustice was sudden and unexpected would be misleading. This is because such ethical dimensions around researching police deviance were expected from the outset of the study and, as advised by Rowe (2007), had already been anticipated before the fieldwork had been carried out. Here the researcher's position, interests and levels of sacrifices had been set. Not only was this done in the mind of Patel herself, but also an indication of this standpoint was given to the PSNI research contacts in meetings at the early stages of the research. It is also assumed that this would have been clear to the PSNI in the background checks that they would have carried out into Patel's work, which is easily available via her academic institution's website. This would have given clear indications to them of her approach as a critical criminologist. In the setting of standards and levels of acceptable sacrifices, the extent to which this position was negotiable had therefore also been considered. Knowledge of similar research projects as well as the culture of the institution under study assisted this process.

All this meant the response of the PSNI was not entirely unexpected and when their requests for data omission and removal were made, they could be acted upon with little hindrance to the release of the overall research message. This message was that the policing of racist incidents were being taken seriously (in terms of resources, specialist posts, introduction of initiatives and with public relations) on a senior level within the PSNI, and that some of this filtered to operational level. In addition, as an organisation the PSNI had in some ways seriously considered anti-racist policing tools, such as the Macpherson Report (1999), and a number of initiatives and active campaigns had been introduced at senior management and MLO levels in recent years to address the problem of increased racist incidents. These were primarily targeted towards protecting members of the black and minority ethnic community who experience racist incidents. However, on an operational level, some underlying assumptions about a racial hierarchy were evident and appeared to impact on views and approaches to the policing of racist incidents. Here operational officers especially tended to equate policing in a racially diverse society with the need to police black and minority ethnic people themselves. There was a tendency to view the black and minority ethnic communities, especially newer migrants, as problematic. This at times led to victim-blaming and even the criminalising of black and minority ethnic people. A consequence of this was a tendency to pay insufficient attention to the racist incidents experienced by black and minority ethnic people at the hands of some members of the local white community, and placed black and minority ethnic people themselves in need of increased surveillance and control

In attempting to pursue the highlighting of this research message, various sites of dissemination, in addition to the international police symposium, were utilised. This took into account the need to release research data in accordance to the interests served by that particular site. This is not an uncommon practice and is a strategy that researchers are familiar with and have come to accept as being a key part of the research process. In the case of the PSNI study, this did not necessarily involve oppressing data, but rather altering the balance of which certain points are emphasised more over others, according to the space, time and context in which they were being reported. In addition, a written report for internal circulation with recommendations for best practice was offered to the institution under study. This was an indication of the genuine desire on the part of the researcher to give something back to the police force under study (Greenhill 1981; Holdaway 1983). This was done with the intent to produce relevant and progressive findings that could be utilised in debates for best practice and policy changes. What this adopted approach indicates, though, is that some degree of diplomacy and tact is needed when such findings are produced in these types of research studies. This involves both the researcher and the police engaging in open dialogue when the findings emerge, not only with regard to the content of the findings, but also with regard to how this is rightfully and most usefully presented. Open dialogue allows both sets of interpretations and interests, those of the criminological researcher and that of the criminal justice agency that is being researched (not to mention whose behaviour is being scrutinised and often criticised), to inform the analysis process, and even in those situations where there is inevitable disagreement, open dialogue at the very least allows for each case to be presented. This is important in studies where the issues of concern, such as those in the reported PSNI study, are raised, for example (i) problematic views about race and racism are presented; (ii) potential harm to image and reputation is revealed, as the data shows the police in bad light; and (iii) internal criticism of senior-level management is made by operational officers.

However, can and should critical criminologists pursue such an approach? Surely it would invite accusations of reinforcing the power of the very institution under study. Would it not go against the very core beliefs of the critical criminologist who seeks to give a voice to the marginalised and oppressed victims of institutions such as the police? In response to this, it is argued here that the adopted approach should not be seen as a means of buckling to any institutional pressures, or necessarily going against the grain of meaningful critical criminological research. Neither should it be seen as transferring control of research over to the policing institution under study. Rather it can act as an additional check on the legitimacy and validity of the data produced. It can also act as a way to keep clear the path of research access. For policy development and service delivery purposes, open dialogue could also be seen as a way to bridge the ever increasing gap between criminologists and practitioners, by connecting the work of one with the work of the other. However, a word of caution! On the part of the researcher, it is vital that one does not allow a complete seizing of the research aims or findings. This is because the core code of the critical criminologist should be remembered, this being to reveal institutional state abusive practices and to empower its victims. In terms of the study discussed here, this is especially important because although some genuine efforts by police forces, such as the PSNI, to remove discrimination from its ranks and to offer victims of racist incidents fair police protection and justice delivery are being made, we cannot escape the fact that this is still a society where racism is rife and all to easily penetrates the police ranks.

REVISION QUESTIONS

1 Do black and minority ethnic groups have valid reasons for being suspicious of criminologists?
2 What is the goal of criminological research in race and crime matters? Does this goal change when considering demands by the funding body; the research institution's concerns about reputation; and the researcher's own academic profile?
3 In their pursuit of anti-oppressive practice, racial equality and fair justice, to what degree can criminological research truly assist the well-being of black and minority ethnic groups?
4 What methodological issues are associated with researching criminal justice agencies, such as the police, on matters of racism, crime and legitimacy?
5 Should the criminologist ever engage in 'open dialogue' with criminal justice institutions over presentation of the research findings?

NOTES

1 Criminological research is often carried out on administrative matters, or on researching the relatively powerless in society. However, critical criminology seeks to present the 'view from below'. It is viewed as being concerned with the 'exposé research of dominant elites and institutions' (Sapsford 1996: 73).
2 The bracketed use of the term '(hi)story' here refers to the way in which 'history' is an interpretation, construction and presentation of a narrative from a particular point of view, within a particular context, given at a particular point of time. Its presentation is therefore

a largely social and political activity, as it will always involve some sort of reflexive construction of the facts. It is therefore neither wholly factual nor fictional, but a version of the narrator's truth (Patel, 2005).

3 Also included in this category are the social and political works of non-criminologists, including people like Benjamin Zephaniah, Bob Marley and Angela Davies.

4 Although the data from a UK-wide comparative study to support whether this is actually the case has yet to be established.

FURTHER READING

Box, Steven (1983) *Power, Crime and Mystification*. London: Routledge.

Garland, Jon, Spalek, Basia and Chakraborti, Neil (2006) 'Hearing Lost Voices: Issues in Researching "Hidden" Minority Ethnic Communities', *British Journal of Criminology*, 46: 423–437.

Russell, Katheryn K. (1992) 'Development of a Black Criminology and the Role of the Black Criminologist', *Justice Quarterly*, 9(4): 667–683.

10

Conclusion: Re-constructing Race and Crime

We opened Chapter 1 by suggesting that scientific racism has become central to the fields of power between the state and ethnic minorities against which 'race and crime' debates are played out. There is nothing new in the suggestion that dubious ideas about race and racial difference can be shored up by reference to science. Neither is there anything to suggest that scientific racism overshadows other modes of racist expression; the case studies we have discussed throughout this book in fact demonstrate precisely the opposite, namely that cultural racism is alive and well, and that it is thriving. So why did we choose to open this book with a reference to scientific racism when we know that to do so in itself can appear to overstate the importance of one mode of racism while undermining our recognition of its other expressions?

Reconsidering 'scientific' racism

To draw a hard distinction between scientific and non-scientific racisms is contingent upon making a prior judgement concerning what is considered to be science (and what is not). Such a question may appear fairly straightforwardly resoluable through some sort of commonsense fudge: after all, in lay parlance, some things are scientific and others not. But commonsense racisms defy straightforward, super-ficial distinctions between scientific and non-scientific knowledge. Even when expressed in terms of cultural difference, the idea that people exist in bounded racial groups draws upon sedimented notions of phenotypal difference. As Hall (2000) has reminded us, racist discourse has its cultural and its biological registers. Let us think of this another way: the distinction between scientific and non-scientific racisms can be conceived of as an epistemological twist concerning what sort of rules are followed when constructing racist knowledges. It can also be understood in terms of the appeals which are made in an attempt to ground prob-lematic ideas of racial difference in some kind of 'real', tangible truth claims. That is, whether racial ideas appeal to scientific foundation, or to other knowledges (such as cultural difference). Race is slippery – it is, as we have established, discursive – and its shifting meanings are fixed through hegemonic operations to stabilise its shifting meanings. Thus, the attempt to connect ideas of racial difference to science or non-science simply reflect different ways of attempting to fix racial meanings, some grounding themselves in appeals to science. Although it is widely acknowledged that other forms of racism, such as new racism, are constructed through a cultural logic (Solomos and Back, 1996: 27), in fact all racisms express a cultural logic in the sense that they infuse meaning and influence 'explicitly or implicitly, in every social conflict and institution, and in every act of social signification' (Winant, 1993: 122). At the same time, even the most unscientific of cultural racisms direct us to the idea that difference is hard-wired into people.

Hard distinctions between scientific and non-scientific racisms can over-simplify because they rely ultimately on the ability to clearly distinguish 'science' from 'non-science'. While this appears relatively straightforward in respect of how ideas about racial difference may appeal to 'science' or 'culture', in practice, it is far harder to draw such a distinction. Would social-sciences work be included under the rubric of 'scientific' racism? And how would we account for the ways in which scientific racism is conveyed through its ability to access dominant cultural codes that enable us to decode it in the correct way? Let us consider an example drawn from the zenith of scientific racism – whiteness and American eugenics policies. We have already introduced the idea that race is socially constructed. This means that racial labels such as 'white' and 'black', and the characteristics to which they supposedly refer, have no basis in science. Rather, we are dealing with the power of a particular set of ideas, and how they become a basis for ordering society. For example, David Roediger has highlighted how people in the US – a country of immigrants – came to be seen as being white through a number of historical processes, as poor European immigrants were given various racial labels which categorised them as somehow not being fully white: '"becoming white," "white by law," "white on arrival," "white before coming," "conditionally white," "situationally white," "inbetween peoples," "probationary whites," "offwhiteness," or even … "our temporary Negroes"' (Roediger, 2008: 140–141). Research has demonstrated the close relationship between invented ideas about whiteness and socio-economic status, and academics have demonstrated that the processes through which people come to be labelled as white have very often been related to wider economic processes and the ways in which the population is organised, disciplined and governed (Nayak, 2007: 739).

The social construction of whiteness involved excluding those who were thought of as falling short of those standards and characteristics stereotypically associated with these new, invented, ideas of what it meant to be 'white'. This occurred most obviously by denying even the most basic rights to the groups of people who were labelled as non-white. However, it also occurred through the invention of a range of racial labels which white people used to describe lower-class white people who appeared not to match the middle-class ideals of whiteness. The best-publicised of these labels was 'white trash', but other labels included 'poor white', 'cracker', 'linthead', 'okie', 'hillbilly' and 'ridge runner' (Hartigan, 1997: 53). These labels were constructed as a way of policing the boundaries of whiteness and explaining away why it was that the supposedly 'superior' invented race ('whites') seemed to contain people who undermined the myth of white superiority (Yukins, 2003: 167).

Those against whom such labels as 'white trash' were applied thus became represented as being somehow 'less than' properly 'white', and in turn became the focus of nationwide moral panics as a result of the threat they posed to ideas about the purity and advancement of whiteness. At the heart of these moral panics lay the work of middle-class industries – most notably, the media which whipped up the moral panics, and the medical professions which sought to explain the degeneracy and racial impurity of the 'white trash'. There followed the creation of a system for dealing with 'white trash' which focused on eugenics practices seeking to identify the source of the defective gene which was seen as lying at the root of the condition of being 'white trash'. The family history studies which took place often attempted to trace poor whites back to a black ancestor who could be blamed for their subsequent genetic decline. Debates focused on the economic cost posed by 'white trash' – one 1877 study claimed a single family had cost 'over a million and a quarter dollars of loss in 75 years' (Dugdale, 1975 [1877], cited in Yukins, 2003: 168) – and the proposed answer increasingly involved their forced sterilisation to prevent further breeding. The most famous of these cases involved the sterilisation of Carrie Buck, a single mother as a result of rape (Wray, 2006). But the work of the assorted scientific racists from the state lunacy commissions and the Eugenics Records Office may well have been justified through appeals to the idea of defective gene pools, but the articulation of this racism also occurred through cultural registers, and it is largely through this articulation through the registers of culture that its greatest legacy remains with us today – the term 'white trash', a notion rooted in scientific notions of racism but which works equally through cultural registers and the cultural hegemony of classed notions of whiteness (Wray and Newitz, 1997: 144).

This case study illustrates that we can speak of scientific racism without diminishing the importance of the relationship between cultural and scientific registers of racism. This is important at a time of the continued spread of 'new racism' (Barker, 1981) and its various cultural correlates such as 'xeno-racism' (Fekete, 2001; Sivanandan, 2006), 'new popular racism' (Kundnani, 2001) and Islamophobia (Meer, 2007). When we suggest that fields of power between ethnic minorities and the state are increasingly couched in scientific terms this does not mean that there is a necessary essentialist distinction between cultural and scientific racism. Let us take, for example, the case of Islamophobia, which has flourished precisely at this nexus between scientific and cultural racisms: it was allowed to spread by the failure to adequately recognise Islamophobia *qua* racism, with anti-racist legislation predicated on biological definitions of race and quite widespread opposition to the idea that Muslims should receive protection against racism since they are not a real (read biological) race. Of course, since race is socially constructed, Muslims are no more (or less) a biological race than any other group on the planet. But if the retreat into ideas of race as phenotype enabled anti-Muslim racism to prosper, it was popularised through its expression via registers of culture, particularly at the hands of a far right which has politicised around anti-Muslim hate expressed in cultural terms that stay (just) on the legal side of anti-racism legislation. The legacies of scientific and cultural thinking on race intertwine in contemporary Islamophobia, as they do in all forms of racism.

Scientific racism can, then, be comprehended in our terms as a register for the expression of racism. When we suggest this we are mindful that the expression of racism in this register is contingent not eternal (thus the same racisms can find expression through different registers). The expression of racism in this register is tactical, and is determined not by the essential nature of the racism itself (within the terms of our anti-essentialism, nothing is essential), but on the basis of political expediency. Returning to our example of Islamophobia, this expedience is illustrated by the appeal to scientific racism as a way of discounting the cultural racism of Islamophobia. The appeal to science here takes as its very object the denial of protection to a racialised minority. This scientific racism is nothing if not a racism born of cynical reason.

To speak of contemporary scientific racism can also mean something more in a context in which attempts are made to identify DNA markers of criminality which can be linked to race. If postmodern science is associated with indeterminacy, chaos and complexity rather than determinism, immutable order and certainty (Best and Kellner, 1997: 225), then we need to account for key features of contemporary expressions of race through scientific registers. Racism today is less concerned with fixing races into a Darwinian schema or into hierarchies than with implicitly acknowledging the mutability of racial identities identities and working within these to stabilise contested racial meanings. This is a response to the discrediting of older ideas of scientific race, and involves a shift from attempts to arrange immutable races into an evolutionary framework (which characterised Darwinian racism) based on certainty of both racial category and its 'objective' capacities, towards attempts to recuperate race while denying that racism is the effect of the exercise. In other words, this is a racism of what we could term, appropriating Peter Sloterdijk's (1987) term, 'cynical reason': one which denies and effects racism, both entirely through cynical logics.

Contemporary scientific racism effects this move by shifting from biological hierarchies to registers of risk and likelihood of offending. Thus, the logics of 'risk reduction', 'pre-emptive immobilisation' and imprisonment before the act emerge from the construction of risk profiles 'using aggregate information about suspect populations, and applied through information technologies' (Wilson and Weber, 2008: 127), and are implemented both by servants of the state and by its sub-contractors. DNA profiling, genome research, risk measurements based on data-mining from a variety of sources of social and psychological data effectively reconstitute the threatening racialised body of the other as a digitised ensemble – or, as Jasbir Puar (2007) would put it, as an assemblage of the organic and the non-organic. This illustrates a shift in today's scientific racism: surveillance is not simply about placing the racialised into disciplinary enclosures (or putting them on display in museums, galleries and 'freak shows'), but is equally undertaken through the capture and analysis of digital data and through the ability to turn the dividualised-digitised racialised body inside and out in constructing the profile to match the citizen.

The stamp placed upon racialised subjects simultaneously marks risk and bio-metrics, and is bound up with the authentication of 'safe' and 'risky' subjects (Ceyhan, 2008: 113) so that racialised interventions against those communities can be enacted while simultaneously denying their racial content: 'we are just responding to statistical risk' was the logic we discussed in Chapters 1 and 2. Scientific racism shifts, then, to underpin an order which makes increasing use of profiling practices which do not just discriminate against racialised minorities, but centrally constitute them as racialised. As French notes in work on a Canadian context but equally relevant to any advanced capitalist state, 'whether it is called risk management or racial profiling, the practice of singling out communities, of classing groups of people as deserving of increased scrutiny because of their race, ethnicity, or apparent community affiliation, is prevalent' (French, 2007: 60).

This logic is underpinned by contemporary iterations of race science, and is centrally biopolitical. As Duffield (2007: 229) notes, all attempts to divide popu-lations racially ultimately appeal to ideas of biological difference, since they emerge from a common biopolitical impulse irrespective of their cultural or bio-logical outward expression. It is therefore worth noting that profiling works not just with the essentialist ideals of 'biological race' upon which our anti-racist legislation is based, but also through the very fluid categories which the state does not recognise under such legislation: Fekete (2004) notes practices such as religious profiling.

The question of races

Profiling practices play important roles in 'filtering' space (Khoury 2009), distin-guishing between those 'in-' and 'out-' of place (racially). Such practices underpin both the surveillances of minorities by the state, and their surveillances amid a broadened politics of hate as racists and extremists struggle over the raciality of space, as we saw in Chapter 3. But while they rely on the idea that the different racial groups can be fairly easily recognised, in practice this is not necessarily the case. For example, the shooting of Jean Charles de Menezes illustrates some of the tensions and difficulties around the fluid nature of race and the problems of assuming straightforward racial recognition. The misrecognition of Menezes for a terrorist has posed questions about race and recognition which are of interest both in the context of state-profiling practices and in the light of a range of racist attacks in which non-Muslim victims have been subjected to Islamophobic violence. Moeckli (2007: 667) has suggested that it is not unreasonable to wonder whether race was involved in the misidentification of Menezes, while Garner (2007: 13) has gone still further, suggesting that 'had Menezes been a blue-eyed blond he would not have been mistaken for a terrorist'. The idea that race was at work in the case was underlined by early media coverage of the shooting which saw news outlets broadcast putative eye-witness accounts which described Menezes in clearly racial terms as an 'Asian', and which alleged he had been suspiciously dressed in a bulky jacket with protruding wires, and that he had fled police and vaulted a ticket barrier (Pugliese, 2006). These false accounts helped cement the incident as being somehow racial, but also pose questions about how race works.

Pugliese (2006) has read the shooting in terms of an 'invisibilised systemacity' of racial profiling, and has suggested that a racialised regime of visuality was central to the misrecognition, with Menezes morphing into an Asian as a result of his skin and hair colour, officers' readings of his movements as suspicious, and the racialised construction of his clothing as redolent of terrorism. In Pugliese's reading, visuality is central to the discursive construction of race. This contrasts from hegemonic ideas about race which tend to de-emphasise the discursive construction of race and instead focus on seeing as a technology for reading unproblematised racial meanings. An academic example of this can be found in Waddington et al.'s (2004) consideration of stop and search. The authors' consideration of how low-visibility conditions affect the ability to perform discriminatory stop and searches, presupposes that while external conditions can problematise the reading of racial meanings, the meanings themselves are stable. In other words, the idea is that racial meanings are constructed outside the encounter between police and racialised minorities, and that the success of the recognition is in part contingent upon it taking place in conditions which allow those meanings to be read.

In contrast to this, Pugliese's theoretical position foregrounds the discursive construction of these racial meanings. This is helpful in two respects which can assist us in thinking through contemporary issues around race. First, Pugliese's position helps maintain an awareness of how race is constructed through the encounter, rather than perpetuating the unhelpful idea that race is constructed prior to it. For instance, if an officer stops an individual on the basis of conflating their ethnicity with particular forms of criminality, this does not simply reproduce static racial meanings which are constructing prior to the encounter, but it actively contributes to their very construction. All meaningful activities can be bound up in the discursive construction of ideas about race. Second, Pugliese's position underlines that it is not the conditions within which racial meanings are interpreted or struggled over which makes them slippery, but actually that race itself is a slippery and contested matter.

The shooting of Menezes illustrates beyond doubt the slipperiness of race. In fact, it is worth noting that the misrecognition of Menezes was multi-layered, as a reading of the Independent Police Complaints Commission's investigations (IPCC 2007a; 2007b) can show us. In the retrospective accounts offered to IPCC, Menezes was variously described as 'IC1' (white) (IPCC, 2007a: 55), 'light skinned' North African (2007a: 55), as having 'Mongolian eyes' (2007a: 56) and as being an Asian wearing a bulky jacket (2007a: 64). Some of the harrowing eye-witness statements provided at the Coroner's inquest add to the sense of uncertainty. For instance, one witness describes fleeing a fellow passenger who is first described as 'mixed race' with 'light' 'olive' skin and a 'dark brown or black' beard (Stockwell Inquest 2008a: 64), before then being as a 'tall Asian' (2008a: 65) who provoked such anxiety in the witness that she had to leave the carriage: 'I knew I would panic if I didn't get off straight away' (2008a: 67). In fact, this frightening passenger was neither Asian, nor even Brazilian, but a member of the police surveillance team, who was also described by another officer as being 'olive skinned' and matching the suspect's description (Stockwell Inquest, 2008b: 2). At one point, this officer is reported as being pinned to the floor of the carriage by another armed officer who had mistaken him for the suspect, while elsewhere on the train, the driver risked death to flee into the tunnel, certain that he had witnessed an attack by 'fanatics' when the shooting actually occurred (Stockwell Inquest 2008a: 3). Race is nothing if not slippery, and to compound the confusion, Pugliese arguably adds another misrecognition: strictly speaking, Menezes had only been mistaken for an Asian by the spurious eye-witness accounts presented to the media and by an unidentified call to the surveillance control room. In fact, he was mistaken for the North African terrorist Hussain Osman, and the various mistaken identifications which occurred were undercut by a further, fundamental one: Menezes was simultaneously being identified as being a Muslim; a category which works as 'quasi-ethnic' in terms of its deployment by Muslims (Meer, 2007) but which is also racialised as a bounded group in contemporary racist discourse of Islamophobia.

The Menezes case is of interest to us for a number of reasons. First, it illustrates the slipperiness and contestedness of race. Second, it helps illustrate the phantasmatic way in which ideas about Muslims infuse and complicate the traditional terms on which we ascribe racial categories to individuals. Third, it also illustrates an important affective dynamic of contemporary workings of race. In Chapter 3 we noted that affect and emotion are central to the expression of a contemporary racial politics. The Menezes case illustrates this, occurring at a time of great fear and anxiety during a hunt for fleeing terrorists. In fact, the retrospective accounts of the various misrecognitions are striking for their affective richness: Menezes was, for example, 'twitchy', jumpy (IPCC, 2007a: 57) and nervous (2007a: 56), and in our analysis the signification of these affective and emotional states as likely markers of suspicious otherness appears to play a significant role in the racial misrecognitions which occur. For this reason it is interesting to read Pugliese's conceptualisation of the systemacity of visual racial profiling against recent work by Jasbir Puar (2007), who has theorised the role of affect in contemporary profiling. Puar's emphasis on affect is particularly interesting since it seeks to explain the misrecognitions which have punctuated the war on terror – involving racist assaults as much as profiling exercise – in the context of a shift from the visual to the affective, or from 'looks like' to 'seems like' and 'feels like' (Puar 2007: 187). While we are not entirely convinced by this reading for a number of reasons, it is significant in helping us further problematise the idea of uncontested visibility which very often underlies writings on race and stop and search, and in incorporating a recognition of the affective dimensions of everyday practices. For instance, an officer might not simply stop somebody simply because they have a particular racial 'look', but because they have a sense that the individual poses a threat or presents cause for suspicion. What it means to arouse suspicion or to present threat or risk is coded in many ways, and in the context of the management of racialised populations through risk can well be used to signify racial difference. However, within the discipline of criminology there is still more scope to incorporate a reading of affect, both in work on race and in broader research agendas.

The Menezes case is also significant because it can help qualify what we mean when we speak of the systemacity of race. To speak of race as being in some way systematic can often create the impression that one is suggesting it as somehow part of a grand design, or some form of intelligent conspiracy for organising society. This is not the case at all, and we have attempted to show this throughout this book by drawing attention to the instability of the racial order. But this instability is not simply a result of the slippery and contested nature of race. Rather, it is because any racial order is ultimately constructed on the basis of fabrication and held in place through the potential for force, as we have seen. It is therefore unsurprising that Deleuze and Guattari suggest of racism that 'its cruelty is equaled only by its incompetence and naivete' (Deleuze and Guattari, 2004: 198). This vicious incompetence of race is reflected in words uttered by Richard Horwell, QC for the Metropolitan Police Force, to the inquest on 20 November 2008:

> You cannot use the eyewitness evidence to construct what happened, because if you did, you would have people firing into the carriage from outside, you would have Arabs firing into the roof of the carriage, and many other actions and words spoken that cannot have happened or cannot have been said at the time before the shooting.

The Menezes affair thus highlights a further dimension to our conception of the ways in which scientific and cultural racisms come together in contemporary racism. That is, race is fluid. If today's cynical racisms appeal to race while claiming not to be racist – a central logic since the emergence of new racism (Barker, 1981) – then they also appear to accept the contestedness and slipperiness of race itself. Even the far right's cynical attempts to mobilise around

Islamophobia because it has traditionally gone unrecognised *qua* racism reflect an acknowledgement of the ways in which traditional racial vocabularies have been decentred. This interruption of race as being something stable and immutable leaves us with forms of race which, whether expressed through appeals to cultural difference or scientific risk, mirror this instability. Postmodern race is fundamentally incompetent: less a rigid set of classifications into which racialised subjects can be arranged, than a shifting, fractured ethnoscape which can create the impression of lacking systemic notions of race through the complex and contradictory ways in which race is reworked. What better illustration of this putative incompetence of race can there be than the repeated cases of mistaken identity/misrecognition which have sutured the war on terror?

Biopolitics

We considered the importance of scientific racism to contemporary fields of relations between the state and ethnic minorities in relation to the question of crime and policing. But how can we reconcile this tension between notions of scientific racism reworked through risk profiles and so forth, with the profoundly unscientific and frequently incompetent ways in which race appears to work. The answer to this question is provided by connecting our understanding of scientific racism to questions of racialised governmentality which we posed in Chapters 3 and 8. Biopolitics places racism at the centre of contemporary state power practices (Terranova, 2007: 135). In other words, race is less incidental to biopolitics than central to it (Reid, 2006: 29). Biopolitical practices are therefore centrally racialised, and invoke both scientific and cultural modes of racism. They are scientific to the extent that they concern themselves with bodies and continue to emphasise phenotype, and increasingly organise bodies in relation to social space and disciplinary enclosures by classifying them through reference to a range of data that it underwritten by appeals to science. Thus, they are scientific and cultural in the sense that phenotypal referents are deployed alongside DNA data, risk calculations, biometric fingerprinting, a surveillance footprint which bears affective and somatic knowledges, and because they are framed by a more general conception of cultural separateness and difference and express hegemonic cultural values. It would be impossible to have racism without a cultural dimension, for it is the cultural dimensions of racism which provide its popular hold. This intersection of the cultural and the scientific illustrates Jasbir Puar's consideration of the ways in which, through contemporary biopolitical practice such as racial profiling, the racialised body becomes an assemblage of the organic and the non-organic, while being simultaneously digitised/dividualised (Puar, 2007).

This nexus between cultural and scientific modes of racism also emerges as a locus for the exercise of biopolitical power by the state. The responsibility of the racialised subject now includes innate physical, somatic and affective alignments which are intended to organise the subject in relation to her/his emotional attachments towards Britain as much as they seek to reposition in relation to disciplinary enclosures. One important aspect of this is the state's ability to strike down suddenly, as occurred with Jean Charles de Menezes. This striking down is what Nick Vaughan-Williams (2007) has referred to as the 'lightning strike' of sovereignty. But this ability to strike suddenly, and from nowhere relates to our awareness of scientific racism *qua* profiling: for example, although Amoore (2008) notes that in fact risk practices involve lengthy calculation, at the same time, the perceived risk of inaction becomes the justifying feature of the desire to strike pre-emptively where there is felt to be a risk, and the 'practices of data mining, social network analysis, risk profiling, identity management and so on diffuse security decisions into algorithmic calculation' (Amoore, 2008: 116). The diffuseness of the calculation matches the radical dispersal of biopolitical function across the social field: thus, the sovereign lightning strike which saw Hicham Yezza imprisoned after downloading files from the website of the US Department of Justice occurred when he was flagged as a risk by monitoring systems within his university. This transforms the spatialities of fields of power between ethnicised minorities and the state, and their temporal framings: if classic works on the disorders of the early 1980s highlighted the negotiation of simmering tensions in 'frontline' urban localities, contemporary practices indicate the centrality of the bolt from the blue – as occurred in Forest Gate, to Yezza, and to Raissi – across dispersed localities. There is nothing new in such miscarriages, but we suggest that they are transformative because of their effects in drawing attention to the state's complicated relationship with Muslim minorities and in influencing confidence in the war on terror. Thus, while state actions during the war on terror have helped fuel anti-Muslim racism, they have also had the unintended effect of highlighting its institutionalised forms.

If contemporary risk is constituted at the level of populations to be controlled (Nadesan, 2008), then this links closely to our early point about the mutability of contemporary notions of risk-conscious scientific racism, for the model subjects on whom this is enacted during the war on terror are, in traditional racial terms, racially indeterminate: Muslims and asylum seekers. It is therefore in relation to these groups in particular that we see the sovereign lightning strike most visible. We discussed instances of this in Chapter 7, when we considered control orders and asylum detention. These instances add to our understanding of the lightning strike of sovereignty by underlining the importance of incorporating a conception of sovereign power into analyses of race and crime.

Certainly, insofar as contemporary bioracism increasingly entails decisions over the right to live, it is also a question about sovereign power. The shooting of Menezes entailed the drawing of a distinction around who can be killed without the act being considered as a murder or sacrifice which falls within the scope of Agamben's (1998, 2005) conceptions of bare life and sovereign power. The decision to use violence against Menezes was bound up with a concern for the capacity, and right, to live, and 'in the name of the life of the population – its health longevity but also its ways of life and thought' (Terranova, 2007: 135). Thus, state violence was at one and the same time a question of sovereignty and biopolitics. But how can we connect the affective of biopolitics with the question of sovereign violence? In order to engage this question, we begin from Agamben's recognition that the state of exception, as 'a space devoid of law … in which all legal determinations – and above all the very distinction between public and private – are deactivated' (Agamben, 2005: 50) has become a dominant paradigm for government (Agamben, 2005: 2) and centrally structures sovereignty (Agamben, 1998: 21). Gulli (2007: 235) has clarified that violence figures in relation to the exception not simply consequentially (because there is a state of exception, the state will enact violence) but constitutively. In other words, it is not the case that violence occurs simply because there is a state of exception, but rather that there is a state of exception because of the violence through which sovereignty is established and maintained. The state of exception is not just a legal determination, but a logic of government for which the condition of possibility is state violence. It does not work through a legal deliberation through which law is suspended – for example, the passing of a law such as the Patriot Act – but rather, these are passed because of the constitutive violence of the state. This violence can signal law's suspension in other ways; for example, as we saw, Vaughan-Williams (2007: 188) describes the Menezes shooting as one such 'lightning strike' of sovereignty. This marks a useful addition to Agamben's conception of sovereignty, since it deals with acts of violence with are reached – seemingly – without deliberation (which is viewed as a sign of weakness). What Vaughan-Williams could add is that such 'lightning strikes' of violence are, of course, intended as affective experiences ('shock and awe'). This 'lightning strike' conception articulates with an affective reading of biopolitics, and with a focus on sovereignty. In this analysis it forms an important links since the attempt to exceptionalise the incident as a means of exculpating the state also proceeds in part from a misreading of an event engineered in any case to be experienced as exceptional (albeit in a different sense). Thus, the affective technologies of control do not just reach into our lives, but also into those of the victim.

A conception of sovereignty can link incidents otherwise separated by their exceptionalisation around a recognition of the logic of government which unites them. In the Menezes affair, this can restore the association with a wider context in which race and questions about misidentification of terrorists also figured. The most notorious incident in the UK involving mistaken identity was that of Lotfi Raissi, an Algerian-born pilot interned in the high-security Belmarsh Prison after a photographic image of a relative was misidentified as that of a 9/11 terrorist. In March 2005 Home Office minister Hazel Blears declared it was a 'fact of life' that Asians and Muslims would be targeted more under anti-terrorism stop and search powers (Kundnani, 2006). A month after the shooting of Menezes, Blears distanced herself from Ian Johnston, Chief Constable of British Transport Police, after he expressed similar views (Lippert-Rasmussen, 2007: 385). Speaking to the House of Commons Home Affairs Committee in 2005, Lord Hope repeated the suggestion that terrorist suspects would be linked to particular communities (Moeckli, 2007: 667). In the global war on terror more widely, racial profiling in the US gained support despite being accompanied by similar 'misidentifications' as a basis for racist attacks against minorities such as Sikhs (Puar, 2005: 136–137), and by sweeping anti-terror interventions by the state against immigration violators and people of 'Middle Eastern appearance', resulting in the questioning, incarceration and deportation of significant numbers of people innocent of involvement in terrorism (Meeropol, 2005). Such incidents – 'lightning strikes' of sovereignty themselves – were linked to the context in which the Menezes case occurred, both by the idea of global war on terror, and because the practices of control and surveillance associated with racial profiling linked the domestic pursuit of the war on terror in the USA with a wider context and politics (Maira, 2007: 48).

Racialised governmentality and the legacy of institutional racism

We introduced a conception of state of exception to help counter the criticism that Foucaultian approaches to power dissolve it into myriad power relations. But in analysing racism we also face the difficulty that governmentality is expressed across diverse social agents and that it often takes contradictory forms in doing so. An understanding of hegemony can help us to conceive of how contested and dispersed practices and meanings are lent the impression of fixity across dispersed sites. This can help us understand institutional racism in some key respects. In Chapters 2 and 4 we considered a range of examples of institutionalised racisms, but included in these discussions some consideration of attempts to challenge the hold of institutional racism. How, then, can we conceive of the continuation of racism alongside its putative demise? Our conception of white governmentality takes, after Hesse (1997), the idea that its exercise is framed by the hegemony of whiteness. This rejects a static and essentialist understanding of whiteness and instead emphasises how hegemonic practices attempt to stabilise contested notions of whiteness around an authoritative conception of whiteness. This notion allows us to therefore consider the presence of challenges to racism. For example, Bethan Loftus's work on institutional change in policing highlights the retrenchment of traditional white masculine professional subjectivities in resistance to change is bound up with struggle over institutional change more broadly (Loftus, 2008). Whiteness in this sense is not something static, but bound up with wider struggles over power, and discursively linked to ideas of the old way being under threat. The white victimhood we noted as central to far-right racism and the sense of victimhood expressed in these institutional contexts are in many ways different, but both reflect the hegemonic attempt to construct a whiteness which unifies these different actors around a hegemonised idea of whiteness *qua* victimhood. It is also important to note that once we read whiteness in these terms, we are shifting beyond the essentialist/racist assumption that whiteness and blackness are ontic. Here, they instead refer to a particular set of ideas about what whiteness means, and how it can be universalised. Thus, white subjects do work to challenge racism, as Patel's work on policing in Northern Ireland demonstrates, because to challenge the hegemonic of whiteness which underpins racism is not a question of attacking white people, but rather of challenging a particular set of hegemonic ideas and practices which prop up white privilege (and black subordinacy).

At the same time, white governmentality can help us to understand how particular technologies of power authorised by hegemonic ideas about whiteness act upon racialised subjects. But white governmentality does not just work upon black and minority ethnic people (by disciplining them as deviant, extremist, and so forth). It also works upon white people, disciplining them to act in ways which subjectify them in terms of hegemonic notions of whiteness. An example of this is the politics of hate we considered in Chapter 3: this does not just involve the labelling of black and minority ethnic people as other, but also affirms the whiteness of the perpetrators. Similarly, racist practices within the criminal justice system render hyper-visible their black and minority ethnic victims while rendering invisible and natural the whiteness of perpetrators. In this sense, Holdaway and O'Neill (2007) refer to the essentialist positions adopted by some respondents in their research on the persistence of covert racism among police officers, and use this as the basis for turning away from 'postmodern' conceptions as a result of the finding that 'the underlife of constabularies we have documented reveals a more stable, dare we say normative understanding of the construction of race and ethnicity' (Holdaway and O'Neill, 2007: 412). But to emphasise governmentality and hegemony enables us to analyse how it is that these contested, often contradictory racial categories take on the appearance of fixity and how their stabilisation is a hegemonic operation, rather than just assuming them to be relatively unchanged. This in turn opens critical spaces for researching and documenting the kinds of changes which take place within police culture, as these seemingly 'stable' labels are contested and challenged. Thus, as Holdaway and O'Neill (2006) find in their research, essentialism is evidence of the presence of institutional racism in the police: we suggest that retaining anti-essentialist conceptions of identity – what the authors describe as 'relative' (Holdaway and O'Neill, 2007) – enables us to unpick these, and to analyse how they are able to assume a notion of fixity within the context of a wider racialised social order. As Jenny Bourne has noted:

> The fight against institutional racism is part of the larger fight against state racism, against asylum laws, against deportations, against stop and search, against deaths in custody, against school exclusions, against miscarriages of justice. You cannot combat popular racism without combating the state racism which gives popular racism its fillip ... state racism contaminates civil society. (Bourne, 2001: 20)

Bourne's recognition of the linkages between different modes of racist discourse is helpful since it reintroduces the state into our understanding of institutional racism. This problematises the definition of institutional racism adopted by the Macpherson report and locates this within the maintenance of a wider field of power relations between minorities and the state. As Hesse (2004: 141) notes, institutional racism accounts for racism as being either a residue from the past, or exceptional, rather than mundane. Thus, this conception of institutional racism becomes enmeshed within the 'routine pragmatics of racist government' (Hesse, 2004: 144). This reading thus establishes the terms of the hegemonic conception of institutional racism within the exercise of white governmentality. This is an important framing because managerialism is a mode of neo-liberal governmental-ity and the neo-liberal state's solution to the problem of institutional racism itself retreats into managerialism, with its targets, performance indicators, centring of hegemonic actors as agents of change, and its retreat into a conservative, fixed understanding of ethnic identities (Rojek, 2003: 183). This regime saves for itself the right to include, exclude, celebrate or oversee members of racialised minori-ties: the very functions outlined by Hesse as being bound up with the surveillance practices of white governmentality (Hesse, 1997); the problem we mentioned of employing 'token' minorities perfectly illustrates this. It is also worth drawing attention to Kundnani's (2001) suggestion that the anti-asylum racism of new popular racism is predicated around appeals to managerialism. The managerialisa-tion of equalities work also helps frame the particular forms adopted by those who seek to resist change.

There is no doubt that the Macpherson report does not provide a radical chal-lenge to institutional racism. By locating its liberal reformism within the context of the governmental regime which frames it, we can understand the ways in which informal modes of state racism can persist despite being formally debunked. Thus, when we discuss questions such as racial discrimination in policing and courts practice, we are discussing processes which do not step outside of estab-lished practices of governing populations. It is for this reason that racism persists in spite of Macpherson; the foreclosure of alternatives (such as anti-racism) underwrites this process. This racism is, as we have noted earlier in this chapter, a racism of cynical reason.

Resistance

We have considered forms of resistance, ranging from attempts to challenge rac-ism in the police service, to the identity politics of Muslim young people. This is important, for resistance transforms racist expression and forces the develop-ment of new strategies for racism. Thus, we cannot understand racism without taking account of the opposition with which it meets. We also need to recognise resistance because accounts of black and minority ethnic people tend too often to collapse their lived experiences into the monolithic aggregate categories and racial classifications they are often represented as inhabiting. In other words, minorities are often only represented through their subjection to white power regimes. To take account of their resistances offers something of a corrective to this, and illustrates Omi and Winant's (1994) argument that the racial order is always unstable, and thus always open to challenge. It is also important to recognise the ways in which members of other groups challenge racism. Whiteness is not an ontic category; its hegemony can be challenged by those whom it positions as 'white'. Unfortunately, however, the hold of racism persists. We therefore find it important to consider the ways in which resistances are articulated which step outside the Eurocentric horizons afforded by essentialist conceptions of identities. In doing so, we emphasised the political nature of the boundary drawing which goes into all articulations of identities. In this sense, the question of race is always political, and the shift from essentialist conceptions of 'race relations' or 'community cohesion' to analysis of the ways in which an anti-essentialist conception of political identities can help us to understand the struggles over the racial (political) frontiers of British society.

Racism has proved remarkably resistant to challenge. One of the reasons for this is because it is closely bound up with organisation and regulation of populations. While the post-Macpherson context has provided opportunities to highlight the tensions and cracks within this racial terrain, they do not fundamentally alter the nature of the terrain itself. For this reason, while the reformism of statist approaches to challenging racism is important, the resistance of black and minority ethnic subjects still represents the most far-reaching critique of the rationalities of racialised governance. Our consideration of race, crime and resistance therefore ends with the suggestion that managerialist reformism alone will not dismantle racism; in order to achieve this end we need to be able to learn from the ways in which the political agency of black and minority ethnic people reveals the limits of the racialised social boundaries which in turn mark the limits of the collective horizons against which racism finds its compass and racists (institutional, individual, collective, unwitting, banal and exceptional) their orientation. This does not mean we seek a return to the old-school anti-racism, with its belief in essential racial identities, but rather that we seek the emergence of anti-racisms which take into account the fluidity of race and the ways in which even everyday practices and logics place under scrutiny the attempts to organise the lives of subjects along racial lives. The fault-line in these efforts will, we believe, continue to be a criminal justice system which still acts as a point of condensation for grievances of minorities with the state, and which continues to over-determine the fields of power between the state and minorities.

Plus ça change, plus c'est la même chose – the more things change, the more they remain the same.

1 What does the case of Jean Charles de Menezes tell us about the fluid and contested nature of race and how it is constructed through encounters with others?
2 In what ways are issues about racialised biopolitical practices raised by the Menezes case?
3 How does the changing nature of biopolitical racism reflect the changing nature of race?
4 Why is it always important to remember resistance as well as racism?
5 How does the intensification of control in the post-Macpherson period problematise the legacies of the Macpherson report in challenging institutionalised state racism?

Kundnani, Arun (2009) *Spooked! How Not to Prevent Violent Extremism*. London: Institute of Race Relations.
Lentin, Alana (2008) 'Europe and the Silence about Race', *European Journal of Social Theory*, 11: 487–503.
O'Driscoll, Cian (2008) 'Fear and Trust: The Shooting of Jean Charles de Menezes and the War on Terror', *Millennium – Journal of International Studies*, 36: 339–360.

Revision Question Answers

The following offers guidance on what a good answer to the revision questions (given at the end of each chapter) should include. This list should be consulted once you have attempted to work through the revision questions for yourself.

1 Introduction: Constructing the Race–Crime Problem

1   In crime matters, why do we talk about the racial profile of suspects/offenders?
  - Identification process
  - Racial profiling
  - Blame
  - Generate fear and panic

2   How is the notion of 'black criminality' sold to us?
  - Media presentations
  - Political speak
  - News ordering
  - Language and emotion

3   Does 'white governmentality' exist in the criminal justice system? If so, where can it be found? How is it allowed to exist? What are the repercussions of its existence?
  - White law
  - Racialised hierarchy
  - Power and authority
  - Discrimination or privilege throughout the criminal justice system

4   What are the key forms of 'race talk' in a post-Macpherson era?
  - New popular racism
  - Xeno-racism
  - Palatable terms of reference
  - Citizenship, community cohesion and self-segregation

5   What do criminologists seek to offer to the study of racism?
  - Prevalence of racism
  - Racist practices that are enabled and legitimated by the state
  - Continued racist practices by agents of a criminal justice system that is uncontested and unchallenged

2 Crime Science?

1 Given a lack of evidence, it is argued that the relationships between criminality and race/ ethnicity are mythical. Yet these ideas persist. Why?
   - Provide easy points of reference due to embedded historical fear of 'foreign other'
   - Impact of social conditioning
   - Images are delivered in a simple and readily digestible way
   - Serves majority's position of privilege, power and authority

2 How has social science been used to legitimate racist oppressive practices?
   - Failure to consider beliefs, make-up and actions of criminal justice institutions themselves
   - Eurocentric history and dominance in criminology
   - Biological criminology
   - Scientific racism

3 What legislative protection is offered against racism? Does this prevent racist human rights violations from occurring?
   - Human Rights Act (1998)
   - Race Relations [Amendments] Act (2000)
   - Victimisation and violations of Acts widespread and under-reported
   - War on terror and detention (Guantanamo and Abu Ghraib)
   - Stereotypes in racial profiling and over-use of stop and search

4 What key theories and concepts have been used to explain data showing high rates of 'black crime'?
   - Subculture of violence (Comer, 1985; Silberman, 1980; Wolfgang and Ferracuti, 1967)
   - Underclass thesis (Calvin, 1981; Wilson, 1987)
   - New left realism (Lea and Young, 1984)
   - Critical Race Theory (Delgado and Stefancic, 2001)
   - Social conditions of violence (Benyon and Solomos, 1987)
   - Invisibility of whiteness (Dyer, 1997)
   - Xeno-racism (Fekete, 2001)
   - New popular racism (Kundnani, 2001)

5 How can Critical Race Theory contribute to the study of race and crime?
   - Consider racist underpinnings of state policy on crime control
   - Examine the response of criminal justice institutions in crime matters
   - Consider the relationship between race, racism and power
   - Diversity of race
   - Intersectionality

3 The Politics of Hate

1 How does an understanding of hate as political help frame our understanding of its role in structuring the boundaries of the social?
   - Hate as a form of antagonism
   - Struggles over social boundaries

- Struggles over race
- Contests over what is meant by hate and who are its 'true' victims

2 What does it mean to suggest that hegemonic responses 'racism' and 'hate' tend to exceptionalise them in order to conceal their importance?
  - Viewed as 'exceptional' not widespread
  - Recognised at the margins of society
  - Not as readily acknowledged among 'elite' groups or in routine state practices

3 How can an understanding of white governmentality help us to explore the complexities of the relationship between populist discourse on race and the commission of race hate at marginalised and exceptionalised sites?
  - Occurs across dispersed sites
  - Unified by hegemonic ideas about 'race' and 'whiteness'
  - Hate not exceptional but a strategy to defend a particular racial order
  - Part of a web of practices which mark racial others as dangerous and determine access to space, resources, power

4 How are emotions (such as hate, resentment) mobilised through the exercise of racialised power?
  - Important way of drawing them/us boundaries
  - Racial difference is recoded in terms of natural human emotions
  - Appeals to ordinary people on emotive terms

5 Why has white victimhood become such a powerful way of popularising racism?
  - Offers a critique of racism
  - Sometimes used to parody black and minority ethnic people
  - Represents certain actions – e.g. far right mobilisation – as behaviour of victims, not perpetrators, of racism

4 Policing Racism or Policing Race?

1 Account for the existence of institutional racism in the criminal justice system.
  - White law
  - Racist culture and normality, i.e. cop culture
  - History of criminal justice system and its agents, i.e. originally set up to serve the interests of the powerful
  - Unchallenged racist views

2 What are the *real* consequences of the Macpherson Report (1999)?
  - Tokenism
  - Continued institutional racism in masked, reworked and excused forms
  - Hidden views, not spoken but acted upon

3 Was the successful policing of the Anthony Walker murder driven by a police force genuinely free from racism or a police force wanting to *appear* to be free from racism? Does it matter?
  - The removal of racism may be impossible to achieve
  - Problem of determining a shared desirable outcome

- Relationship between representation (public) and reality (private)
- Determining markers of success

4 What attempts have been made to deal with the lack of black and minority ethnic officers in the police force? What is the impact of these?
- Recruitment initiatives
- Monitoring numbers and progression
- Tokenistic appointments where merits are questioned or resentment caused
- Race is still being used as a marker of difference
- Poor retention and career progression

5 An inquiry into the police shooting of Jean Charles de Menezes in 2005 stated that officers were working under the state's pressures of policing in an 'atmosphere of fear' (Independent Police Complaints Commission, 2007a: 16). Is this response an acceptable reason for the series of police actions that took place on that day?
- Victimisation
- Fear, panic and pressure to perform
- Police accountability
- Organisation and capability of officers with power
- Reaction of de Menezes family

5 Courtin' Justice

1 Does everyone experience the right to a fair trial?
- Bias
- Misrepresentation
- Infringement and denial of rights in practice
- Powerlessness and little access to resources

2 What does the evidence say about the existence of racial bias in the court?
- Over-sentencing
- White law
- White masks

3 Given that it is one part of a wider criminal justice system, can racism ever be eradicated in the court system?
- Impossible to achieve due to the roots, authority and positions of power
- Recommendations of Macpherson (1999)

4 Will the appointment of black and minority ethnic court personnel and judges mean fairness in court practices and sentencing decisions?
- Tokenism
- Over-compensation
- Conforming to the court's white law to prove worth and belonging

5 How and why was Satpal Ram a victim of unfair justice?
- Victim status denied
- Self-defence questioned

- Offender motives and background not fully considered
- Poor representation and short pre-court consultation with barrister
- Continued victimisation after sentencing (i.e. life licence release by the Home Office)

6 Proportionate Punishment?

1 Does a punitive practice have to be disproportional to be racialised?
   - Race not simply about proportionality
   - Assumptions, racial beliefs important

2 What do control orders tell us about the intensification of state power?
   - Similar to house arrest
   - Extensive restrictions on liberty
   - Secret evidence
   - Associated with risk management

3 What is the relationship between exceptional measures used to police the war on terror and those used to detain asylum seekers?
   - Intensification of power
   - Securitisation of immigration and asylum
   - Convergence of war on terror and war on asylum

4 How does the racism experienced by asylum seekers problematise the role of the state?
   - Lack of citizenship status
   - Criminalisation of asylum seekers

7 Victims' Rights and the Challenge of Discrimination

1 What kind of obstacles have black and minority ethnic groups faced in 'mainstream' political organisation?
   - Institutional racism
   - Historical emphasis upon white workers' needs and problems as universal
   - Struggles for recognition
   - Representation of black and minority ethnic political identities as threatening, corrupt, or militant

2 How do forms of autonomous resistance by black and minority ethnic people reflect challenges to, and redrawing of, racialised boundaries?
   - Challenge terms of racist discourse
   - Emphasise agency of black and minority ethnic people
   - Struggles over racialised identities
   - Challenge how we think of race and racism

3 How has resistance to racism by black and minority ethnic women's groups unsettled traditional conceptions of racial politics?
- Challenges stereotypes about 'silent' and 'oppressed' black and minority ethnic women
- Challenges idea that white women's experiences are universal within feminist movement
- Challenges idea that black and minority ethnic men's experiences are universal within anti-racist movements

4 What is the significance of the concept of 'intersectionality' in explaining the relationship of class, race and gender?
- Challenges idea that one of either race, gender or class will always have primacy
- Helps us to understand how particular experiences of oppression occur through the intersections of race, gender and social class

8 Forms of Resistance

1 Given the extent of the state power brought to bear on terrorism suspects, what are the problems of thinking through the resistance of victims of miscarriages of justice during the war on terror?
- Cases often shrouded in secrecy or followed by deportations
- 'No smoke without fire' assumption
- Extent of the power brought to bear on individuals

2 What do the experiences of Maher Arar, Lotfi Raissi and Hicham Yezza tell us about the problems of resisting racism?
- Opposition of the state to challenging injustices
- Demonisation of victims in the media
- Presumption of guilt

3 How have Muslim young people been stereotyped as extremists?
- Assumption that Muslim young people are extremist
- Assumption that any political activity by Muslims is likely to be radical

4 What is the significance of the anti-essentialism to our understanding of the complexities of the identity work which goes into resisting ascribed racial labels and racialised markers of deviance?
- Moves away from fixed understandings of identities
- Rejects idea that people mobilise as they do for racial reasons; instead focuses on contingency of political behaviour

9 Researching the Agenda

1 Do black and minority ethnic groups have valid reasons for being suspicious of criminologists?
- History of black and minority ethnic representation by criminology
- Eurocentric history of criminology

- Bias (to meet funders interests)
- Reputation and results

2 What is the goal of criminological research in race and crime matters? Does this goal change when considering demands by the funding body; the research institution's concerns about reputation; and the researcher's own academic profile?
- Truth
- Representation of voice, narratives, story and experience
- Uncovering problems
- Providing solutions
- Conflict and goals of funders
- Legacy of research on academia, researcher and institution's reputation, especially if research is too political, critical or radical

3 In their pursuit of anti-oppressive practice, racial equality and fair justice, to what degree can criminological research truly assist the well-being of black and minority ethnic groups?
- Removal of bias and personal goals
- Dissemination and use of data
- Penetrate discussions of key policy makers
- Continued dominance of powerful, via 'us' and 'them' defining

4 What methodological issues are associated with researching criminal justice agencies, such as the police, on matters of racism, crime and legitimacy?
- Truth and bias
- Ethics
- Access and gate-keeping
- Power, control and politics

5 Should the criminologist ever engage in 'open dialogue' with criminal justice institutions over presentation of the research findings?
- Acts as an additional check on the legitimacy and validity of data
- A way forward
- Suitable to some studies
- Balance of power and interests
- At odds with the core belief of criminology, especially critical criminology
- Re-negotiate relationship between criminology and criminal justice institutions

10 Conclusion: Re-constructing Race and Crime

1 What does the case of Jean Charles de Menezes tell us about the fluid and contested nature of race and how it is constructed through encounters with others?
- Problematic nature of racial identification
- Fluidity of ideas and labels of racial difference

2 In what ways are issues about racialised biopolitical practices raised by the Menezes case?
- Debates over racial profiling (was it/wasn't it?)
- Debates about use of state power (shoot to kill)

3 How does the changing nature of biopolitical racism reflect the changing nature of race?
- Different racial labels
- Different suspect groups
- Changing moral panics
- Role of emotion and affect

4 Why is it always important to remember resistance as well as racism?
- Importance of recognising agency of black and minority ethnic people
- Importance of acknowledging contributions made by black and minority ethnic people
- Moving beyond looking at black and minority ethnic people simply as victims
- Racist strategies transform in response to the resistance of black and minority ethnic people

5 How does the intensification of control in the post-Macpherson period problematise the legacies of the Macpherson report in challenging institutionalised state racism?
- Does Macpherson report provide a wholesale, radical challenge to racism?
- Importance of acknowledging power
- Strategies for governing racialised populations persist

References

Abrams, David S., Bertrand, Marianne and Mullainathan, Sendhil (2008) 'Do Judges Vary in Their Treatment of Race?', *American Law and Economics Association Annual Meetings*, 93: 1–44.

Adkins, Lisa (2005) 'Social Capital: The Anatomy of a Troubled Concept', *Feminist Theory*, 6(2): 195–211.

Afshar, Haleh, Aitken, Rob and Franks, Myfanwy (2005) 'Feminisms, Islamophobia and Identities', *Political Studies*, 53: 262–283.

Afshar, Haleh, Franks, Myfanwy, Maynard, Mary Ann and Wray, Sharon (2002) 'Issues of Ethnicity in Researching Older Women', *ESRC Growing Older Programme Newsletter*, 4: 8–9.

Agamben, Giorgio (1998) *Homo Sacer: Sovereign Power and Bare Life*. Stanford: Stanford University Press.

Agamben, Giorgio (2000) *Means Without End: Notes on Politics*. Minneapolis: University of Minnesota Press.

Agamben, Giorgio (2005) *State of Exception*. London: University of Chicago Press.

Agozino, Biko (1997) *Black Women and the Criminal Justice System*. Aldershot: Ashgate.

Agozino, Biko (2000) 'Theorizing Otherness: The War on Drugs and Incarceration', *Theoretical Criminology*, 4(3): 359–376.

Agozino, Biko (2008) 'Foreign Women in Prison', *African Journal of Criminology and Justice Studies*, 3(2): 1–33.

Ahmed, Sara (2004) 'Affective economies', *Social Text*, 22(2): 117–139.

Alexander, Claire (2005) 'Embodying Violence: 'Riots', Dis/order and the Private Lives of the Asian Gang', in Claire Alexander and Caroline Knowles (eds), *Making Race Matter: Bodies, Space and Identity*. Hampshire: Palgrave Macmillan. pp. 199–217.

Alexander, Claire, Edwards, Rosalind and Temple, Bogusia (2007) 'Contesting Cultural Communities: Language, Ethnicity and Citizenship in Britain', *Journal of Ethnic and Migration Studies*, 33(5): 783–800.

Allen, Chris (2003) *Fair Justice: The Bradford Disturbances, the Sentencing and the Impact*. Bradford: Forum Against Islamophobia and Racism.

Alleyne, Brian, W. (2002) *Radicals Against Race: Black Activism and Cultural Politics*. Oxford: Berg.

Amin, Ash (2002) Ethnicity and the Multicultural City: Living with Diversity Draft Report for the ESRC CITIES Programme and the Department of Transport, Local Government and the Regions. www.aulaintercultural.org/IMG/pdf/ash_amin.pdf.

Amin, Ash (2003) 'Unruly Strangers? The 2001 Urban Riots in Britain', *International Journal of Urban and Regional Research*, 27(2): 460–463.

Amnesty International (2006) *UK: Human Rights: A Broken Promise*. www.amnesty.org/en/library/info/EUR45/004/2006.

Amoore, Louise (2008) 'Consulting, Culture, the Camp: On the Economics of the Exception', in L. Amoore and M. de Goede (eds), *Risk and the War on Terror*. Abingdon: Routledge. pp. 112–130.

Anthias, Floya (2001) 'The Concept of "Social Division" and Theorising Social Stratification: Looking at Ethnicity and Class', *Sociology*, 35(4): 835–854.

Anzaldua, Gloria (ed.) (1998) *Making Face, Making Soul*. San Francisco: Aunt Lute Foundation.

Apena, Feyishola (2007) 'Being Black and in Trouble: The Role of Self-perception in the Offending Behaviour of Black Youth', *The National Association for Youth Justice*, 7(3): 211–228.

Appadurai, Arjun (1990) 'Disjunctive and Difference in the Global Cultural Economy', in M. Featherstone (ed.), *Global Culture*. London: Sage.

Arora, Ranjit K. (2005) *Race, Ethnicity and Education*. Aldershot: Ashgate.

Asad, Talal (1993) *Genealogies of Religion*. London: Johns Hopkins University Press.

Athwal, Harmit and Bourne, Jenny (2007) 'Driven to Despair: Asylum Deaths in the UK', *Race and Class*, 48(4): 106–114.

Austin, Roy L. and Allen, Mark D. (2000) 'Racial Disparities in Arrest Rates as an Explanation of Racial Disparity in Commitment to Pennsylvania's Prisons', *Journal of Research in Crime and Delinquency*, 37: 200–220.

Baldus, David C., Woodworth, George, Zuckerman, David, Weiner, Neil A. and Broffitt, Barbara (1998) 'Racial Discrimination and the Death Penalty in the Post-Furman Era: An Empirical and Legal Overview, with Recent Findings from Philadelphia', *Cornell Law Review*, 83: 1638–1770.

Bano, Samia (2011) 'Asking the Law Questions: Agency and Muslim women' in Sayyid, Salman and Vakil, Abdool Karim (eds), *Thinking Through Islamophobia: Global Perspective*. London: C. Hurst & Co., pp. 135–156.

Barker, Martin (1981) *The New Racism: Conservatives and the Ideology of the Tribe*. London: Junction Books.

Bartol, Curt R. and Bartol, Anne M. (2005) *Criminal Behavior: A Psychosocial Approach*. New Jersey: Pearson-Prentice Hall.

Bates, Ed (2009) 'Anti-terrorism Control Orders: Liberty and Security Still in the Balance', *Legal Studies*, 29(1): 99–126.

Batty, David (2011) 'Lady Warsi Claims Islamophobia is Now Socially Acceptable in Britain', *Guardian*, 20 January, www.guardian.co.uk/2011/jan/20/lady-warsi-islamophobia-muslims-prejudice.

BBC News (2006) 'Three jailed for racist bombing', 26 October 2006. news.bbc.co.uk/1/hi/england/norfolk/6089480.stm.

BBC News (2009) 'Murder Police Name Wanted Youth', 17 August 2009. news.bbc.co.uk/1/hi/england/manchester/8204657.stm.

BBC News (2009) 'Race Hate Murder Man Found guilty', 10 November 2009. news.bbc.co.uk/1/hi/scotland/glasgow_and_west/8352458.stm.

BBC News (2008) 'Entering the "baby father" debate', 16 July 2008. news.bbc.co.uk/1/hi/uk/7509142.stm.

BBC News (2010) 'Man Punched after Racial Abuse', 3 February 2010. news.bbc.co.uk/1/hi/northern_ireland/foyle_and_west/8495157.stm.

BBC News (2010) 'Identity Cards Scheme will be Axed "within 100 days"', 27 May 2010. news.bbc.co.uk/1/hi/uk_politics/8707355.stm.

BBC News (2010) 'Thousands of Anti-terror Searches Were Illegal', 10 June 2010. news.bbc.co.uk/1/hi/politics/10283701.stm.

Begg, Moazzam (2006) *Enemy Combatant: The Terrifying True Story of a Briton in Guantanamo*. London: Pocket Books.

Bell, Kathryn, Jarman, Neil and Lefebvre, Thomas (2004) *Migrant Workers in Northern Ireland*. Belfast: Institute for Conflict Research.

Benyon, John and Solomos, John (eds) (1987) *The Roots of Urban Unrest*. New York: Pergamon.

Berger, Ronald J. (2008) *Hoop Dreams on Wheels: Disability and the Competitive Wheelchair Athlete*. Abingdon: Routledge.

Best, Steven and Kellner, Douglas (1997) *The Postmodern Turn*. New York: Guilford Press.

Bethnal Green and Stepney Trades Council (1978) *Blood on the Streets: A Report on Racial Attacks in East London*. London: Bethnal Green and Stepney Trades Council

Bhavnani, Reena, Mirza, Heidi Safia and Meetoo, Veena (2005) *Tackling the Roots of Racism: Lessons for Success*. Bristol: Policy Press.

Birnberg Peirce and Partners, Medical Justice and NCADC (2008) 'Outsourcing Abuse: The Use and Misuse of State-sanctioned Force during the Detention and Removal of Asylum Seekers', London: Medical Justice Network.

Birt, Jonathan (2005) 'Lobbying and Marching: British Muslims and the State', in T. Abbas (ed.), *Muslim Britain: Communities Under Pressure*. London: Zed Books. pp. 92–106.

Birt, Jonathan (2006) 'Good Imam, Bad Imam: Civic Religion and National Integration in Britain post-9/11', *The Muslim World*, 96: 687–705.

Birt, Yahya (2009) 'Promoting Virulent Envy? Reconsidering the UK's Terrorist Prevention Strategy', *The RUSI Journal*, 154(4): 52–58.

Bjorgo, Tore and Witte, Rob (1993) 'Introduction', in T. Bjorgo and R. Witte (eds), *Racist Violence in Europe*. London: St Martin's Press. pp. 1–16.

Black, Edwin (2003) *War against the Weak: Eugenics and America's Campaign to Create a Master Race*. New York: Thunder's Mouth Press.

Blair, Irene V., Judd, Charles M. and Chapleau, Kristine M. (2004) 'The Influence of Afrocentric Facial Features in Criminal Sentencing', *Psychological Science*, 15: 674–679.

Bolton, Kenneth Jr. (2003) 'Shared Perceptions: Black Officers Discuss Continuing Barriers in Policing', *Policing: An International Journal of Police Strategies and Management*, 26(3): 386–399.

Bonger, William A. (1943) *Race and Crime*. New York: Columbia University Press.

Bonham, Vence L., Warshauer-Baker, Esther and Collins, Francis S. (2005) 'Race and Ethnicity in the Genome Era: The Complexity of the Constructs', *American Psychologist*, 60(1): 9–15.

Bonilla-Silva, Eduarda and Baiocchi, Gianpaolo (2001) 'Anything but Racism: How Sociologists Limit the Significance of Racism', *Race and Society*, 4: 117–131.

Bonnett, Alistair (2000) *Anti-racism*. London: Routledge.

Booth, Robert, Taylor, Matthew and Lewis, Paul (2009) 'English Defence League: Chaotic Alliance Stirs Up Trouble on Streets', *Guardian*, 12 September 2009. www.guardian.co.uk/world/2009/sep/11/english-defence-league-chaotic-alliance.

Bourne, Jenny (2001) 'The Life and Times of Institutional Racism', *Race and Class*, 43(2): 7–22.

Bowling, Benjamin (1996) 'The Emergence of Violent Racism as a Public Issue in Britain, 1945–81', in P. Panayi (ed.), *Racial Violence in Britain in the 19 and 20 Century*. Leicester: Leicester University Press. pp. 185–220.

Bowling, Benjamin (1999) *Violent Racism: Victimisation, Policing and Social Context*. Oxford: Oxford University Press.

Bowling, Benjamin and Phillips, Coretta (2002) *Racism, Crime and Justice*. Harlow: Longman.

Bowling, Benjamin and Phillips, Coretta (2007) 'Disproportionate and Discriminatory: Reviewing the Evidence on Police Stop and Search', *Modern Law Review*, 70(6): 936–961.

Box, Steven (1983) *Power, Crime and Mystification*. London: Routledge.

Brah, Avtar (1996) *Cartographies of Diaspora: Contesting Identities*. London: Routledge.

Brah, Avtar (1999) 'The Scent of Memory: Strangers, Our Own, and Others', *Feminist Review*, 61: 4–26.

Brah, Avtar (2006) 'The 'Asian' in Britain', in K. Ali and A. Sayyid (eds), *A Postcolonial People: Asians in Britain*. London: Hurst. pp. 35–61.

Braithwaite, John (1989) *Crime, Shame and Reintegration*. Cambridge: Cambridge University Press.

Brewer, John, D. and Magee, Kathleen (1991) *Inside the RUC: Routing Policing in a Divided Society*. Gloucestershire: Clarendon Press.

Bright, M. (1995) 'Politics and Prejudice', *Guardian Education*, 7 November 1995.

Brittain, Victoria (2007) 'Racism, Liberty and the War of Terror: Guantanamo', *Race and Class*, 48(4): 60–63.

Brook, Stephen (2007) 'Mail and Express Deny Asylum Bias', *Guardian*, 23 January 2007. www.guardian.co.uk/media/2007/jan/23/pressandpublishing.immigrationasylumandrefugees.

Britton, Joanne Nadia (2000) 'Race and Policing: A Study of Police Custody', *British Journal of Criminology*, 40: 639–658.

Britton, Nadia Joanne (2002) *Race, Ethnicity and Social Class in the Legal Profession: The Careers of Lawyers from Minority Ethnic Groups*. Sociological Studies Seminar Series, University of Sheffield, 2 November (unpublished).

Bryan, Beverly, Dadzie, Stella and Scafe, Suzanne (1985) *The Heart of the Race – Black Women's Lives in Britain*. London: Virago.

Burlet, Stacey and Reid, Helen (1998) 'A Gendered Uprising: Political Representation and Minority Ethnic Communities', *Ethnic and Racial Studies*, 21(2): 270–287.

Burnett, Jonathan (2004) 'Community, Cohesion and the State', *Race and Class*, 45(3): 1–18.

Burnley Express (2007) '"Explosives Plot": Pair Face New Trial', 3 July 2007. www.burnleyexpress.net/burnleynews/39Explosives-plot39-pair-face-new.2998885.jp.

Burr, Vivien (1995) *An Introduction to Social Constructionism*. London: Routledge.

Butt, Jabeer and O'Neil, Alex (2004) 'Let's Move On', *Black and Minority Ethnic Older People's Views on Research Findings*. York: Joseph Rowntree Foundation.

Byrne, David (2000) *Social Exclusion*. Buckingham: Open University Press.

Cain, Maureen (1973) *Society and the Policeman's Role*. London: Kegan Paul.

Calverly, Adam, Cole, Bankole, Kaur, Gurpreet, Lewis, Sam, Raynor, Peter, Sadeghi, Sohheila, Smith, David, Vanstone, Maurice and Wardak, Ali (2004) *Black and Asian Offenders on Probation*. Home Office Research Study 277. London: Home Office.

Calvin, Allen D. (1981) 'Unemployment among Black Youths: Demographics and Crime', *Crime and Delinquency*, 27: 234–244.

Cameron, Deborah (1993) '"What It Is We Could Call Equal": Cultural Politics, Language, and the Law', *American Literary History*, 5(4): 735–749.

Cantle, Ted (2001) *Community Cohesion: A Report of the Independent Review Team*. London: Home Office.

Carby, Hazel V. (1982) 'White Woman Listen! Black Feminism and the Boundaries of Sisterhood', in CCCS, *The Empire Strikes Back: Race and Racism in 70s Britain*. London, Hutchinson. pp. 211–234.

Carling, Alan, Davies, Darrell, Fernandes-Bakshi, Amritha, Jarman, Neil and Nias, Peter (2004) *Fair Justice for All? The Response of the Criminal Justice System to the Bradford Disturbances of July 2001*, Bradford: Programme for a Peaceful City/University of Bradford. betterbradford.org.uk/Documents/Fair%20Justice%20For%20All.pdf.

Cashmore, Ellis (2002) 'Behind the Window Dressing: Ethnic Minority Police Perspectives on Cultural Diversity', *Journal of Ethnic and Migration Studies*, 28(2): 327–341.

Ceyhan, Ayse (2008) 'Technologization of Security: Management of Uncertainty and Risk in the Age of Biometrics', *Surveillance and Society*, 5(2): 102–123.

Chadwick, Katherine and Scraton, Phil (2001) 'Criminalization' in Eugene McLaughlin and John Muncie (eds), *The Sage Dictionary of Criminology*. London, Sage. pp. 68–69.

Chakraborti, Neil and Garland, John (2009) *Hate Crime: Impact, Causes and Responses*. London: Sage.

Cheong, Pauline, H., Edwards, Rosalind, Goulbourne, Harry and Solomos, John (2007) 'Immigration, Social Cohesion and Social Capital: A Critical Review', *Critical Social Policy*, 27(1): 24–49.

Clark, Tom (2008) '"We're Over-Researched Here!": Exploring Accounts of Research Fatigue within Qualitative Research Engagements', *Sociology*, 42: 953–970.

Clough, Patricia T. (2003) 'Affect and Control: Rethinking the Body "Beyond Sex and Gender"', *Feminist Theory*, 4(3): 359–364.

Clydebank Post (2009) 'Racists Attack Asian Shopkeeper Wearing Klan Hoods', 9 December 2009. www.clydebankpost.co.uk/news/thisweek/articles/2009/12/09/394876-racists-attacked-shopkeeper-wearing-klan-hoods/.

Cohen, Phil (1997) 'Labouring under Whiteness', in R. Frankenberg (ed.), *Displacing Whiteness: Essays in Social and Cultural Criticism*, Durham, NC: Duke University Press. pp. 244–282,

Cohen, Stanley (1973) *Folk Devils and Moral Panics*. St Albans: Paladin.

Cole, Bankole and Wardak, Ali (2006) 'Black and Asian Men on Probation: Social Exclusion, Discrimination and Experiences of Criminal Justice', in Sam Lewis, Peter Raynor, David Smith and Ali Wardak (eds), *Race and Probation*. Devon: Willan. pp. 81–99.

Coleraine Times (2009) 'Taxi Driver has Speeding Conviction Thrown Out of Court', 17 December 2009. www.colerainetimes.co.uk/news/Taxi-driver-has-speeding-conviction.5911585.jp.

Colic-Peisker, Val (2005) 'At Least You're the Right Colour': Identity and Social Inclusion of Bosnian Refugees in Australia', *Journal of Ethnic and Migration Studies*, 31(4): 615–638.

Collins, Patricia Hill (1990) *Black Feminist Thought: Knowledge, Consciousness and the Politics of Empowerment*. London: Routledge.

Collins, Patricia Hill (1998) *Fighting Words: Black Women and the Search for Justice*. Minneapolis: University of Minneapolis.

Comaz-Diaz, Lillian and Greene, Beverly (1994) 'Women of Color with Professional Status', in Lillian Comaz-Diaz and Beverly Greene (eds), *Women of Color: Integrating Ethnic and Gender Identities in Psychotherapy*. New York: Guildford Press. pp. 347–388.

Comer, James (1985) 'Black Violence and Public Policy', in Lynn Curtis (ed.), *American Violence and Public Policy*. Yale University Press: New Haven. pp. 63–86.

Commission for Racial Equality (2003) *A Formal Investigation by the CRE into HM Prison Service, England and Wales, Part I, The Murder of Zahid Mubarek; Part II, Racial Equality in Prisons*. London: Commission for Racial Equality.

Commission for Racial Equality (2005) *The Police Service in England and Wales: Final Report of a Formal Investigation by the Commission for Racial Equality*. London: Commission for Racial Equality.

Communities and Local Government (2009) 'Connecting Communities Programme Triples in Size – John Denham', 14 December 2009. www.communities.gov.uk/news/corporate/1412643.

Covington, Jeanette (1995) 'Racial Classification in Criminology: The Reproduction of Racialized Crime', *Sociological Forum*, 10(4): 547–568.

Crown Prosecution Service (2001) *Report of an Independent Inquiry into Race Discrimination in the Crown Court Prosecution Service [The 'Denman Report']*. London: CPS.

Crowther, Chris (2007) *An Introduction to Criminology and Criminal Justice*. Hampshire: Palgrave Macmillan.

D'Alessio, Stewart and Stolzenberg, Lisa (2008) 'Race and the Probability of Arrest', in A. Walsh and C. Hemmens (eds), *Introduction to Criminology*. Sage: Los Angeles. pp. 59–68.

Daily Mail (2009) 'Nick Griffin Defends BNP Leaflet that Says Black and Asian Britons "Do Not Exist"', 23 April 2009. www.dailymail.co.uk/news/article-1172801/Nick-Griffin-defends-BNP-leaflet-says-black-Asian-Britons-exist.html.

Daily Post (2005) 'Family Have Nothing but Praise for Merseyside Police', *Daily Post*, 1 December.

Daly, Mark (2003) *The Secret Policeman*. BBC Television, 21 October.

Darwin, Charles (1859) *On the Origin of Species by Means of Natural Selection, or the Preservation of Favoured Races in the Struggle for Life*. London: John Murray.

Daulatzi, Sohail (2007) 'Protect Ya Neck: Muslims and the Carceral Imagination in the Age of Guantanamo', *Souls: A Critical Journal of Black Politics, Culture, and Society*, 9(2): 132–147.

Davies, Malcolm, Croall, Hazel and Tyrer, Jane (2005) *Criminal Justice: An Introduction to the Criminal Justice System in England and Wales*. Harlow, Longman Pearson.

Davis, Gwynn and Vennard, Julie (2006) 'Racism in Court: The Experience of Ethnic Minority Magistrates', *The Howard Journal*, 45(5): 485–501.

De Schutter, Oliver and Ringelheim, Julie (2008) 'Ethnic Profiling: A Rising Challenge for European Human Rights Law', *Modern Law Review*, 78(3): 358–384.

Deleuze, Gilles (1992) 'Postscript on the Societies of Control' October, 59: 3–7.

Deleuze, Giles and Guattari, Felix (2004) *A Thousand Plateaus and Schizophrenia*. London: Continuum.

Delgado, Richard (1989) 'Storytelling for Oppositionists and Others: A Plea for Narrative', *Michigan Law Review*, 87: 2411–2441.

Delgado, Richard and Stefancic, Jean (2001) *Critical Race Theory – An Introduction*. New York: New York University Press.

Delgado, Richard and Stefancic, Jean (eds) (1991) *Critical White Studies: Looking Behind the Mirror*. Philadelphia: Temple University Press.

DeLisi, Matt and Regoli, Robert (2005) 'Race, Conventional Crime, and Criminal justice', in Shaun L. Gabbidon and Helen T. Greene (eds), *Race, Crime, and Justice: A Reader*. New York: Routledge. pp. 87–96.

Denham, John (2002) *Building Cohesive Communities: A Report of the Ministerial Group on Public Order and Community Cohesion*. London: Home Office.

Diken, Bulent and Laustsen, Carsten B. (2005) *The Culture of Exception: Sociology Facing the Camp*. Abingdon: Routledge.

Dilulio, John J. Jr. (2005) 'My Black Crime Problem, and Ours', in S.L. Gabbidon and H.T. Greene (eds), *Race, Crime, and Justice: A Reader*. New York: Routledge. pp. 73–86.

DuBois, William Edward Burghardt (1899) *The Philadelphia Negro*. Atlanta: Atlanta University Press.

DuBois, William Edward Burghardt (1901) 'The Relations of Negroes to Whites in the South', *Annals of the American Academy of Political and Social Sciences*, 18: 121–140.

DuBois, William Edward Burghardt (1904) *Notes on the Negro Crime, Particularly in Georgia*. Atlanta: Atlanta University Press.

Duffield, Mark (2007) *Development, Security and Unending War: Governing the World of Peoples*. Cambridge: Polity Press.

Dugdale, Richard (1877) *The Jukes in Crime, Pauperism and Heredity*. New York: Putnam.

Dwyer, Claire, Shah, Bindi and Sanghera, Gurchathen (2008) 'From Cricket Lover to Terror Suspect – Challenging Representations of Young British Muslim Men', *Gender, Place and Culture*, 15(2): 117–136.

Dyer, Richard (1997) *White*. London: Routledge.

Eades, Chris, Grimshaw, Roger, Silvestri, Arianna and Solomon, Enver (2007) *Knife Crime: A Review of Evidence and Policy*. London: Centre for Crime and Justice Studies.

Eberhardt, Jennifer L., Davies, Paul G., Purdie-Vaughns, Valerie J. and Lynn Johnson, S. (2006) *Looking Deathworthy: Perceived Stereotypicality of Black Defendants Predicts Capital-Sentencing Outcomes*, Research Report 06-012. New York: Cornell Law School.

Eberhardt, Jennifer L., Goff, Phillip A., Purdie, Valerie J. and Davies, Paul G. (2004) 'Seeing Black: Race, Crime and Visual Processing', *Journal of Personality and Social Psychology*, 87: 876–893.

Economist, The (2008) 'Race and the Police: No Quick Fix', *The Economist*, 388(8598): 72–73.

Edkins, Jenny (2003) *Trauma and the Memory of Politics*. Cambridge: Cambridge University Press.

Edkins, Jenny, Pin-Fat, Véronique and Shapiro, Michael J. (eds) (2004) *Sovereign Lives: Power in Global Politics*. New York: Routledge.

Ely, Peter and Denney, David (1987) *Social Work in a Multi Racial Society*. Aldershot: Gower Publishing.

Essed Philomena and Goldberg, David T. (eds) (2002) *Race: Critical Theories*. Oxford: Blackwell.

Evening Standard (2009) 'Wedding Emails Sparked Terror Swoop', 14 August 2009.

Fanon, Franz (1952) *Black Skins, White Masks*. New York: Grove.

Faulks, Keith (2006) 'Education for Citizenship in England's Secondary Schools: A Critique of Current Principle and Practice', *Journal of Education Policy*, 21(1): 59–74.

Fawcett, Liz (1998) 'Fitting In: Ethnic Minorities and the News Media', in P. Hainsworth (ed.), *Divided Society: Ethnic Minorities and Racism in Northern Ireland*. London: Pluto Press. pp. 104–126.

Feagin, Joe R. (2006) *Systemic Racism: A Theory of Oppression*. New York: Routledge.

Fekete, Liz (2001) 'The Emergence of Xeno-racism', *Race and Class*, 43(2): 23–40.

Fekete, Liz (2003) 'Racism and the Courts', *Institute of Race Relations*, 29 July 2003. www.irr.org.uk/cgi-bin/news/open.pl?id=5553.

Fekete, Liz (2004) 'Anti-Muslim Racism and the European Security state', *Race and Class*, 46(1): 3–29.

Fekete, Liz (2005) 'The Deportation Machine: Europe, Asylum and Human Rights', *Race and Class*', 47(1): 64–91.

Fitzgerald, Marian (1998) '"Race" and the criminal justice system', in T. Blackstone, B. Parekh and P. Sanders (eds), *Race Relations in Britain: A Developing Agenda*. London: Routledge. pp. 159–179.

ForsterLee, Robert, ForsterLee, Lynne, Horowitz, Irwin A. and King, Ellen (2006) 'The Effects of Defendant Race, Victim Race, and Juror Gender on Evidence Processing in a Murder Trial', *Behavioral Sciences and the Law*, 24(2): 179–198.

French, Martin (2007) 'In the Shadow of Canada's Camps', *Social and Legal Studies*, 16(1): 49–69.

Frost, Diane (2008) 'Islamophobia: Examining Causal Links between the Media and "race hate" from "below"', *International Journal of Sociology and Social Policy*, 28 (11/12): 564–578.

Gabbidon, Shaun L., Penn, Everett B., Jordan, Kareem L, and Higgins, George E. (2009) 'The Influence of Race/Ethnicity on the Perceived Prevalence and Support for Racial Profiling at Airports', Criminal Justice Policy Review, 20(3): 344–358.

Gardham, Duncan (2010) 'Control Orders Were Unlawful Says Judge', *Daily Telegraph*, 18 January 2010. www.telegraph.co.uk/news/uknews/terrorism-in-the-uk/7018629/Control-orders-were-unlawful-says-judge.html.

Garland, Jon, Spalek, Basia and Chakraborti, Neil (2006) 'Hearing Lost Voices: Issues in Researching "Hidden" Minority Ethnic Communities', *British Journal of Criminology*, 46: 423–437.

Garner, Steve (2006) 'The Uses of Whiteness: What Sociologists Working on Europe Can Draw from US Research on Whiteness', *Sociology*, 40(2): 257–275.

Garner, Steve (2007) *Whiteness: An Introduction*. Abingdon: Oxford.

Garner, Steve (2010) *Racisms: An Introduction*. London: Sage.

Gaskell, George and Smith, Patten (1985) 'Young Blacks' Hostility to the Police: An Investigation into Its Causes', *New Community*, (9)2: 182–193.

Gates, Henry Louis and Jarrett, Gene Andrew (eds) (2007) *The New Negro: Readings on Race, Representation, and African American Culture, 1892–1938*. Woodstock: Princeton University Press.

Gifford, [Lord] Anthony, Brown, Wally and Bundey, Ruth (1989) *Loosen the Shackles: First Report of the Liverpool 8 Inquiry into Race Relations in Liverpool*. London: Karia.

Gill, Aisha and Rehman, Gulshan (2004) 'Empowerment through Activism: Responding to Domestic Violence in the South Asian Community in London', *Gender and Development*, 12(1): 75–82.

Gilroy, Paul (1982) 'The Myth of Black Criminality', in Martin Eve and David Musson (eds), *The Socialist Register*. Monmouth: Merlin. pp. 47–56.

Gilroy, Paul (1987) *There Ain't No Black in the Union Jack*. First Edition. London: Hutchinson.

Gilroy, Paul (2002) *There Ain't No Black in the Union Jack*. Introduction to the Routledge Classics Reprint. London: Routledge.

Gilroy, Paul (2004) *After Empire. Melancholia or Convivial Culture?* London: Routledge.

Githens-Mazer, Jonathan and Lambert, Robert (2010) *Islamophobia and Anti-Muslim Hate Crime: A London Case Study*. Exeter: European Muslim Research Centre.

Goffman, Erving (1963) *Stigma: Notes on the Management of a Spoilt Identity*. London: Penguin.

Goldberg, David T. (1993) *Racist Culture*. Oxford: Blackwell.

Goodey, Jo (2001) 'The Criminalization of British Asian Youth: Research from Bradford and Sheffield', *Journal of Youth Studies*, 4(4): 429–450.

Gordon, Neve (2004) 'Introduction: Human Rights as Being-Marginal-in-the-World', in N. Gordon (ed.), *From the Margins of Globalization: Critical Perspectives on Human Rights*. Oxford: Lexington Books. pp. 1–24.

Gordon, Paul (1990) *Racial Violence and Harassment*. London: Runnymede Trust.

Gordon, Paul (1993) *White Law: Racism in the Police, Courts and Prisons*. London, Pluto Press.

Gordon, Robert (1976) 'Prevalence: The Rare Datum in Delinquency Measurement and its Implications for the Theory of Delinquency', in Malcolm Klein (ed.), *The Juvenile Justice System*. Beverly Hills, Sage. pp. 201–284.

Gordon, Thomas (1973) 'Notes on White and Black Psychology', *Journal of Social Issues*, 29(1): 87–95.

Gorz, Andre (1982) *Farewell to the Working Class*. London: Pluto.

Goulbourne, Harry and Solomos, John (2003) 'Families, Ethnicities and Social Capital', *Social Policy and Society*, 2(4): 329–338.

Graef, Roger (1989) *Talking Blues*. London: Collins.

Greenhill, Norman (1981) 'The Value of Sociology in Policing', in D. Pope and N. Weiner (eds), *Modern Policing*. London: Croom Held Ltd. pp. 91–109.

Gregory, Derek and Pred, Allan R. (2007) *Violent Geographies: Fear, Terror, and Political Violence*. Abingdon: Routledge.

Grillo, Ralph (2007) 'An Excess of Alterity? Debating Difference in a Multicultural Society', *Ethnic and Racial Studies*, 30(6): 979–998.

Guardian (2002) 'Asian who Killed Man in Race Row Freed after 15 Years', reported by Vikram Dodd, 15 June 2002. www.guardian.co.uk/uk_news/story/0,3604,737722,00.html.

Guardian (2004) 'Afghan Detainees Routinely Tortured and Humiliated by US Troops', reported by Duncan Campbell and Suzanne Goldenberg, 23 June 2004. www.guardian.co.uk/world/2004/jun/23/usa.afghanistan3.

Guardian (2005) 'Fear and Loathing', reported by Mary O'Hara, 29 June 2005. www.guardian.co.uk/society/2005/jun/29/socialexclusion.guardiansocietysupplement.

Guardian (2005) Britain *'Sleepwalking to Segregation'*, 19 September 2005. www.guardian.co.uk/world/2005/sep/19/race.socialexclusion.

Guardian (2009) 'Police Launch Appeal to Find Gangland Murder Suspect', reported by Helen Carter, 17 August 2009.

Guardian (2010) 'Anti-terror Stop and Search Powers to be Scrapped', reported by Alan Travis, 8 July 2010.

Guild, Elspeth (2005) 'Cultural and Identity Security', in E. Guild and J. van Selm (eds), *International Migration and Security: Opportunities and Challenges*. Abingdon: Routledge. pp. 101–112.

Gulli, Bruno (2007) 'The Ontology and Politics of Exception: Reflections on the Work of Giorgio Agamben', in M. Calarco and S. DeCaroli (eds), *Giorgio Agamben: Sovereignty and Life*. Stanford: Stanford University Press. pp. 219–242.

Halifax Courier (2010) 'Man Jailed for Repeated Racist Attacks', 27 May 2010. www.halifax-courier.co.uk/news/Man-jailed-for-racist-attack.6323683.jp.

Hall, Stuart, Critcher, Chas, Jefferson, Tony, Clarke, John and Roberts, Brian (1978) *Policing the Crisis*. London: Macmillan.

Hall, Stuart (1995) 'The Whites in their Eyes', in G. Dines and J. Humez (eds), *Gender, Race and Class in Media*. London: Sage. pp. 89–93.

Hall, Stuart (2000) 'Conclusion: the Multi-cultural Question', in B. Hesse (ed.), *Un/settled Multiculturalisms: Diasporas, Entanglements, 'Transruptions'*. London: Zed Books. pp. 209–241.

Hall, Stuart (2002) 'Reflections on Race, Articulation, and Societies Structured in Dominance', in P. Essed and D.T. Goldberg (eds), *Race: Critical Theories*. Oxford: Blackwell. pp. 449–454.

Halliday, Fred (1999) 'Islamophobia' reconsidered', *Ethnic and Racial Studies*, 22(5): 892–902.

Harding, Luke and Wilsher, Kim (2006) 'Anger as Papers Reprint Cartoons of Muhammad', *Guardian*. www.guardian.co.uk/world/2006/feb/02/raceandreligion.pressandpublishing.

Hari, John (2008) 'Ken Livingstone: The Interview', 13 April 2008. www.johannhari.com/archive/article.php?id=1285.

Harriss, John (2002) *Depoliticizing Development: The World Bank and Social Capital*. London: Anthem Press.

Harry Goulbourne and John Solomos (2003) 'Families, Ethnicity and Social Capital', *Social Policy and Society*, 2: 329–338.

Hartigan, John Jr. (1997) 'Name Calling: Objectifying "Poor Whites" and "White Trash" in Detroit', in M. Wray and A. Newitz (eds), *White Trash: Race and Class in America*. New York: Routledge. pp. 41–56.

Haskins, Ron (2009) 'Moynihan Was Right: Now What?', *Annals of the American Academy of Political and Social Science*, 621(6): 281–314.

Hazelton, Liz (2009) 'BNP Leader Nick Griffin in Fresh Storm after Claiming London has been "Ethnically Cleansed" as he Defends *Question Time* Debut', *Daily Mail*, 23 October 2009. www.dailymail.co.uk/news/article-1222521/BNP-leader-Nick-Griffin-claims-London-ethnically-cleansed-defends-shambolic-Question-Time-debut.html.

Heldman, Caroline (2007) '"Burnin" and "Lootin": Race and Media Coverage of Hurricane Katrina', paper presented at the Annual Meeting of the Western Political Science Association, Nevada.

Her Majesty's Courts Service (2009) *Standards for Equality and Diversity*. Birmingham: HMCS. www.hmcourts-service.gov.uk/cms/files/HMCSStandardForEqualityAndDiversity.pdf.

Herrnstein, Richard and Murray, Charles (1994) *The Bell Curve*. New York: Basic Books.

Hesse, Barnor (1997) 'White Governmentality: Urbanism, Nationalism, Racism', in S. Westwood and J.M. Williams (eds), *Imagining Cities: Scripts, Signs, Memory*. London: Routledge. pp. 85–102.

Hesse, Barnor (2004) 'Discourse on Institutional Racism, the Genealogy of a Concept', in I. Law, D. Phillips and L. Turney (eds), *Institutional Racism in Higher Education*. Stoke-on-Trent: Trentham. pp. 131–148.

Hillier, Jean (2007) *Stretching Beyond the Horizon: A Multiplanar Theory of Spatial Planning and Governance*. Aldershot: Ashgate.

Hillyard, Paddy (2009) 'The 'Exceptional' State', in D. Whyte, R. Coleman, S. Tombs and J. Sim (eds), *State, Power, Crime*. London: Sage. pp. 129–144.

Hines, Nico and Pitas, Costas (2009) 'Far-Right Group, the English Defence League, indisarray after Birmingham fracas', *The Sunday Times*, August 10, *Times Online*, www.timesonline.co.uk/tol/news/uk/article6790067.ece.

HM Inspectorate of Prisons (2005) *Parallel Worlds: A Thematic Review of Race Relations in Prisons*. London: HMIP.

HM Inspectorate of Prisons (2007) *Report on an Unannounced Short Follow-up Inspection of: Lindholme Immigration Removal Centre 16–18 July 2007*. London: HMIP.

Holdaway, Simon and O'Neill, Megan (2006) 'Institutional Racism after Macpherson: An Analysis of Police Views', *Policing and Society*, 16(4): 349–369.

Holdaway, Simon and O'Neill, Megan (2007) 'Where Has All the racism Gone? Views of Racism within Constabularies after Macpherson', *Ethnic and Racial Studies*, 30(3): 397–415.

Holdaway, Simon (1983) *Inside the British Police Force: A Force at Work*. Oxford: Basil Blackwell.

Holdaway, Simon (1996) *The Racialisation of British Policing*. Basingstoke: Palgrave Macmillan.

Holdaway, Simon (1997) 'Some Recent Approaches to the Study of Race in Criminological Research: Race as Social Process', *British Journal of Criminology*, 37(5): 383–400.

Home Office (2004) *Statistics on Race and the Criminal Justice System*. London: Home Office.

Home Office (2005) *Hate Crime: Delivering a Quality Service – Good Practice and Tactical Guidance*. London: ACPO and Home Office.

Home Office (2009) *Statistics on Terrorism Arrests and Outcomes – Great Britain: 11 September 2001 to 31 March 2008*. London: Home Office. http://rds.homeoffice.gov.uk/rds/pdfs09/hosb0409.pdf.

Home Office (1998) *Fairer, Faster, Firmer, A Modern Approach to Immigration and Asylum*. Cm. 4018. London: Home Office. www.archive.official-documents.co.uk/document/cm40/4018/4018.htm.

Hood, Roger (1992) *Race and Sentencing: A Study in the Crown Court*. Oxford: Clarendon Press.

hooks, bell (2008) *Belonging: A Culture of Place*. Abingdon: Routledge.

hooks, bell (1992) 'Representing Whiteness in the Black Imagination', in L. Grossberg, C. Nelson and P. Treichler (eds), *Cultural Studies*. New York: Routledge. pp. 338–346.

hooks, bell (2003) *Rock My Soul: Black People and Self-esteem*. New York: Washington Square Press.

Hooper, John (2009) 'Italian Court Finds CIA Agents Guilty of Kidnapping Terrorism Suspect', *Guardian*, 4 November 2009. www.guardian.co.uk/world/2009/nov/04/cia-guilty-rendition-abu-omar.

Howarth, David and Stavrakakis, Yannis (2000) 'Introducing Discourse Theory and Political Analysis', in D.R. Howarth, A.J. Norval and Y. Stavrakakis (eds), *Discourse Theory and Political Analysis: Identities, Hegemonies, and Social Change*. Manchester: Manchester University Press. pp. 1–24.

Howarth, D.R., Norval, A.J. and Stavrakakis, Y. (eds), *Discourse Theory and Political Analysis: Identities, Hegemonies, and Social Change*. Manchester: Manchester University Press.

Howarth, David R. (2000) *Discourse*. Buckingham: Open University Press.

Howe, Darcus (2000) 'Where the Asians and Caribbeans Now Wage Bloody War', *New Statesman*, 4 September 2000. www.newstatesman.com/200009040016.

Hudson, Barbara (1987) *Justice through Punishment: A Critique of the 'Justice' Model of Corrections*. London: Macmillan Education.

Hudson, Barbara (2001) 'Social Justice', in Eugenie McClaughlin and John Muncie (eds), *The Sage Dictionary of Criminology*. London: Sage. pp. 278–279.

Hudson, Barbara (2007) 'Diversity, Crime and Criminal Justice', in Mike Maguire, Rod Morgan and Robert Reiner (eds), *The Oxford Handbook of Criminology*. Oxford: Oxford University Press. pp. 158–175.

Huey, Jacklyn and Lynch, Michael, J. (2005) 'The Image of Black Women in Criminology: Historical Stereotypes as Theoretical Foundation', in Shaun L. Gabbidon and Helen T. Greene (eds), *Race, Crime, and Justice: A Reader*. New York: Routledge. pp. 127–140.

Hunt, Alan (1990) 'Rights and Social Movements: Counter-Hegemonic Strategies', *Journal of Law and Society*, 17(3): 309–328.

Iganski, Paul (2008) *Hate Crime and the City*. Bristol: Policy Press.

Independent Police Complaints Commission (2007a) *Stockwell One: Investigation into the Shooting of Jean Charles de Menezes at Stockwell Underground Station on 22 July 2005*. London: IPCC.

Independent Police Complaints Commission (2007b) *Stockwell Two: An Investigation into Complaints about the Metropolitan Police Service's Handling of Public Statements Following the Shooting of Jean Charles de Menezes on 22 July 2005*. London: IPCC.

Institute of Race Relations (2002) 'IRR Expresses Concern Over Excessive Sentencing of Bradford Rioters'. *Institute of Race Relations*, 5 July 2002. www.irr.org.uk/2002/july/ak000003.html.

Jäger, Siegfried and Maier, Florentine (2009) 'Theoretical and Methodological Aspects of Foucauldian Critical Discourse Analysis and Dispositive Analysis', in Ruth Wodak and Michael Meyer (eds), *Methods of Critical Discourse Analysis*. London: Sage. pp. 34–61.

Jarman, Neil and Monaghan, Rachel (2003) *Analysis of Incidents of Racist incident Recorded by the Police in Northern Ireland*. Belfast: Institute for Conflict Research.

Jensen, Tina Gudrun (2009) 'The Cartoon Affair and the Question of Cultural Diversity in Denmark', *e-cadernos CES, no.3 The European Imaginary in the Cartoons Controversy: Drawing Civilisations?* pp. 64–73. www.ces.uc.pt/e-cadernos/media/e-cadernos%203.pdf.

Jenson, Arthur (1969) 'How Much Can We Boost IQ and Scholastic Achievement?', *Harvard Educational Review*, 39: 1–123.

Jones, Stephen (2001) *Criminology*. Third edition. Oxford: Oxford University Press.

Joyce, Peter (2006) *Criminal Justice: An Introduction to Crime and the Criminal Justice System*. Devon: Willan.

Judicial Studies Board (1999) *Race and the Courts*. London: JSB.

Judicial Studies Board (2001) *Equality Before the Courts*. London: JSB.

Jupp, Victor (1989) *Methods of Criminological Research*. London: Routledge.

Kalra, Virinder (2003) 'Police Lore and Community Disorder: Diversity in the Criminal Justice System', in D. Mason (ed.), *Explaining Ethnic Differences: Changing Patterns of Disadvantage in Britain*. Bristol: Policy Press. pp. 139–152.

Kanter, Rosabeth Moss (1977) 'Some Effects of Proportions on Group Life: Skewed Sex Ratios and Responses to Token Women', *American Journal of Sociology*, 82(5): 965–990.

Keith, Michael (1993) *Race, Riots and Policing: Lore and Disorder in a Multiracist Society*. London: UCL Press.

Kelley, Robin D.G. (1998) 'House Negroes on the Loose: Malcolm X and the Black Bourgeoisie, *Callaloo*, 21(2): 419–435.

Kelso, Paul (2000) 'Sick Institution in Urgent Need of Cure', *Guardian*, 3 November 2000. www.guardian.co.uk/uk/2000/nov/03/race.prisonsandprobation1.

Kemp, Charles, Norris, Clive and Fielding, Nigel (1992) *Negotiating Nothing: Police Decision-Making in Disputes*. Aldershot: Avebury.

Kennedy, Maeve (2010) 'Lord Carlile Finds 'No Alternative' to Control Orders for Terrorism Suspects', *Guardian*, 1 February 2010. www.guardian.co.uk/politics/2010/feb/01/carlile-control-orders-terrorism-suspects.

Khan, Shehla (2006) 'Muslims!', in N. Ali, V.S. Kalra and S. Sayyid (2006) *A Postcolonial People: South Asians in Britain*. London: Hurst.

Khiabany, Gohlam and Williamson, Milly (2008) 'Veiled Bodies, Naked Racism: Culture, Politics and Race in the Sun', *Race and Class*, 50(2): 69–88.

Khoury, Laura J. (2009) 'Racial Profiling as Dressage: A Social Control Regime!', *African Identities*, 7(1): 55–70.

Knowles, Caroline and Mercer, Sharmilla (1992) 'Feminism and Antiracism: An Exploration of the Political Possibilities', in J. Donald and A. Rattansi (eds), *'Race', Culture, and Difference*. London: Sage, pp. 104–125.

Kramer, John and Steffensmeier, Darrell (1993) 'Race and Imprisonment Decisions', *The Sociological Quarterly*, 34(2): 357–376.

Kundnani, Arun (2007) *The End of Tolerance*. London: Pluto Press.

Kundnani, Arun (2006) *Racial Profiling and Anti–terror Stop and Search*. London: Institute of Race Relations. www.irr.org.uk/2006/january/ha000025.html.

Kundnani, Arun (2001) 'In a Foreign Land: The New Popular Racism', *Race and Class*, 43(2): 41–60.

Kundnani, Arun (2001) From Oldham to Bradford: The Violence of the Violated', *Institute of Race Relations*, 1 October 2001. www.irr.org.uk/2001/october/ak000003.html.

Kundnani, Arun (2009) *Spooked! How Not to Prevent Violent Extremism*. London: Institute of Race Relations.

Laclau, Ernesto and Mouffe, Chantal (1985) *Hegemony and Socialist Strategy*. London: Verso.

Lambert, John (1970) *Crime, Police and Race Relations*. London: Oxford University Press.

Lawrence, Errol (1982a) 'In the Abundance of Water the Fool is Thirsty: Sociology and Black "Pathology"', *The Empire Strikes Back: Race and Racism in 70s Britain*. London: Hutchinson. pp. 95–142.

Lawrence, Errol (1982b) 'Just Plain Common Sense: The 'Roots' of Racism', *The Empire Strikes Back*. London: Hutchinson. pp. 47–94.

Lawrence, Doreen (2006) *And Still I Rise: Seeking Justice for Stephen*. London: Faber and Faber.

Lea, John and Young, Jock (1984) *What is to be Done about Law and Order?* Harmondsworth: Penguin.

Lippert-Rasmussen, Kasper (2007) 'Nothing Personal: On Statistical Discrimination', *Journal of Political Philosophy*, 15(4): 385–403.

Liverpool Daily Post (2010) 'Liverpool Judge Reprimanded by Lord Chief Justice for "Immigration Tirade"'. 10 May 2010. www.liverpooldailypost.co.uk/liverpool-news/regional-news/2010/05/19/liverpool-judge-reprimanded-by-lord-chief-justice-for-immigration-tirade-92534-26474435/.

Local Government Association (2009) *Prevent All Extremism*. London: LGA. www.lga.gov.uk/lga/core/page.do?pageId=6461823.

Loftus, Bethan (2008) 'Dominant Culture Interrupted: Recognition, Resentment and the Politics of Change in an English Police Force', *British Journal of Criminology*, 48: 756–777.

Lombroso, Cesare (1876) *The Criminal Man*. Translated with a New Introduction by M. Gibson and N.H. Rafter. North Carolina: Duke University Press.

Lynn, Nick and Lea, Susan (2003) '"A Phantom Menace and the New Apartheid": The Social Construction of Asylum–Seekers in the United Kingdom', *Discourse and Society*, 14(4): 425–452.

Macpherson of Cluny, Sir William. (1999) *The Stephen Lawrence Inquiry*. Cm. 4262–1. London: Home Office. www.archive.official-documents.co.uk/document/cm42/4262/4262.htm.

MacPherson Watt, Steven (2005) 'Torture, "Stress and Duress," and Rendition as Counterterrorism Tools', in R. Meeropol, with R. Brody (eds), *America's Disappeared: Detainees, Secret Imprisonment, and the 'War on Terror'*. NY: Seven Stories Press. pp. 72–112.

Maira, Sunaina (2009) 'Deporting Radicals, Deporting La Migra: The Hayat Case in Lodi', *Cultural Dynamis*, 19(1): 39–66.

Malik, Sirita (2002) *Representing Black Britain: Black and Asian Images on Television*. London: Sage.

Mama, Amina (1989) *The Hidden Struggle: Statutory and Voluntary Sector Responses to Violence Against Black Women in the Home*. London: Runnymede.

Marks, Monique (2004) 'Researching Police Transformation: The Ethnographic Imperative', *British Journal of Criminology*, 44: 866–888.

Mason, David (2000) *Race and Ethnicity in Modern Britain*. Oxford: Open University Press.

Mathur, Shubh (2006) 'Surviving the Dragnet: 'Special Interest' Detainees in the US after 9/11', *Race and Class*, 47(3): 31–46.

Mauer, Marc and King, Ryan S. (2007) *Uneven Justice: State Rates of Incarceration by Race and Ethnicity*. Washington: The Sentencing Project.

Mawby, Richard (1979) *Policing the City*. Farnborough: Gower.

Maynard, Warwick and Read, Tim (1997) *Policing Racially Motivated Incidents*. Crime Detection and Prevention Series – Paper 84. London, Home Office/Police Research Group.

Mccann-Mortimer, Patricia, Augoustinos, Martha and Leocouteur, Amanda (2004) '"Race" and the Human Genome Project: Constructions of Scientific Legitimacy', Discourse and Society, 409–432.

McGhee, Derek (2005) *Intolerant Britain? Hate, Citizenship and Difference*. Berkshire: Open University Press.

McGhee, Derek (2007) 'The Paths to Citizenship: A Critical Examination of Immigration Policy in Britain Since 2001', *Patterns of Prejudice*, 43(1): 41–64.

McGhee, Derek (2009) 'The Paths to Citizenship: A Critical Examination of Immigration Policy in Britain Since 2001', *Patterns of Prejudice*, 43(1): 41–64.

McNamee, Eegene (2007) 'In the Midst of Death We Are in Life ... Biopolitics and Beginning Again in Rwanda', *Social and Legal Studies*, 16(4): 483–508.

McSmith, Andy (2010) 'Tory MP Proposes Law to Ban Wearing Burkas', *Independent*, 18 May 2010. www.independent.co.uk/news/uk/politics/tory-mp-proposes-law-to-ban-wearing-burkas-2015267.html.

Meer, Nasar (2007) 'Less Equal than Others', *Index on Censorship*, 36(2): 114–118.

Meer, Nasar (2008) 'The Politics of Voluntary and Involuntary Identities: Are Muslims in Britain an Ethnic, Racial or Religious Minority?', *Patterns of Prejudice*, 42(1): 61–81.

Meeropol, Rachel (ed.) (2005) *America's Disappeared: Detainees, Secret Imprisonment, and the 'War on Terror'*. New York: Seven Stories Press.

Mercer, Jane (1972) 'IQ: The Lethal Label', *Psychology Today*, September. pp. 44–47.

Metropolitan Police Force (1999) *Protect and Respect: The Met's Diversity Strategy*. London: Metropolitan Police.

Metropolitan Police Force (2010) *Stephen Lawrence Inquiry Report – Ten Years On*. www.met. police.uk/stephenlawrence/representative_workforce.htm.

Metro (2010) *Handyman? Pest Controller? Bomb Maker?* 17 March 2010.

Miles, Robert (1989) *Racism*. London: Routledge.

Ministry of Justice (2008) *Race and the Criminal Justice System 2006–07*. London: Ministry of Justice.

Ministry of Justice (2010) *Statistics on Race and the Criminal Justice System 2008/09*. London: Ministry of Justice.

Mitchell, Tara, Haw, Ryann, M., Pfeifer, Jeffrey, E. and, Meissner, Christian A. (2005) 'Racial Bias in Mock Juror Decision-making: A Meta-analytic Review of Defendant Treatment', *Law and Human Behaviour*, 29(6): 621–637.

Modood, Tariq (1992) 'British Asian Muslims and the Rushdie Affair', in J. Donald and A. Rattansi (eds), *Race, Culture, and Difference*. London: Sage. pp. 260–277.

Modood, Tariq (2006) 'The Liberal Dilemma: Integration or Vilification?', *International Migration*, 44(5): 4–7.

Moeckli, Daniel (2007) 'Stop and Search Under the Terrorism Act 2000: A Comment on R (Gillan) v Commissioner of Police for the Metropolis', *Modern Law Review*, 70(4): 659–670.

Morris, Sir William (2004) *The Case for Change: People in the Metropolitan Police Service, The Report of the Morris Inquiry*. London, Metropolitan Police Authority.

Mouffe, Chantal (2005) *On the Political*. Abingdon: Routledge.

Moynihan, Daniel Patrick (1965) *The Negro Family: The Case for National Action*. United States Department of Labor.

Muir, William Ker Jr., (1977) *Police: Street Corner Politicians*. Chicago: Chicago University Press.

Müller, Marion G, Özcana, Esra and Seizova, Ognyan (2009) 'Dangerous Depictions: A Visual Case Study of Contemporary Cartoon Controversies', *Popular Communication*, 7(1): 28–39.

Murji, Karim (2007) 'Sociological Engagements: Institutional Racism and Beyond', *Sociology*, 41(5): 843–855.

Murray, Nancy (2004) 'Profiled: Arabs, Muslims, and the Post-9/11 Hunt for the "Enemy Within"', in E.C. Hagopian (ed.), *Civil Rights in Peril: The Targeting of Arabs and Muslims*. London: Pluto. pp. 27–68.

Nabi, Shaida (2009) *Racialised Governmentality: Institutionalised Islamophobia and Muslim Students in British Higher Education*, Unpublished draft working paper, University of Manchester.

NACRO (1991) *Black People's Experience of Criminal Justice*. London: NACRO.

Nadesan, Majia Holmer (2008) *Governmentality, Biopower, and Everyday Life*. Abingdon: Routledge.

National Offender Management Service (2008) *Race Review 2008 Implementing Race Equality in Prisons – Five Years On*. London: Ministry of Justice.

National Statistics (2005) *Prison Population: Record Number of Prisoners in 2003*. Newport: Office for National Statistics.

Nayak, Anoop (2007) 'Critical Whiteness Studies', *Sociology Compass*, 1(2): 737–755.

Nelson Leader/Pendle Today (2006) 'Chemicals Find: Two in Court', 6 October 2006. www.pendletoday.co.uk/nelsonnews/Chemicals-Find-Two-In-Court.1806619.jp.

New York Times (2005) 'Who's a Looter? In Storm's Aftermath, Pictures Kick Up a Different Kind of Tempest', 5 September 2005. www.nytimes.com/2005/09/05/business/05caption.html.

Nottinghamshire Police (2010) *Positive Action*. www.nottinghamshire.police.uk/jobs/police_staff/positive_action/.

O'Neil, Megan (2005) *Policing Football: Social Interaction and Negotiated Order*. Basingstoke: Palgrave Macmillan.

Omi, Michael and Winant, Howard (1994) *Racial Formation in the United States: from the 1960s to the 1990s*. London: Routledge.

Ong, Aihwa (2006) *Neoliberalism as Exception: Mutations in Citizenship and Sovereignty*. Durham: Duke University Press.

O'Neill, Megan and Holdaway, Simon (2007) 'Examining "Window Dressing": The Views of Black Police Associations on Recruitment and Training', *Journal of Ethnic and Migration Studies*, 33(3): 483–500.

O'Nions, Helen (1995) 'The Marginalisation of Gypsies', *Web Journal of Current Legal Issues*. http://webjcli.ncl.ac.uk/articles3/onions3.html.

Ouseley, Herman (2008) *Independent Review into Disproportionate Regulatory Outcomes for Black and Minority Ethnic Solicitors*. London: The Solicitor's Regulatory Authority.

Owusu-Bempah, Kwame and Howitt, Dennis (2000) *Psychology Beyond Western Perspectives*. Leicester: British Psychological Society.

Pantazis, Christina and Pemberton, Simon (2009) 'From the 'Old' to the 'New' Suspect Community: Examining the Impacts of Recent UK Counter-Terrorist Legislation', *British Journal of Criminology*, 49: 646–666.

Park, Shelley M. and Green, Cheryl E. (2000) 'Is Transracial Adoption in the Best Interests of Ethnic Minority Children? Questions Concerning Legal and Scientific Interpretations of a Child's Best Interests', *Adoption Quarterly*, 3(4): 5–34.

Parrott, Roxanne, Silk, Karri, Dollow, Megan, Krieger, Janice L., Harris, Tina M. and Condit, Celeste (2005) 'Development and Validation of Tools to Assess Genetic Discrimination and Genetically Based Racism', *Journal of the National Medical Association*, 97(7): 1–11.

Patel, Tina (2005) 'The Usefulness of Oral Life (Hi)story to Understand and Empower: The Case of Trans-racial Adoption', *Qualitative Social Work*, 4(3): 327–345.

Patel, Tina G. (2011) 'Policing Racist Incidents: Views and Experiences of Officers within the Police Service of Northern Ireland', *Journal of Criminal Justice Research*, 1(2): 1–16.

Patten, Christopher (1999) *A New Beginning: Policing in Northern Ireland*. Belfast: Independent Commission on Policing for Northern Ireland.

Perry, Barbara (2001) *In the Name of Hate: Understanding Hate Crimes*. New York: Routledge.

Phillips, Coretta and Bowling, Benjamin (2003) Racism, Ethnicity and Criminology. Developing Minority Perspectives, *British Journal of Criminology*, 43: 269–290.

Phillips, Coretta (2005) 'Facing Inwards and Outwards? Institutional Racism, Race Equality and the Role of Black and Asian Professional Associations', *Criminal Justice*. 5(4): 357–377.

Phillips, Coretta and Bowling, Benjamin (2003) 'Racism, Ethnicity and Criminology: Developing Minority Perspectives', *British Journal of Criminology*, 43: 269–290.

Phizacklea, Annie and Miles, Robert (1980) *Labour and Racism*. London: Routledge and Kegan Paul.

Pilkington, Andrew (2003) *Racial Disadvantage and Ethnic Diversity in Britain*. Hampshire, Palgrave.

Police Ombudsman for Northern Ireland (2009) *Annual Reports and Accounts for the Year Ended 31 March 2009*. London: The Stationery Office.

Power, Colm (2003) '"Telling It Like It Is"? Power, Prejudice and People in the Qualitative Process', in Steve Tombs and David Whyte (eds), *Unmasking Crimes of the Powerful: Scrutinising States and Corporations*. London: Peter Lang. pp. 189–215.

Poynting, Scot and Mason, Victoria (2006) '"Tolerance, Freedom, Justice and Peace": Britain, Australia and Anti-Muslim Racism Since 11 September 2001', *Journal of Intercultural Studies*, 27: 4, 369–391.

Prisons and Probation Ombudsman for England and Wales (2004) *Report of the Inquiry into the Disturbance and Fire at Yarl's Wood Removal Centre*. London: Prisons and Probation Ombudsman.

Prisons and Probation Ombudsman for England and Wales (2005) *Inquiry into Allegations of Racism and Mistreatment of Detainees at Oakington Immigration Reception Centre and while Under Escort*. London: Prisons and Probation Ombudsman.

PSNI (2007a) *Chief Constable's Annual Report*, 20 April 2008. www.psni.police.uk/psni_cc_report_06-07.pdf.

PSNI (2007b) *District Command Unit Initiatives*. Belfast: PSNI.

Puar, Jasbir K. and Rai, Amit S. (2002) 'Monster, Terrorist, Fag: The War on Terrorism and the Production of Docile Patriots', *Social Text*, 20(3): 117–148.

Puar, Jasbir K. (2005) 'Queer Times, Queer Assemblages', *Social Text*, 23 (3–4): 121–140.

Puar, Jasbir K. (2007) *Terrorist Assemblages Homonationalism in Queer Times*. Durham: Duke University Press.

Pugliese, Joseph (2006) 'Asymmetries of Terror: Visual Regimes of Racial Profiling', *Borderlands*, 5(1). www.borderlands.net.au/vol5no1_2006/pugliese.htm.

Punch, Maurice (1979) *Policing the Inner City*. London: Macmillan.

Punch, Maurice (1989) 'Researching Police Deviance: A Personal Encounter with the Limitations and Liabilities of Field-work', *British Journal of Sociology*, 40(2): 177–204.

Punch, Maurice (1993) 'Observation and the Police: The Research Experience', in Martyn Hammersley (ed.), *Social Research: Philosophy, Politics and Practice*. London: Sage. pp. 181–199.

Purdham, Kingsley (2001) 'Democracy in Practice: Muslims and the Labour Party at the Local Level', *Politics*, 21(3): 147–157.

Putnam, Robert D. (2000) *Bowling Alone The Collapse and Revival of American Community*. New York: Simon and Schuster.

Quraishi, Muzammil (2005) *Muslims and Crime: A Comparative Study*. Aldershot: Ashgate.

Ramamurthy, Anandi (2006) 'The Politics of Britain's Asian Youth Movements', *Race and Class*, 48(2): 38–60.

Ramsay, Donald (2006) *Lothian and Borders Police: Black and Minority Ethnic Study*, February 2006. Edinburgh: Lothian and Borders Police. www.lbp.police.uk/freedom-of-information/publications/TLReport/Final_Report.pdf.

Ray, Larry and Smith, David (2004) 'Racist Offending, Policing and Community Conflict', *Sociology*, 38(4): 681–699.

Reid, Julian (2006) *The Biopolitics of the War on Terror: Life Struggles, Liberal Modernity, and the Defence of Logistical Societies*. Manchester: Manchester University Press.

Reiner, Robert (1978) *The Blue Coated Worker*. Cambridge: Cambridge University Press.

Reiner, Robert (2000) *The Politics of the Police*. Oxford: Oxford University Press.

Reiner, Robert and Newburn, Tim (2000) 'Police Research', in Roy King and Emma Wincup (eds), *Doing Research on Crime and Justice*. Oxford: Oxford University Press. pp. 343–374.

Renton, David (2003) 'Examining the Success of the British National Party 1999-2003', *Race and Class*, 45(2): 75–85.

Renton, David (2005) '"A day to make history"? The 2004 elections and the British National Party', *Patterns of Prejudice*, 39(1): 25–45.

Rex, John and Tomlinson, Sally (1979) *Colonial Immigrants in a British City: A Class Analysis*. London: Routledge and Kegan Paul.

Rhodes, James (2009) 'Revisiting the 2001 Riots: New Labour and the Rise of "Colour Blind Racism"', *Sociological Research Online*, November 2009. www.socresonline.org.uk/14/5/3.html.

Ridanpää, Juha (2009) 'Geopolitics of Humour: The Muhammad Cartoon Crisis and the ITKaltioIT Comic Strip Episode in Finland, *Geopolitics*, 14(4): 729–749.

Riley, James, Cassidy, Davnet and, Becker, Jane (2009) *Statistics on Race and the Criminal Justice System 2007/8*. London: Home Office. www.justice.gov.uk/publications/docs/stats-race-criminal-justice-system-07-08-revised.pdf.

Roach, Kent and Trotter, Gary (2004) 'Miscarriages of Justice in the War against Terror', *Penn State Law Review*, 109(4): 967–1040.

Rodriguez, Dalia (2006) 'Un/masking Identity: Healing our Wounded Souls', *Qualitative Enquiry*, 12: 1067–1090.

Roediger, David R. (2008) *How Race Survived US History: From Settlement and Slavery to the Obama Phenomenon*. New York: Verso.

Rojek, Chris (2003) *Stuart Hall*. Cambridge: Polity Press.

Romero, Mary (2008) 'Crossing the Immigration and Race Border: A Critical Race Theory Approach to Immigration Studies', *Contemporary Justice Review*, 11(1): 23–37.

Root, Marcia P.P. (2001) 'On the Development of the Bill of Rights for Racially Mixed people', in D. Goldberg and P. Essed (eds), *Race Critical Theories*. New York: Blackwell. pp. 355–368.

Rowe, Michael (2004) *Policing Race and Racism*. London: Willan.

Rowe, Michael (2007) 'Tripping Over Molehills: Ethics and the Ethnography of Police Work', *International Journal of Social Research Methodology*, 10(1): 37–48.

Rowe, Michael (2009) 'Policing and Race Equality: Thinking Outside the (Tick) Box', in H. Singh Bhui (ed.), *Race and Criminal Justice*. London: Sage. pp. 49–65.

Runneymede Trust, 1995 'Echoes over the Years', *The Runnymede Bulletin*, July/August: 1.

Runnymede Trust (1997) *Report on British Muslims and Islamophobia*. London: Runnymede Trust Commission.

Russell, Katheryn K. (1992) 'Development of a Black Criminology and the Role of the Black Criminologist', *Justice Quarterly*, 9(4): 667–683.

Ryder, Matthew (2011) 'Control Orders Have Been Rebranded. Big Problems Remain', *Guardian*, 28 January, www.guardian.co.uk/commentisfree/libertycentral/2011/jan/28/control-orders-protection-of-freedoms-bill.

Said, Edward (1978) *Orientalism*. London: Penguin.

Sapsford, Roger (1996) 'The Politics of Criminological Research', in Roger Sapsford (ed.), *Researching Crime and Criminal Justice*. Milton Keynes: Open University Press. pp. 57–106.

Savage, Stephen P., Grieve, John and Poyser, Sam (2007) 'Putting Wrongs to Right: Campaigns against Miscarriages of Justice', *Criminology and Criminal Justice*, 7(83): 83–105.

Sayyid, Bobby and Zac, Lillian (1998) 'Political Analysis in a World Without Foundations', in E. Scarbrough and E. Tanenbaum (eds), *Research Strategies in the Social Sciences: A Guide to New Approaches*. Oxford: Oxford University Press. pp. 249–268.

Sayyid, Salman (2004) 'Slippery People: The Immigrant Imaginary and the Grammar of Colours', in I. Law, D. Phillips and L. Turney (eds), *Institutional Racism in Higher Education*. Stoke-on-Trent: Trentham Books. pp. 149–160.

Sayyid, Salman and Vakil, AbdoolKarim (eds) (2011 forthcoming) *Thinking Through Islamophobia*: Global Perspectives. London: C. Hurst and Co.

Scraton, Phil (2007) *Power, Conflict and Criminalisation*. London: Routledge.

Scraton, Phil and Chadwick, Katherine (2001) 'Critical Research' in Eugene McLaughlin and John Muncie (eds), *The Sage Dictionary of Criminology*. London: Sage. pp. 72–73.

Scraton, Phil and Moore, Linda (2004) *The Hurt Inside: The Imprisonment of Women and Girls in Northern Ireland*. Belfast: Northern Ireland Human Rights Commission.

Scraton, Sheila, Caudwell, Jayne and Holland, Samantha (2005) ''Bend it like Patel' Centring "Race" Ethnicity and Gender in Feminist Analyses of Women's Football in England', *International Review for the Sociology of Sport*, 40(1): 71–88.

Selmeczi, Anna (2009) '"... we are being left to burn because we do not count": Biopolitics, Abandonment, and Resistance', *Global Society*, 23(4): 519–538.

Sen, Puma (1999) 'Domestic Violence, Deportation, and Women's Resistance: Notes on Managing Inter-Sectionality', *Development in Practice*, 9(1/2): 178–183.

Sharp, Douglas (2002) 'Policing after Macpherson: Some Experiences of Muslim Police Officers', in Basia Spalek (ed.), *Islam, Crime and Criminal Justice*. Devon: Willan. pp. 76–95.

Sharp, Douglas and Atherton, Susie (2007) 'To Serve and Protect: The Experiences of Policing in the Community of Young People from Black and Other Ethnic Minority Groups', *British Journal of Criminology*, 7 June.

Sheffield Star (2010) 'Policeman Found Guilty of Racial Abuse', 28 May 2010. www.thestar.co.uk/news/Policeman-guilty-of-racial-abuse.6327198.jp.

Siddiqui, Hannana (2000) 'Black Women's Activism: Coming of Age?', *Feminist Review*, 64: 83–96.

Silberman, Charles E. (1980) *Criminal Violence, Criminal Justice*. New York: Vintage.

Sinha, Shamser (2008) 'Seeking Sanctuary: Exploring the Changing Postcolonial and Racialised Politics of Belonging in East London', *Sociological Research Online*, 13(5). www.socresonline.org.uk/13/5/6.html.

Sivanandan, Ambalavaner (1982) *A Different Hunger: Writings on Black Resistance*. London: Pluto.

Sivanandan, Ambalavaner (1991) *Institute of Race Relations Comment – Deadly Silence: Black Deaths in Custody*. www.irr.org.uk/1991/january/ak000003.html.

Sivanandan, Ambalavaner (2006) 'Race, Terror and Civil Society', *Race and Class*, 47(1): 1–8.

Skellington, Richard (1996) *Race in Britain Today*. London: Sage.

Skogan, Wesley G. (1994) *Contacts Between Police and Public: Findings from the 1992 British Crime Survey*. Home Office Research Study 132. London: Home Office.

Sloterdijk, Peter (1987) *Critique of Cynical Reason*. Minneapolis: University of Minnesota Press.

Smiljanic, Natassja (2002) 'Human Rights and Muslims in Britain', in Basia Spalek (ed.), *Islam, Crime and Criminal Justice*. Devon: Willan. pp. 118–132.

Smith, David (2009) 'Criminology, Contemporary Society, and Race Issues', in Hindpal Singh Bhui (ed.), *Race and Criminal Justice*. London: Sage. pp. 30–48.

Smith, David J. (1983) *A Survey of Police Officers*. London: Policy Studies Institute.

Smith, David J. and Gray, Jeremy (1985) *Police and People in London IV: The Police in Action*. London: Policy Studies Institute.

Socialist Worker (2002) 'Satpal Ram – 16 Years in Jail: I Kept Fighting to Win Freedom'. *Socialist Worker*, 1807, 6 July 2002. www.socialistworker.co.uk/print_art.php?id=5297.

Soguk, Nevzat (2007) 'Border's Capture: Insurrectional Politics, Border-Crossing Humans, and the New Political', in P.K. Rajaram and C. Grundy-Warr (eds), *Borderscapes: Hidden Geographies and Politics at Territory's Edge*. Minneapolis: University of Minnesota Press. pp. 284–308.

Sollund, Ragnhild (2007) 'Canteen Banter or Racism: Is There a Relationship Between Oslo Police's Use of Derogatory Terms and Their Attitudes Towards Ethnic Minorities?', *Journal of Scandinavian Studies in Criminology and Crime Prevention*, 8: 77–96.

Solomos, John and Back, Les (1995) *Race, Politics, and Social Change*. London: Routledge.

Solomos, John and Back, Les (1996) *Racism and Society*. Basingstoke: Palgrave Macmillan.

Sommers, Samuel R., Apfelbaum, Evan P., Dukes, Kristin N., Toosi, Negin and Wang, Elsie J. (2006) 'Race and Media Coverage of Hurricane Katrina: Analysis, Implications, and Future Research Questions', *Analyses of Social Issues and Public Policy*, 6(1): 1–17.

Spencer, Stephen (2006) *Race and Ethnicity: Culture, Identity and Representation*. London: Routledge.

Steffensmeier, Darrell and Britt, Chester L. (2001) 'Judges' Race and Judicial Decision Making: Do Black Judges Sentence Differently?', *Social Science Quarterly*, 82(4): 749–764.

Steffensmeier, Darrell and Demuth, Stephen (2000) 'Ethnicity and sentencing outcomes in U.S. Federal Courts: Who is punished more harshly?, *American Sociological Review*, 65: 705–729.

Steffensmeier, Darrell, Ulmer, Jeffrey, and Kramer, John (1998) 'The Interaction of Race, Gender, and Age in Criminal Sentencing: The Punishment Cost of Being Young, Black, and Male', *Criminology*, 36(4): 763–798.

Stockwell Inquest (2008a) *Hearing Transcript – 4/11/2008*. www.stockwellinquest.org.uk/hearing_transcripts/nov_04.pdf.

Stockwell Inquest (2008b) *Hearing Transcript – 29/10/2008*. www.stockwellinquest.org.uk/hearing_transcripts/oct_29.pdf.

Stone, Alison (2004) 'Essentialism and Anti-Essentialism in Feminist Philosophy', *Journal of Moral Philosophy*, 1(2): 135–153.

Street Weapons Commission (2009) *The Street Weapons Commission Report*. London: Channel Four.

Sunday Times (2006) 'The Enemy Within', 13 August 2006. www.timesonline.co.uk/tol/comment/article607432.ece.

Sunday Times (2006) 'BNP Chief Told Pub Rally of "Muslim rape gangs"', 18 January 2006. www.timesonline.co.uk/tol/news/uk/article789545.ece.

Taylor, Matthew (2009) 'Archbishop Condemns BNP Leader's 'Bloodless Genocide' Claim', *Guardian*, 23 April 2009. www.guardian.co.uk/politics/2009/apr/23/bnp-nick-griffin-john-sentamu.

Taylor, Matthew (2010) 'English Defence League: Inside the Violent World of Britain's New Far Right', *Guardian*, 28 May 2010. www.guardian.co.uk/uk/2010/may/28/english-defence-league-guardian-investigation.

Terranova, Tiziana (2007) 'Futurepublic on Information Warfare, Bio-racism and Hegemony as Nonpolitics', *Theory, Culture and Society*, 24(3): 125–145.

Thames Valley Police (2009) *Community Recruitment Network Team*. www.thamesvalley.police.uk/joinus/join-diversity.htm.

Thomas, Jim and Marquart, James (1987) 'Dirty Information and Clean Conscious: Communication Problems in Studying "Bad Guys"', in Carl Crouch and David Mains (eds), *Communication and Social Structure*. Springfield: Charles Thomas Publisher. pp. 81–96.

Tizard, Barbara and Phoenix, Ann (2002) *Black, White or Mixed-Race? Race and Racism in the Lives of Young People of Mixed Parentage*. London: Routledge.

Townsend, Mark (2009) 'English Defence League Marchers Clash with Police in Nottingham', *Guardian*, 5 December 2009. www.guardian.co.uk/uk/2009/dec/05/edl-march-violence-nottingham.

Townsend, Mark (2010) 'Immigration Bosses to be Quizzed after Asylum Seekers were 'Beaten' by Guards', *Observer*, 28 February 2010. www.guardian.co.uk/uk/2010/feb/28/yarls-wood-assaults.

Travis, Alan (2010a) 'Judge Rules Compensation Can be Paid to Terror Suspects over Control Orders', *Guardian*, 18 January 2010. www.guardian.co.uk/politics/2010/jan/18/control-orders-ruling-compensation.

Travis, Alan (2010b) 'Terror Suspects Could Win Damages after Control Orders Ruling', *Guardian*, 28 July 2010. www.guardian.co.uk/law/2010/jul/28/terror-suspects-control-orders-quashed.

Travis, Alan (2011) 'Control Orders: Home Secretary Tables Watered-Down Regime', *Guardian*, 26 January. www.guardian.co.uk/law/2011/jan/26/control-order-review-theresa-may.

Treviño, A. Javier (2003) 'Introduction: Erving Goffman and the Interaction Order', in A. Treviño (ed.), *Goffman's Legacy*. Lanham, MD: Rowman and Littlefield. pp. 1–49.

Trivedi, Parita (1984) 'To Deny Our Fullness: Asian Women in the Making of History', *Feminist Review*, 17, Autumn: 37–50.

Troyna, Barry and Carrington, Barry (1990) *Education, Racism and Reform*. London: Routledge.

Tsoukala, Anastassia (2008) 'Defining the Terrorist Threat in the Post-September 11 Era', in D. Bigo and A. Tsoukala (eds), *Terror, Insecurity and Liberty: Illiberal Practices of Liberal Regimes After 9/11*. Abingdon: Routledge. pp. 49–99.

Tye, Deborah (2009) *Children and Young People in Custody 2008–2009: An Analysis of the Experiences of 15–18 year olds in Prison*. London: HM Inspectorate of Prisons/Youth Justice Board.

Tyler, Imogen (2006) 'Welcome to Britain: The Cultural Politics of Asylum', *European Journal of Cultural Studies*, 9(2): 185–202.

Tyrer, David (2011) "Flooding the Embankments': Race, Bio-Politics and Sovereignty', in S. Sayyid and A. Vakil (eds), *Thinking Through Islamophobia: Global Perspectives*. London: C. Hurst & Co., pp. 93–110.

Tyrer, David and Ahmad, Fauzia (2004) *Muslim Women and Higher Education: Identities, Experiences, and Prospects: A Summary Report*. Liverpool: Liverpool John Moores University. www.mywf.org.uk/uploads/projects/borderlines/Archive/2007/muslimwomen.pdf.

Valentine, Simon R. (2006) *Muslims in Bradford*. Oxford: COMPAS – University of Oxford. www.compas.ox.ac.uk/fileadmin/files/pdfs/Research/Bradford%20Background%20Paper%200506b.pdf.

Van Dijk, Teun A. (1992) 'Discourse and the Denial of Racism', *Discourse and Society*, 3: 87–118.

Van Dijk, Teun A. (1993) 'Elite Discourse and Racism', in I.M Zavala (ed.), *Approaches to Discourse Poetics and Psychiatry*. California: Newbury Park. pp. 81–124.

Van Maanen, John (1988) *Tales of the Field: On Writing Ethnography*. Chicago: University of Chicago Press.

Vaughan-Williams, Nick (2007) 'The Shooting of Jean Charles de Menezes: New Border Politics?', *Alternatives*, 32: 177–195.

Vaughan-Williams, Nick (2009) 'Lines in the Sand? Towards an Agenda for Critical Border Studies', *Geopolitics*, 14(3): 582–587.

Vaught, Sabina E. (2008) 'Writing Against Racism: Telling White Lies and Reclaiming Culture', *Qualitative Enquiry*, 14(4): 566–589.

Verkaik, Robert (2009) 'Ministers to Spend £12m Fighting White Working-class Extremism', *Independent*, 15 October 2009. www.independent.co.uk/news/uk/home-news/ministers-to-spend-16312m-fighting-white-workingclass-extremism-1802824.html.

Virdee, Satnam (1995) *Racial Violence and Harassment*. London, Policy Studies Institute.

Virdee, Satnam (2000) 'A Marxist Critique of Black Radical Theories of Trade-union Racism', *Sociology*, 34(3): 545–565.

Voorhees, Courte C.W., Vick, John and Perkins, Douglas D. (2007) 'Came Hell and High Water': The Intersection of Hurricane Katrina, the News Media, Race and Poverty', *Journal of Community and Applied Social Psychology*, 17: 415–429.

Wacquant, Loïc (2001) 'Deadly Symbiosis: When Ghetto and Prison Meet and Mesh', *Punishment and Society*, 3(1): 95–133.

Wacquant, Loïc (2005) 'Race as Civic Felony', *International Social Science Journal*, 57(183), pp. 127–142.

Waddington, P.A.J., Stenson, Kevin and Don, David (2004) 'In Proportion: Race, and Police Stop and Search', *British Journal of Criminology*, 44(6): 889–914.

Waddington, David (2010) 'Applying the Flashpoints Model of Public Disorder to the 2001 Bradford Riot', *British Journal of Criminology*, 50(2): 342–359.

Walker, Hilary (2002) *A Genealogy of Equality: The Curriculum for Social Work Education and Training*. London: Woburn Press.

Walsh, Anthony (2008) 'African Americans and Serial Killing in the Media', in Anthony Walsh and Craig Hemmens (eds), *Introduction to Criminology*. Los Angeles: Sage. pp. 385–398.

Watt, Nicholas (2010) 'Immigration Cap to be Put on Skilled Workers from Outside EU', *Guardian*, 25 June 2010, www.guardian.co.uk/uk/2010/jun/25/conservatives-against-dropping-immigration-cap.

Wanstead and Woodford Guardian (2009) 'Wanstead: BNP by-election campaigner arrested over "racist attack"', 15 April 2009. www.guardian-series.co.uk/news/rbnews/4292232.WANSTEAD__BNP_by_election_campaigner_arrested_o/.

Wray, Matt (2006) *Not Quite White: White Trash and the Boundaries of Whiteness*. Durham: Duke University Press.

Wardak, Ali (2000) *Social Control and Deviance: A South Asian Community in Scotland*. Aldershot: Ashgate.

Watters, Charles (2008) *Refugee Children: Towards the Next Horizon*. Abingdon: Routledge.

Webster, Colin (2003) 'Race, Space and Fear: Imagined Geographies of Racism, Crime, Violence and Disorder in Northern England', *Capital and Class*, 27(2): 95–122.

Webster, Colin (1997) 'The Construction of British Asian Criminality', *International Journal of the Sociology of Law*, 25: 65-86.

Webster, Colin (2007) *Understanding Race and Crime*. Berkshire: McGraw Hill–Open University Press.

Webster, Colin (2008) 'Marginalized White Ethnicity, Race and Crime', *Theoretical Criminology*, 12(3): 293–312.

Weedon, Chris (2004) *Identity and Culture: Narratives of Difference and Belonging*. Berkshire: Open University Press.

Weis, Michelle Fine Lois (1998) 'Crime Stories: A Critical Look Through Race, Ethnicity and Gender', *International Journal of Qualitative Studies in Education*, 11(3): 435–459.

Werbner, Pnina and Anwar, Muhammad (eds) (1991) *Black and Ethnic Leaderships: The Cultural Dimensions of Political Action*. London: Routledge.

Werbner, Pnina (1994) 'Islamic Radicalism and the Gulf War: Lay Preachers and Political Dissent among British Pakistanis', in B. Lewis and D. Schnapper (eds), *Muslims in Europe*. London: Pinter. pp. 98–115.

Westwood, Sallie (1991) 'Red Star over Leicester: Racism, the Politics of Identity, and Black Youth in Britain', in P. Werbner and M. Anwar (eds), *Black and Ethnic Leaderships in Britain: The Cultural Dimensions of Political Action*. London: Routledge. pp. 101–116.

Williams, Katherine S. (2008) *Textbook on Criminology*. Second edition. Oxford: Oxford University Press.

Whyte, David (2007) 'Market Patriotism and the War on Terror', *Social Justice* 35(2–3): 111–131.

Wilson, Amrit (1981) 'Trials in Bradford: Whose Conspiracy?', *Economic and Political Weekly*, 16(38): 1527–1528.

Wilson, Dean and Weber, Leanne (2008) 'Surveillance, Risk and Preemption on the Australian Border', *Surveillance and Society*, 5(2): 124–141.

Wilson, William J. (1987) *The Truly Disadvantaged*. Chicago: University of Chicago Press.

Winant, Howard (2001) 'White Racial Projects', in B. Rasmussin, B.E. Klingenberg, I. Nexica and M. Wray (eds), *The Making and Unmaking of Whiteness*. Durham: Duke University Press. pp. 97–112.

Winston, George T. (1901) 'The Relations of the Whites to the Negroes', *Annals of the American Academy of Political and Social Science*, XVII: 108–109.

Wolfgang, Marvin E. and Ferracuti, Franco (1967) *The Subculture of Violence*. London: Tavistock.

Wood, Rebecca (2009) 'Returned Iraqi Asylum Seekers on Hunger Strike', Institute of Race Relations. www.irr.org.uk/2009/october/bw000045.html.

Worley, Claire (2005) '"It's not about Race, it's about the Community": New Labour and Community Cohesion', *Critical Social Policy*, 25(4): 483–496.

Wray, Matt (2006) *Not Quite White: White Trash and the boundaries of Whiteness*. Durham: Duke University Press.

Wray, Matt and Newitz, Annalee (eds) (1997) *White Trash: Race and Class in America*. New York: Routledge.

Wright, Cecile, Standen, Penny and Patel, Tina (2009) *Black Youth Matters: From Transitions to Success*. London, Routledge.

Youmans, W. (2004) 'The New Cold Warriors' in Hagopian, Elaine C. (ed.), *Civil Rights* in Peril: The Targeting of Arabs and Muslims. London: Pluto Press. pp. 105–130.

Young, Lola (2000) 'What is Black British Feminism?', *Women: A Cultural Review*, 11(1/2): 45–60.

Younge, Gary (2009a) 'When You Watch the BNP on TV, Just Remember: Jack Straw Started All This', 21 October 2009. www.guardian.co.uk/commentisfree/2009/oct/21/jack-straw-bnp-griffin-hain.

Younge, Gary (2009b) 'I've changed my mind about racism', 28 December 2009. www.guardian.co.uk/commentisfree/2009/dec/28/goodbye-noughties-race-relations.

Yukins, Elizabeth (2003) '"Feeble-Minded" White Women and the Spectre of Proliferating Perversity in American Eugenics Narratives', in L.A. Cuddy and C.M. Roche (eds), *Evolution and Eugenics in American Literature and Culture, 1880–1940: Essays on Ideological Conflict and Complicity*. Massachusetts: Rosemont Publishing. pp. 164–186.

Yuval-Davis, Nira (2006) 'Intersectionality and Feminist Politics', *European Journal of Women's Studies*, 13(3): 193–209.

Yuval-Davis, Nira, Anthias, Floya and Kofman, Eleanor (2005) 'Secure Borders and Safe Haven and the Gendered Politics of Belonging: Beyond Social Cohesion', *Ethnic and Racial Studies*, 28(3): 513–535.

Zahid Mubarek Inquiry (2006) *Report of the Zahid Mubarek Inquiry Volume 1*. London: The Stationery Office.

Zembylas, Michalinos (2010) 'Agamben's Theory of Biopower and Immigrants' Asylum Seekers' Discourses of Citizenship and the Implications for Curriculum Theorizing', *Journal of Curriculum Theorizing*, 26(2): 31–4.

Zylinska, Joanne (2005) *The Ethics of Cultural Studies*. London: Symposium.

Index